Islamic Principles

ISLAMIC PRINCIPLES

M. Husain

Reference Press

4831/24, Ansari Road
Darya Ganj
New Delhi-110 002
Phone: 51563444
Fax: 51563334
E-mail: info@essessreference.com
url: http://www.essessreference.com

First Published 2005

ISBN: 81-88583-83-9

Rs.700/-

Published by:
Reference Press
4831/24, Ansari Road, Darya Ganj,
New Delhi-110 002.
Phone: 51563444
Fax: 51563334
E-mail: info@essessreference.com
url: http://www.essessreference.com

Printed in India at:
Mehra Offset Press, New Delhi

Contents

Preface

The book 'Islamic Principles, makes a sincere and painstaking attempt to delve deep into almost all aspects of Islamic way of life. This author has touched upon many a dimension of Islam as a religion, such as ; the faith, its backdrop, basis of belief, the preaching, religious practices, philosophical basis, ethical dimensions, moral codes, believers' unity, institution of family, social life and scientific approach. These fundamental aspects of the religion are presented chapter by chapter.

The fundamentals of the faith such as; basic principles, principles of unity, holy angels, holy books, the messengers and life-after-death are explained in a very interesting way. The reader will undoubtedly find interest and keenness, while advancing to the second chapter of the book in which, world before Islam, the birth and emergence of Islam, preaching of faith, Holy Prophet's proclamation and basic ideology etc., are dealt with. The very next chapter provides the reader getting understanding of the holy book and Prophet's tradition. It can be said, without a second thought that no other book in this area of subject has ever touched upon the thorny issues like invitation to faith, the faithfulness, law and protocol, rules, the polity, status of minorities, law of faith and the struggle for God's sake, the way this author has done. One would enjoy and surely take a sharp look at the religious planks, such as Iman (the belief), Salat (the prayer) Saum (the fast) Zakat (the alms) and Hajj (the pilgrimage).

The basis on which the Islamic philosophy stands, would evince one's interest, and sense of investigation. The philosophical basis mainly consists of basic ideology, heavenly knowledge, academic standards, the perception, practical aspects, almighty's kindness and search for knowledge. Taking a digression from normal practice of writing a religious book, I have set aside a chapter on ethical dimensions, which covers among other topics, the determination, the reality, the toleration, discrimination and patience.

The moral codes are also explained in an elaborate and understanding way. Ethical values, universal perfection, perception of peace, social justice, liberty to speak, social levelling, equality for all, peaceful dealings, way of learning, rules and regulations, the goals, the evaluation and values and traditions are the major tips of the moral codes covered in the book.

I suggest some practical ways to maintain unity among believers. It is strictly insisted in the book that the aspects like, way of life, status of non-believers, no show-off and lessons in economy should be taken into account as far as the unity is concerned. The book also authoritatively speaks of the relationship and domestic life in the family. The major aspects of the social life are also elaborated. It puts a major stress on the aspects of the scientific approach towards religion, such as scholarly percept, educational development and holy Prophet's tradition.

Definitely, this book will find a place in the shelves of many libraries, institutions and homes.

Author

1

The Faith

Basic Principles

The fundamental beliefs, which serve as the foundation of a religion, are called its doctrines or articles of faith. All the prophets of Allah, in their attempts to reform mankind, concentrated mainly on transferring their beliefs to their followers. The Holy Prophet (PBUH), too, began propagating his message by focusing attention on these beliefs.

These beliefs are stated in Iman-e-Mufassal which says:

> "I believe in Allah, in His angels, in His books, in His messengers, in the Last Day and in the fact that everything, good or bad, is decided by Allah, the Almighty, and in life after Death."

The Holy Quran says:

> "O you who believe! Believe in Allah and His messenger and the scripture which He hath sent to His messenger and the scripture which He sent to those before (him). Any who denieth Allah, His angels, His books, His messengers and the Day of Judgement hath gone far, far astray. " (4:136)

And also:

> "... It is righteousness to believe in Allah and the Last Day and the angels and the book and the messengers."
> (2:177)

The fundamental beliefs or articles of faith are:

1. Unity or Oneness of Allah
2. Angels
3. Revealed books
4. Prophets
5. Life after death.

Principle of Unity

Belief in the Unity and Oneness of Allah - Tauhid is the first and main principle of the Islamic faith. It means that Allah is the Supreme Being, the Creator, Sustainer and Master of the universe, the highest authority and hence exclusively worthy of worship. The first Surah of the Holy Quran begins with the words:

> "Praise be to Allah, the Cherisher and Sustainer of the worlds. " (1:2)

Tauhid is the belief in Allah with all His powers. Allah is All-knowing, All-wise, and All-powerful. He is and will always be. He has no beginning and no end. He is the First and the Last. He has no parents or son. He has no partners of any sort in His attributes, power, work and dominion. The Quran says:

> " Say, praise be to Allah, Who begets no son and has no partner in (His) dominion ..." (17:11)

And also:

> "No son has He begotten, nor has He a partner in His dominion..." (25:2)

The Quran has laid the greatest emphasis on Allah's absolute Unity and Oneness, The concept has been summed up in Surah Ikhlas of the Holy Quran, which says:

> "Say He is Allah, the One and Only Allah, the Eternal, the Absolute. He begetteth not, nor is He begotten. And there is none like unto Him. " (112:1-4)

At another place, we are told:

> "Allah! There is no god but He the Living, the Self-subsisting, Eternal." (2:255)

And again:

> "There is nothing whatever like unto Him and He is the One that hears and sees (all things)." (42:11)

Islam emphatically proclaims that Allah, the Creator is not bound by any of the limitations of human beings or of anything else He has created. He has no body, nor form, no physical attributes, nor characteristics. He is the Originator and Fashioner of the universe with its vast and perfect system, the One Who sustains it and keeps it functioning according to His laws and plans.

Allah is beyond anything which the mind or senses of man can grasp or comprehend or imagine. He is above having any similarity to any of His creations for He alone is the Creator and everything else is created by Him. He alone is Divine and no other human being or any other creature can share His Divinity or His unique attributes. Allah is always concerned and involved with every single part of His creation. All His creations exist and fulfil their functions by His command and will. For His concern is not only in creating, but also in sustaining and providing for His creatures, in guiding, regulating and maintaining them.

The vast universe with its flawless system clearly indicates that there is one Creator and one Controller. The sun, the moon, the galaxy and the whole universe obey the laws of the Supreme Authority. There is complete harmony and everything is set perfectly in the system. There is no flaw and no need for improvement in it. Had there been more than one Creator and Controller, there would have been chaos and confusion as the Quran says:

> "If there were in the heavens and the earth other gods besides Allah, there would have been confusion in both." (21:22)

But there is no conflict and disorder in the universe. This perfect order and combination is the proof of the presence of one powerful Creator and Regulator.

Allah has created everything in the earth and heavens for the service of mankind. When a person surrenders himself to Allah's commands, he gains superiority over all other creatures in the universe.

Tauhid shapes and regulates the entire course of a Muslim's life. A believer in Tauhid is sure that Allah knows and sees everything, so he is restrained from committing a sin either secretly or in the darkness of the night because of his firm conviction that Allah sees everything all the time.

A person who truly and whole heartedly believes that Allah alone is the Master of the universe, the sole Authority and Law-giver and he himself is a humble servant before Him, will not obey or give his devotion or allegiance to other deities besides Allah. He would reject them all and submit himself to Allah alone and strive with all his might and energies against serving any deities other than Allah.

Holy Angels

Allah conveyed His revelation to prophets including Hadrat Muhammad (PBUH) through an angel, Hadrat Jibbrail. In the Holy Quran, angels are spoken of as 'messengers' which denotes their spiritual function of Divine messengers. The Quran says:

> "He doth send down His angels with inspiration of His command to such of His servants as He pleaseth ...."
> (16:2)

Because of this important role of angels as bringers of Divine revelation to prophets, the belief in them is so important as to form a fundamental article of faith in Islam.

Angels act as Allah's agents and serve Him in many ways. They are created of light and unlike jinn and men have not been endowed with a free will. They are absolutely obedient to Allah's commands and are engaged in worship and service to Him. They are sent to protect men, to administer Allah's punishments, to carry His messages and to perform various other functions.

Angels are heavenly beings not visible to ordinary mortals and thus, belong to the category of the unseen unless they appear in human form. They were sent by Allah to bring messages to Hadrat Zakriya and to Hadrat Maryam before whom the angels appeared in human form. Angels also appeared in human form before Hadrat Ibrahim to give him the glad tidings of the birth of a son. Hadrat Lut was also warned by angels in human form of the impending doom of his wicked people and told to leave the town that was going to be destroyed.

Angels are one of Allah's creation. They have been given the necessary qualities and powers to carry out their duties They are not His daughters nor are they objects of worship. They have no knowledge except what Allah has taught them, they obey Allah and act on His commands. They prostrated before Adam when Allah commanded them to do so. Angels glorify and praise Allah. They never get tired. They do not need sleep, nor do they require the things needed by human beings.

Angels have various functions and duties. They act as Allah's messengers but do not descend except by Allah's command. They strengthen the hearts of the righteous believers and are their protectors. At the Battle of Badr, they helped and strengthened the hearts of the believers and put terror into the hearts of the unbelievers. They implore forgiveness for the believers but they can offer no intercession for them. They send blessings on the Holy Prophet (PBUH) and the believers.

Angels are the guardians of Hell-fire. They will welcome in Heaven all those who obey Allah's commands and will throw the wrong doers into Hell.

Angels record man's words and deeds. Each human is attended by two angels who record all his deeds upto the moment of his death. This record will be presented to him on the Day of Judgement. They are called the 'respected recorders.' The Quran says:

> "But verily, over you (are appointed angels) to protect you kind and honourable, writing down (your deeds)."
> (82:10-11)

There are many angels, the prominent among them are:

(1) Hadrat Jibbrail who brought revelations from Allah to the prophets including Hadrat Muhammad (PBUH).

(2) Hadrat Israil, also called the angel of death is responsible for taking our souls upon death.

(3) Hadrat Israfil who will blow the trumpet at the time of the end of the world, that is, on the Day of Judgement.

Holy Books

Human beings are the servants of Allah and His agents on earth who need guidance to carry out their various duties and responsibilities. This guidance is contained in the books of revelation sent to mankind through prophets and messengers. Belief in the reality of Allah's guidance to mankind in the form of revealed books is another basic article of faith in Islam.

Allah, who has created for man all things that are on the earth and has made subservient to him all that is in the heavens and on the earth, has provided everything for man's physical needs, has also provided him with spiritual guidance.

Revelation is the name given to the means of communication employed by Allah for conveying His command and messages to prophets and apostles. Revelation is not due to the prophet's own thoughts, intelligence or knowledge, it is not acquired through study or learning nor is it earned through labour but it is a special gift from Allah.

About the various methods employed by Allah for communicating His commandments to His apostles, the Quran says:

> "It is not fitting for a man that Allah should speak to him except by inspiration, or from behind a veil or by the sending of a messenger to reveal with Allah's permission what Allah wills: ...." (42:51)

The guidance sent by Allah from time to time to His messengers was basically the same. The principles of religion relating the unity of Allah, His attributes, prayer, belief in prophethood, the Day of Judgement and the concept of reward and punishment for one's deeds in the life Hereafter are common to all the revealed books. However, as the needs of the people differed in different periods, the details of the Shariat laws given in these books also varied.

Each of the previous apostles and prophets was sent to some particular nation, people or tribe and therefore, the revelation sent to each was intended for the guidance of his people. It was not intended to be universal because humanity had not yet reached the stage of readiness for such a comprehensive and final guidance from Allah. This is clear from what the Quran states concerning the messages given to various prophets.

Moreover, by the time of the advent of the Holy Prophet (PBUH), the books revealed upto that time had either been totally lost, or their original message distorted. The time had, therefore, come for Allah to send a final and complete revelation in the form of the Holy Quran.

The Holy Quran is the only revealed scripture, which has been preserved to the present time in its exact, original form and language. Although parts of the earlier revelations still survive, they are so intermixed with additions and alterations that it is very difficult to determine what part of them actually forms the original message sent by Allah. The Holy Quran does not mention all the prophets nor all the revealed books. It only mentions revelations sent to Hadrat Nuh, Hadrat Ibrahim, Hadrat Ismail, Hadrat Ishaq, Hadrat Daud, Hadrat Musa, Hadrat Isa and the Holy Prophet Muhammad (PBUH).

The revealed books mentioned by name in the Holy Quran are:

(1) Sahuf-e-Ibrahim

(2) Zabur, granted to Hadrat Daud.

(3) Taurat, revealed to Hadrat Musa. About it, the Quran says:

> "And before this was the book of Moses as a guide and a mercy." (46:12)

Thus, according to the Holy Quran, the book that Allah revealed to Hadrat Musa contained guidance, Allah's commands and warnings for the Bani Israel who failed to act according to its teachings. They distorted and perverted Allah's word. No copy of the original Taurat is now available.

(4) Injeel, granted to Hadrat Isa. About this book, the Quran says:

> "And in their footsteps we sent Jesus the son of Mary confirming the law that had come before him: we sent him the gospel therein was guidance and light, and confirmation of the law that had come before him: a guidance and an adomonition to those who fear Allah." (5:46)

The Injeel confirmed the Taurat and contained guidance and light for the Bani Israel. According to the Holy Quran, Allah took a covenant from those who call themselves Christians, but they forgot the message that was sent to them and failed to act according to its teachings.

(5) The Holy Quran is the last and the most comprehensive book revealed by Allah to His last messenger, Hadrat Muhammad (PBUH), through Hadrat Jibbrail. It was not sent down by Allah all at once. Its revelation to the Holy Prophet (PBUH) was spread over a period of twenty-three years. The Holy Quran confirms the previous revelations, and points out and corrects some of the errors that had crept into the earlier revealed books. Thus, the Holy Quran perfects and completes Divine Revelation.

The Quran speaks of the attributes of Allah and His power, of man's relationship and responsibility to Him, of the certainty of the coming of the Last Day and the life hereafter. It contains instructions about the principle of Islam and the method of worship and guides mankind to the right path. It lays down moral and ethical principles to govern all aspects of human life, both individual and collective. It narrates the stories of some of the earlier prophets and nations as an example and encouragement to the Prophet and his community and as a warning to those who deny Allah. Its main theme, repeated again and again is the reality of Allah's Supreme Power and man's position as His slave and vicegerent who is accountable to Him in everything. About the Holy Quran Allah says:

> "This is the Book; in it is guidance sure, without doubt, to those who fear Allah; who believe in the Unseen, are steadfast in prayer and spend out of what we have provided for them; and who believe in the revelation sent to thee and sent before thy time, and (in their hearts) have the assurance of the Hereafter; They are on (true guidance) from their Lord, and it is these who will prosper." (2:2-5)

Quran is undoubtedly the only book in the world that remains in the same form today as it was fourteen hundred years ago. This is because Allah Himself promised to safeguard it from corruption and change. Allah says:

"We have, without doubt, sent down the message and We will assuredly guard it (from corruption)" (15:9)

The Holy Quran is a book for reading, reciting and learning in fact, prayers cannot be complete without the recitation of some parts of the Quran.

The Holy Prophet (PBUH) laid great emphasis on memorizing the Holy Quran. There is authentic proof to show that as soon as the Holy Prophet (PBUH) received a revelation, he would ask his scribes to write it down. The Quran was committed to memory as well as written down during the lifetime of the Holy Prophet (PBUH). The Quran was complete with the same arrangement of chapters and verses that we have now, at the time of the death of the Holy Prophet (PBUH).

The Quran is not only a blessed book, but also a complete code of life. We must, therefore, study it with the object of acting in all matters according to its teachings. We must mould our lives according to the guidance contained in the Holy Quran and abstain from whatever is against its teachings. The success of human beings on this earth and in the life after death depends on obedience to the Quranic teachings and principles which are as valid and binding today as at the time when they were revealed; for although the style and mode of human life have changed, the ultimate realities, the nature of good and evil and man's own nature are unalterable and permanent and are not affected by the passing of time or changes in the world.

The Messengers

Since the beginning of creation, Allah has sent guidance for mankind through His selected people known as prophets or messengers. Belief in prophets forms the fourth ingredient of faith.

The Islamic concept of the role and function of prophethood is different from that of the other religions. In Islam, the word prophet - Nabi - denotes one who is very near to Allah through the total surrender of his entire being to Him and who receives revelation from Him which serve as a source of guidance for men. If the revelation is in the form of a scripture, the prophet is, in addition, a messenger-Rasool-as well.

Islam holds that a prophet possesses the following characteristics: he is absolutely truthful, he is free of all kinds of sins, he delivers the messages from Allah without any omission or concealment and he has the highest order of intelligence and mental ability.

According to the Quran, all the apostles and prophets sent by Allah were men, had wives and children and were mortal. All of them taught in the language of the people to whom they were sent. At the same time, the Quran tells us that they were good and truthful, Allah favoured them above all others, chose them and guided them and conferred His grace upon them. He gave them the Book and prophethood and sent them for the guidance of their people. The unbelievers scoffed at them and persecuted them but they bore it patiently. Some of them were endowed with more gifts than the others, but Muslims are asked to believe in all of them, to respect them and to make no distinction amongst them. The Quran says:

> "We make no distinction between one and another of His messengers." (2:285)

And also:

> "Those who deny Allah and His messengers and (those who) wish to separate Allah from His messengers, saying: "we believe in some but reject others": and (those who) wish to take a course midway - They are in truth (equally), unbelievers;" (4:150-151)

The Quran tells us that Allah always helped His apostles and prophets and punished and destroyed the wicked unbelievers. The apostles and prophets will be questioned on the Day of Judgement about the response of their people to their mission.

Allah sent prophets to mankind from amongst themselves for their guidance and reformation because a man can best serve as an example and a guide for his own race. The message could have been conveyed by the angels, but they belong to a different class of beings and cannot serve as models for men. The Quran says:

> "If there were settled on earth, angels walking about in peace and quiet, we should certainly have sent them down from the heavens an angel for a messenger."
> (17:95)

All the prophets who preceded Hadrat Muhammad (PBUH) were sent with a message of warning and guidance to a particular people. None of their messages was intended to be universal, until the last messenger, Hadrat Muhammad (PBUH) was entrusted with the final and complete guidance for the whole of humanity for all times to come.

The Quran says that Allah sent a warner and guide to every nation and it mentions the names of many of them. At the beginning of the line was Hadrat Adam, who was also the first human being. Allah bestowed prophethood on him and gave him guidance for himself and his descendants. The first human beings on earth were true believers in one Allah, who submitted to His guidance. But, gradually over a period of time, they became idolators, until Allah raised a new messenger from amongst them to recall them to the truth. The Quran mentions Hadrat Nuh, who brought a message of warning to his peoples. They refused to listen and were destroyed by the flood. The next major prophet whose history is narrated in the Quran is Hadrat Ibrahim. Although he grew up among idolators, he surrendered himself to Allah with such total submission that Allah made him an example for people of all times. From Hadrat Ibrahim came a long line of prophets through his two sons - Hadrat Ismail and Hadrat Ishaq. From Hadrat Ishaq a number of prophets came which included Hadrat Yaqub, Hadrat Yusuf, Hadrat Musa, Hadrat Daud, Hadrat Sulaiman, Hadrat Yahya and Hadrat Isa. Hadrat Ismail was the ancestor of the Arabs and Hadrat Muhammad (PBUH) was among his descendants.

The Holy Quran proclaims that Hadrat Muhammad (PBUH) is the last messenger of Allah, 'The seal of the prophets.' He was born in Mecca, Arabia, nearly six hundred years after Hadrat Isa. It was the time when the Arabs practiced idolatory and the society was in a state of extreme corruption and decay.

When Hadrat Muhammad (PBUH) called people to Islam and to a noble and righteous path he was met with intense hostility.

At first he was ridiculed and opposed and then with his small group of followers exposed to abuse, torture, boycott and ultimately the threat of assassination. But all of them remained firm and constant because they were sure of the truth of the message that was delivered to them. At last, after thirteen years of preaching and bearing patiently all the trials, the Holy Prophet (PBUH) with his followers migrated to Medina where he was able to establish the first Islamic state based upon the teachings of the Quran. Soon, the Muslim community although initially small in number and poorly equipped was able to subdue the unbelievers. The Holy Prophet (PBUH) then returned to the city of Mecca from where he had migrated several years ago. He forgave his bitterest enemies and thus, the conquest of Mecca was a peaceful one.

Prophet Muhammad (PBUH) died about a year later. He left behind for all times to come two permanent and unchangeable sources of guidance, the Holy Quran and his Sunnah - that is his own example and practice.

A complete and detailed account of the life of the Holy Prophet (PBUH) has been preserved by his followers. Hence the narrations preserved in the books of Hadith-sayings of the Holy Prophet (PBUH) deal with all aspects of life from the most personal matters to the conduct of war and affairs of the state. The Muslims have before them in every aspect of their lives the living example of the best of human beings as the Quran says:

> "We have indeed in the Messenger of Allah a beautiful pattern (of conduct) for anyone whose hope is in Allah and the Final Day, and who engages much in the praise of Allah." (33:21)

His wife, Aishah said about him that his conduct was the Quran. The Holy Prophet (PBUH) was very close to Allah, but he lived an extremely active and complete life. He was a devoted husband, father, a kind and responsible kinsman, a faithful and affectionate friend, a leader in worship as well as in battle and an excellent ruler and statesman. For the Muslims of his time as well as for the present and the future generations, he was and will always be the model, the teacher, the guide, the leader and the conveyor of Divine Guidance to mankind.

World Hereafter

Belief in life after death, the Day of Judgement, bodily resurrection and Heaven and Hell is one of the articles of faith in Islam. Death is an absolute certainty. According to the Holy Quran, every soul shall have a taste of death, and must pass away. A man's life on this earth ends with his death, after which another life begins. The Qiyamat-e-Sughra or lesser judgement takes place immediately after death. The word 'Barzakh' occurs in verse 100 of Surah al-Mominun:

> "Before them is a partition (Barzakh) till the day they are raised up." (23:100)

Abdullah Yusuf Ali has explained Barzakh: "Barzakh is the place or state in which people will be after death and before judgement. Behind them is the barrier of death and in front of them is the Barzakh, partition, a quiescent state until the judgement comes." Barzakh is therefore, the intermediate state in which the soul is placed after death till the resurrection.

The Holy Quran informs man of the reality of another life of infinite duration which will be very different from the life of this world. For Allah is easily able to transform His creatures from one state of being to another. The Quran speaks again and again of examples of such transformations: the coming to life again of the earth which lies dead and barren in winter or drought; the development of a sperm in the mother's womb into a human being with all the faculties of thinking and feeling. The Quran says:

> "And among His signs is this: thou seest the earth barren and desolate; but when We send down rain to it, it is stirred to life and yields increase. Truly, He who gives life to the (dead) earth can surely give life to (men) who are dead. For He has power over all things."
> (41:39)

Those who denied Allah and rejected His guidance and did evil deeds will be thrown into a fearsome and terrible abode, where they with their companions will be in a state of torment and agony. They will long to have another chance to return to the world to live their lives differently but it will be too late. For such people, the Quran says:

"And on the day that the unbelievers will be placed before the fire (they will be asked) "Is this not the Truth?" they will say "Yea, by our Lord!" (One will say)

"Then taste ye the penalty for that ye were wont to deny (Truth)! " (46:34)

And also :

"The sinners will be in the punishment of hell, to dwell therein ..."

Nowise shall We be unjust to them: But it is they who have been unjust themselves." (43:74, 76)

As for the people who believed in Allah, who obeyed and submitted to Him and lived their lives for His pleasure, and who died in a state of surrender to Him, the Holy Quran says:

"My devotees! No fear shall be on you that Day; nor shall ye grieve - (Being those) who have believed in Our signs and bowed (their will to Ours) in Islam. Enter ye the garden, ye and your wives in (beauty and) rejoicing." (43:68-70)

"Those who have faith and do righteous deeds - they are the best of creatures.

Their reward is with Allah; gardens of Eternity, beneath which rivers flows; they will dwell therein for ever;...." (8:7-8)

The two states of Heaven and Hell are not spiritual. They will be experienced in physical forms by the new bodies with which Allah will raise men up. The Quran describes Hell as a state of intense, fearful burning and agony without respite, among the most horrifying surroundings and companions. For its inhabitants, it will be a temporary or permanent state of torture depending upon the nature and extent of their sins. The worst part of their suffering will be the awareness that they have brought about this punishment upon themselves by rejecting Allah and ignoring the guidance and the clear warnings which He had conveyed to them through His messengers. The Quran says:

> "Those who have earned evil will have a reward of like evil: ignominy will cover their (faces): No defender will they have from (the wrath of) Allah: ... they are companions of the fire: they will abide therein."
> (10:27)

The Quran tells us that the inhabitants of Heaven will experience happiness and joy that will far exceed anything one can imagine. The ultimate triumph and bliss for these people will be their nearness to Allah. The Quran says:

> "To those who do right is a goodly (reward) -yea, more (than in measure)! No darkness nor shame shall cover their faces! They are companions of the garden; they will abide therein." (10:26)

The Quran describes the outline of the events of the Last Day in a very clear and awe-inspiring language. It says that at a time which is known only to Allah, the hour of judgement will come all of a sudden; and it will be like the twinkling of an eye. When the first trumpet of Resurrection is sounded, the earth will be split apart, it will be shaken to its depths, it will be in violent commotion and become as a level stretch. The mountains will crumble to dust and will fly here and there like wool. The sun will be folded up, the moon will be in darkness, the stars will become dim and fall. The oceans will boil over and burst forth. Human souls will be dazed and lose all consciousness of time and place. The world will cease to be in the form which we see now and there will be a new heaven and a new earth. The Quran says:

> "When the sky is rent asunder, and hearkens to (The command of) its Lord and it must needs (Do so) - and when the earth is flattened out, and casts forth what is within it and becomes (clean) empty." (84: 1-4)

On that day, the bodies of the dead will be rejoined with their souls, while those who are alive on earth at that time will die and be joined to this assembly. All men will stand before Allah, each one, alone and helpless, to give an account of their deeds. They will be given their book of deeds, which they will be asked to read. The good will be given their record in their right hands and the sinners in their left hands or from behind their backs. No injustice will be done on that day. People's hands, feet and tongues will bear witness against them. No one shall speak except by Allah's leave, no ransom or compensation will be accepted, there will be no bargaining or friendship and there will be no intercession except by Allah's permission. Parents, children, spouses and relatives will be of no avail.

The Quran says:

> "Then he who is given his record in his right hand, soon will his account be taken by an easy reckoning, and he will turn to his people, rejoicing! But he who is given his record behind his back- soon will he cry for perdition, and he will enter a blazing fire."
>
> (84: 7-12)

And also:

> "At length, when there comes the deafening noise - that Day shall a man flee from his own brother, and from his mother and his father, and from his wife and his children. Each one of them, that Day, will have enough concern (of his own) to make him indifferent to the others. " (80:33-37)

Islam lays the greatest stress on the individual's accountability to Allah. The human being's life in this world is a trial, an examination period, during which he prepares himself, either for reward or punishment, for the next life which is ever lasting.

It is obvious that a person who has lived his life in submission to Allah is in an entirely different state from the one who has lived all his life in rebellion and ingratitude to Allah. Those who do not believe in a future life become immoral and irresponsible because, for them the short life on this earth is everything. On the other hand, those who have a firm belief in life after death fear Allah, follow the straight path, do good deeds and abstain from all evil deeds.

2

The Backdrop

Islam, the Religion of Peace, was not the creation of Muhammad (PBUH) any more than other religions were of those to whom their origins are respectively attributed. No religion is the creation of any single individual, nor does it appear all of a sudden, revealed to this or that Seer as it is always claimed. Islam, like any other religion, was the product of the conditions of the time, and of the surroundings in which it flourished.

Pre-Islamic Era

Though living on the side of the fateful road on which the conquering armies of the Assyrians, Persians, Macedonians and Romans had marched back and forth, the inhabitants of the vast Arabian Peninsula maintained their freedom by virtue of the natural aspects of their country and the mode of life moulded by these aspects. But the fierce love of freedom, together with the exigencies of a nomadic existence, had split the inhabitants of the Arabian desert into a number of tribes perpetually engaged in feuds and warfare.

Separated from the rest of the mankind, the Arabs took the stranger for an enemy. The poverty of his country had added to the growth of that spirit. These two factors went into the making of the codes of law and morality of the Arabs. They believed that, as descendants of the outlawed Ismael, they were doomed to live in a dreary desert while rich and fertile lands were assigned to the other branches of the human family. Consequently, they felt justified in recovering by force a portion of the heritage, they believed, they had been deprived of.

The Roman historian Pliny, six hundred years before the appearance of Muhammad, found the Arabs occupied with two lucrative professions, robbery and trade, in addition to their native calling of sheep-raising and horse-breeding. In the earlier stages of social evolution, these two professions of robbery and trade are usually distinguished by a thin and elastic line of demarcation. The trader makes his profit by purchasing things at the cheapest price and selling them at the highest. The cheaper the price he pays, the greater is his profit. Robbery or theft places him in possession of things at the lowest price. Therefore, once the morality of the fundamental principle of trading is admitted, the right of the trader to act so as to make the greatest possible profit becomes legitimate. Then, competition keeps the price of his wares down. The most convenient way of eliminating competition is to rob the rival. By that stratagem, not only is the competitor kept away from the market, but his goods go there as the property of the more efficient party. Further, robbery is an effective weapon to establish monopoly on trade-routes and markets. In its earlier stages of development, trade is everywhere conducted with these practical policies which must shock a modern merchant. Still, robbery was the weapon with which his less orthodox predecessors established the noble profession ' which he now carries on so righteously with the laudable maxim: Honesty is the best policy.

Besides, robbery imperceptibly ripens into the manly political virtue of war likeness, so much glorified in the savage adolescence of mankind. Given to robbery by the physical aspects of their homeland, the Arabs were naturally destined to develop unusual talent in trade as well as in war. Their bravery and war likeness were almost legendary. The famous historical work, "Ayam al Arab", composed in the most flourishing days of the Saracen Empire, records no less than seventeen hundred memorable battles fought by the Arabs before the rise of the Prophet. So, if the Saracens distinguished themselves as warriors, they did not derive that virtue from their Islamic faith. They had been warriors before they were called to wield the sword in the service of God. The military achievements of Islam should be credited not so much to the religious teachings of the Arabic Prophet as to the social conditions of the country in which it was born.

The wars conducted by the Arabs before the appearance of the Prophet were mostly internecine feuds fought with savage fierceness, but strictly according to the quaint codes of honour, chivalry and nobility. The profuse spilling of blood did not fertilise the sands of Arabia, but it did, eventually, become prejudicial to the profitable economic consequences of robbery, the legitimate profession of trade conducted by the primitive Arabs. Economic necessity demanded termination of the proud but ruinous virtue of internecine wars, and diversion of the traditional Saracen valour in more profitable channels. The, ideas, born out of that necessity, eventually crystallised into the " Religion of Muhammad ".

Itself a vast stretch of sandy wilderness, Arabia, however, is surrounded in three sides by populous countries — homes of ancient civilisations, where industry and agriculture thrived from time immemorial. On the south is the ocean on which navigated vessels carry the trade of India. Thanks to her geographical position, Arabia was intersected by the routes of Caravan trade and maritime commerce, interchanged among India, Persia, Assyria, Syria, Palestine, Egypt and Abyssinia. In earlier days, the trade-routes connecting Africa and Asia lay through the south and north of the Peninsula, avoiding the unknown interior of the sandy wilderness. But the exorbitant taxation of Byzantine despotism, supplemented by the endless extortion of its local officials, drove the traders to hazard the encounter of the fierce but hospitable Beduin in the heart of his home.

In the beginning, the Arab collected his tribute according to his peculiar code of law and morality. But in course of time, he discovered that trade would be more profitable than robbery. Of all the Arabian tribes, the Koreish were the first to exchange the turbulent for a peaceful but more profitable profession. They inhabited the coast-line of the Red Sea and commanded the Abyssinian trade long before the Asiatic traffic also came their way. In the earlier centuries of the Christian era, the capital of the Koreish tribe, Mecca, had become the point where the important trade-routes from south to north and east to west intersected. At Yemen, on the Arabian Sea, the Koreish caravans took over the commodities from India; at a point near modern Aden, their precious burden was increased by the African riches from Abyssinia. The journey northwards terminated at the busy marts of Damascus, where corn and manufactured articles were bought with the exchange of aromatics, pearls, precious stones, tusks, etc. The lucrative exchange diffused plenty of riches in the streets of Mecca. When, later, the east-west trade-route also passed through Mecca, the prosperity of the Koreish became unbounded, and their ambition proportionately grew.

But other Arabian tribes, jealous of their freedom, and envious of the prosperity of the Koreish, stood faithfully by their traditional codes of law and morality, whose profane origin was no longer admitted. They were raised to the nobility of offensive and defensive warfare, on the authority of tribal gods. The old national pastime of robbery which had previously been played at the expense of unwary strangers, turned out ruinous to the new national occupation of trade. Termination of the tribal feuds became an essential condition for further political progress. The task of establishing unity, by the logic of historical events, devolved upon those who controlled the economic forces making for the historically necessary goal. The Koreish appeared as the chosen people of history.

In the midst of their ceaseless feuds, all the Arabian tribes worshipped and sacrificed at the temple of Kaaba near Mecca. The Koreish head seized the control of the seat of national worship, and the sacerdotal office of great power and extensive privilege had been captured by the Hashemites -the most important family of the tribe. The Hashemites, therefore, commanded national respect and veneration, in addition to the opulence derived from trade. Eventually, a scion of the Hashemite family issued the call for unity in the form of a new religion which denied all gods but one.

The severe monotheism of Muhammad not only echoed the yearning for unity on the part of a people torn asunder by internecine feuds; it was also destined to find a ready response from the neighbouring nations, tormented by the intolerance of the Catholic Church. The religious life of the people of Persia, Mesopotamia, Syria, Palestine and Egypt had been hopelessly confused by the conflicts of Magian Mysticism, Jewish conservatism and Christian bigotry. Rigid rites and rituals had taken the place of religion; hypocritical ceremonies had driven away devotion; dogmatic theology had prosecuted faith; and God had disappeared in a confusing crowd of angels, saints and apostles. The stringent cry of the new religion" There is but One God "softened by great toleration, subject to this fundamental creed, was enthusiastically hailed by the distressed multitudes searching for the secure anchor of a simple faith in the stormy sea of social disintegration, intellectual bankruptcy and spiritual chaos. The historic cry was raised by the caravan traders of Arabia who had stood outside the ruinous conflict of arms and beliefs, had prospered economically, and progressed` in spirit, while their older and more civilised neighbours had stagnated, decayed and disintegrated. The propagation of the stern belief in the Oneness of God prepared the ground for the rise of a military State which unified all the social functions — religious, civil, judicial and administrative. The unitarianism of the Saracens laid the foundation of a new social order which rose magnificently out of the ruins of the antique civilisation. Such a creed was sure to attract the attention of the multitudes barbarously persecuted for religious heterodoxy. The new faith allowed freedom of conscience to all who placed themselves under its protection. Islam rose as a protection against religious persecution and refuge for the oppressed.

The accommodating nature, cosmopolitan spirit, democratic policy and the monotheistic creed of Islam were the creation of the geographical position of the land of its birth. Surrounded with countries oppressed by native despotism or devastated by foreign invasions, Arabia maintained her freedom. The persecuted sects from Egypt and Persia as well as from Christendom fled to the free and hospitable desert where they could profess what they thought, and practise what they professed. When the Empire of the Assyrians was conquered by the Persians, and the altars of Babylon subverted by the Magis, the Sabian priests retired to the neighbouring desert with their ancient faith and the precious knowledge of astronomy. Previously, Assyrian invasion had driven many a devout son of Israel in the same hospitable wilderness. All the Hebrew prophets, down to John the Baptist, lived, meditated and preached in the depth of the Arabian desert. The invasion of Alexander having avenged the wrong done to the Assyrians, the more orthodox disciples of Zoroaster, who did not wish to desecrate the purity of their faith by the toleration of Greek idolatry, migrated to the free atmosphere of the Arabian desert to join hands with their Babylonian adversaries.

Gnosticism and Manichxanism-those hybrids of oriental mystic cults-Greek metaphysics and Christian Gospel, all thrived luxuriantly on the sandy soil of free Arabia. Finally, Catholic orthodoxy drove to the same smelting pot of Arabian hospitality the Nestorian Jacobite and Eutychian heretics who preferred the simplicity of the Gospel to the idolatry of the orthodox Church. The freedom of exile brought the representatives of those diverse faiths into closer contact enabling them to see what was common to them all. In the calm atmosphere of toleration, their heterodoxy disappeared, the fire of proselytism died out, and the common essence of the teachings of the learned guests was imparted to the hospitable Beduin. In short, the Barbarians of the desert inherited the best the religions of antiquity had to offer, namely, the faith in the existence of one supreme God who is exalted above all the powers of heaven and earth, but who had revealed himself to mankind from time to time through his Prophets. Here is the essence of Islam crystallised in the spiritual consciousness of the Arabian people before Muhammad appeared with the mission of building a new religion on its basis. The spirit of Islam was not invented by the genius of Muhammad; nor was it revealed to mankind. It was a heritage of history conferred on the Arabian nation. The greatness of Muhammad was his ability to recognise the value of the heritage and make his countrymen conscious of it.

The Arabs had acquired the notion of one supreme God; but out of habit and for tribal interests, they still practised their old polytheistic worship. To be benefited by the positive outcome of earlier religions, delivered to them as a heritage of history, they must change their traditional mode of worship. A supreme effort must be made with the purpose; and Mecca was the most strategic point to lead the attack from.

The particularist freedom and internecine feuds of the Arabian tribes were mutually compromised and composed at Mecca. All routes of trade led there. The unity of the economic interest of the decentralised nation had created at Mecca a symbol of precarious spiritual unity. All the tribes from distant parts of the vast desert, while visiting the market of Mecca, worshipped in the temple of Kaaba. Each had introduced there its own emblem of devotion. The temple had been adorned with no less than three hundred and sixty idols of men, eagles, lions, etc. But the prosperous tribe of Koreish dominated the trade of Mecca, and the powerful family of Hashim had seized control of the temple. It was natural that the new spirit of a rising faith, which would further economic interest through national unity, should be first felt consciously at the heart of the nation. So, it happened that a member of the Hashemite family began to preach the new religion.

Once the family of Hashim and the tribe of Koreish were converted to the new faith, the whole nation would follow soon. All the tribes must visit Mecca for the purposes of trade. Those who controlled the trade of Mecca could easily dictate the faith and conscience of the entire nation. But prejudice and habit induced the Koreish to persecute the innovating zeal of their kinsmen. They were afraid that trade would be driven away from Mecca, should the Pantheon of Kaaba be disturbed. But there were others ready to assume the leadership of the revolution, when the most eligible candidate failed. Medina espoused the cause of the Prophet, and the call of unity found enthusiastic response in other quarters. The supremacy of Mecca was menaced. One family after another defected from the Koreish conservatism, and joined the revolutionary Hashemites. Before long the Koreish capitulated before their exiled kinsmen, but only to capture the sceptre of the "Commander of the Faithful".

As soon as the followers of the Prophet captured Mecca, a perpetual law was passed that no unbeliever should be allowed to set foot on the territory of the Holy City. The new religion was imposed upon the entire nation with the potent weapon of economic boycott. Kaaba was cleared of its idols and became the shrine of " Muhammad's God ". Once the standard of the new religion was raised, the whole nation flocked under it. The ground had been prepared. The faith had unconsciously taken hold of the mind of the nation before it was preached. Economic interest demanded its establishment.

Islam on the Scene

The apparently sudden rise and the dramatic expansion of Mohammedanism constitutes a most fascinating chapter in the history of mankind. A dispassionate study of .this chapter is of great importance in the present fateful period of the history of India. The scientific value of the study by itself is great, and the meritorious quest for knowledge is sure to be handsomely rewarded. But with us, today in India, particularly with the Hindus, a proper understanding of the historical role of Islam and the contribution it has made to human culture has acquired a supreme political importance.

This country has become the home of a very considerable number of the followers of the Arabian Prophet. One seldom realises that many more Mohammedans live in India than in any single purely Islamic country. Still, after the lapse of many centuries, this numerous section of the Indian population is generally considered to be an extraneous element. This curious but extremely regrettable cleft in the loose national structure of India has its historical cause. The Mohammedans originally came to India as invaders. They conquered the country and its rulers for several hundred years. That relation of the conqueror and the subjugated has left its mark on the history of our nation which today embraces both. But the unpleasant memory of the past relation has been progressively eclipsed by the present companionship in slavery. The effect of British Imperialism is no less painful and ruinous for the bulk of the Muslim population than for the masses professing Hinduism. So completely have the Mohammedans become an integral part of the Indian nation that the annals of the Muslim rule are justly recorded as chapters of the history of India. Indeed, nationalism has gone farther in effacing the painful memory of the past.

The practice of seeking consolation for the shame of the present in the real or legendary glory of the past has dressed the Muslim rulers of India in brilliant national colours.

Yet, an Indian, who prides in the prosperity of the reign of an Akbar, or boasts of the architectural accomplishments of a Shahjahan, is even today separated most curiously by an unbridgeable gulf from his next door neighbour belonging to the race, or professing the faith, of those illustrious monarchs who are believed to have glorified the history of India. For the orthodox Hindus who constitute the great majority of the Indian population, the Mussulman, even of noble birth or high education or admirable cultural attainments, is a 'mlechha'-impure barbarian-who does not deserve a social treatment any better than accorded to the lowest of the Hindus.

The cause of this singular situation is to be traced in the prejudice born, in the past, of the hatred a conquered and oppressed people naturally entertained for the foreign invader. The political relation out of which it sprang is a thing of the past. But the prejudice still persists not only as an effective obstacle to national cohesion, but also as a hindrance for a dispassionate view of history. Indeed, there is no other example of two communities living together in the same country for so many hundred years, and yet having so little appreciation of each other's culture. No civilised people in the world are so ignorant of Islamic history and contemptuous of the Mohammedan religion as the Hindus. Spiritual imperialism is an outstanding feature of our nationalist ideology. But this nasty spirit is the most pronounced in relation to Mohammedanism. The current notion of the teachings of the Arabian Prophet is extremely ill-informed. The average educated Hindu has little knowledge of, and no appreciation for, the immense revolutionary significance of Islam, and the great cultural consequences of that revolution. The prevailing notions could be laughed at as ridiculous, were they not so pregnant with harmful consequences. These notions should be combatted for the sake of the Indian people as well as in the interest of science and historical truth. A proper appreciation of the cultural significance of Islam is of supreme importance in this crucial period of the history of India.

The great historian Gibbon describes the rise and expansion of Islam as "one of the most memorable revolutions which has impressed a new and lasting character on the nations of the globe". One is simply amazed to contemplate the incredible rapidity with which the two mightiest empires of the ancient time were subverted by the comparatively small bands of nomads issuing from the Arabian desert, fired with the zeal of a new faith. Hardly fifty years had passed since Muhammad assumed the role of the singular Prophet spreading his Message of Peace at the point of the sword, when his followers victoriously planted the banner of Islam on the confines of India on the one side, and on the shores of the Atlantic on the other. The first Caliphs of Damascus reigned over an Empire which could not be crossed in less than five months on the fleetest camel. At the end of the first century of the Hegira, the " Commanders of the Faithful " were the most powerful rulers of the world.

Every Prophet establishes his pretension by the performance of miracles. On that token, Muhammad must be recognised as by far the greatest of all Prophets, before or after him. The expansion of Islam is the most miraculous of all miracles. The Roman Empire of Augustus, as later enlarged by the valiant Trajan, was the result of great and glorious victories won over a period of seven hundred years. Still, it had not attained the proportions of the Arabian Empire established in less than a century. The Empire of Alexander represented but a fraction of the vast domain of the Caliphs. For nearly a thousand years, the Persian Empire resisted the arms of Rome, only to be subdued by the "Sword of God" in less than a decade. Let a modern historian describe the miracle of the rise of Islam.

"Nowhere was there a vestige of an Arabian state, of a regular army, or of a common political ambition. The Arabs were poets, dreamers, fighters, traders; they were not politicians. Nor had they found in religion a stabilising or unifying power. They practised a low form of polytheism ..... A hundred years later, these obscure savages had achieved for themselves a great world power. They had conquered Syria and Egypt, they had overwhelmed and converted Persia, mastered Western Turkestan and part of the Punjab. They had wrested Africa from the Byzantines and the Berbers, Spain from the Visigoths. In the West they threatened France, in the East Constantinople. Their fleets, built in Alexandria or the Syrian ports, rode the waters of the Mediterranean, pillaged the Greek islands and challenged the naval power of the Byzantine Empire. Their success had been won so easily, the Persians and Berbers of the Atlas Mountains alone offering a serious resistance, that at the beginning of the eighth century it, must have seemed an open question whether any final obstacle could be opposed to their victorious course. The Mediterranean had ceased to be a Roman lake. From one end of Europe to the other, the Christian states found themselves confronted with the challenge of a new Oriental civilisation founded on a new Oriental faith."

How did that stupendous miracle happen ? That has been one of the baffling questions for historians. Today the educated world has rejected the vulgar theory that the rise of Islam was a triumph of fanaticism over sober and tolerant peoples. The phenomenal success of Islam was primarily due to its revolutionary significance and its ability to lead the masses out of the hopeless situation created by the decay of the antique civilisations not only of Greece and Rome but of Persia and China-and of India.

Preaching of Faith

Vulgar interpreters of the Islamic history lay stress upon its military achievements either to praise or to deprecate its far-reaching revolutionary significance. If the undoubtedly brilliant military conquests of the Saracens were the only measure of the historic role of Islam, then it would not be a unique historical phenomenon. The depredations of the barbarians of Tartary and Scythia (Goths, Huns, Vandals, Avars, Mongols etc.) approximated, if not equalled or excelled, their military accomplishments. But there is a vast difference between the tidal waves that occasionally rolled over West, South and East, from the border land of Europe and Asia, and the Arabic eruption of religious frenzy: Like tidal waves the former rolled on in their cataclysmic greatness, only to subside, sooner or later, having distributed death and destruction far and wide. The latter, on the contrary, was an abiding historical phenomenon, which ushered in a brilliant chapter of the cultural annals of mankind. Destruction was only a subsidiary part of its mission. It pulled down the played-out old, to construct a necessary new. It demolished the holy edifices of the Caesars and the Chosroes, only to rescue from their impending ruin the accumulated treasures of human knowledge, to preserve and multiply them for the benefit of posterity.

The prodigious feats of the Saracen horsemen are not the only distinctive features of Islam. They simply captivate our attention which must marvel at them, and impel us to search out and admire the causes of such a tremendously dynamic historical phenomenon. The miraculous performance of the "Army of God " usually dazzles the vision and the more magnificent achievements of the Islamic revolution are seldom known to the average student of history, even if he be a follower of Muhammad. Yet, the martial victories of the followers of the Arabian Prophet were but the prelude to a more magnificent and lasting performance in the social and cultural fields. They only created the conditions for political unity which opened up an era of economic prosperity and spiritual progress. The stupendous ruins of the Roman and Persian Empires had to be cleared away so that a new social order could rise with new ideas and new ideals. The dark superstition of the Magian mysticism, and the corrupt atmosphere of the Greek Church vitiated the spiritual life of the subjects of the decrepit Persian and Byzantine Empires rendering all moral and intellectual progress impossible. The severe monotheism of Muhammad wielded the formidable scimitar of the Saracen not only to destroy the profane idolatry of the Arabian tribes; it also proved to be the invincible instrument of history for freeing a considerable section of mankind from the evil spirit of Zoroaster as well as from degenerate Christianity given to the superstition of miracle-mongering, to the deadly disease of monasticism and to the idolatrous worship of Saints. The amazing achievements of Saracen arms only prove that they were wielded in the service of history-for the progress of humanity.

The rich spiritual legacy of the glorious civilisation of ancient Greece was almost buried under the dreary ruins of the Roman Empire, and lost in the darkness of Christian superstition. The grand mission of rescuing the invaluable patrimony, which eventually enabled the peoples of Europe to emerge from the depressing gloom of the holy middle-ages and build the marvellous monument of modern civilisation, belonged to the Saracen arms, and to the socio-political structure erected on the basis of Islamic Monotheism. The sword of Islam, wielded ostensibly in the service of God, actually contributed to the victory of a new social force - the blossoming of a new intellectual life - which eventually dug the grave of all religions and faiths.

Islam rose rather as a political movement than a religion in the strictest sense of the word. In the initial stages of its history, it was essentially a call for the unity of the nomadic tribes inhabiting the Arabian desert. Upon its speedy realisation, the politico-religious unitarian doctrine became the flag under which the Asiatic and African provinces of the Roman Empire survived the dissolution of the antique social order. The previous revolt had miscarried itself. Christianity had lost its original revolutionary fervour becoming, on the one hand, the ideology of social dissolution (Monasticism), and a prop for the decaying Empire, on the other. But the social crisis continued, aggravated by the degeneration of Christianity. The message of hope and salvation came from the Caravan traders of .Arabia who had stood outside the corrupting atmosphere of the decomposed Roman world, and prospered by their advantageous position. The "Revolt of Islam" saved humanity.

A famous authority on Islamic history writes the following about the mission of Muhammad: "He found a whole nation -in the full tide of rapid improvement, eagerly in search of knowledge and power. The excitement in the public mind of Arabia, which produced the mission of Mahamet, induced many other Prophets to make their appearance during his life time."

The people, for whom Islamic history is summarised in the exploits of fanatical hordes, dramatically offering the dismayed world the choice between the Koran and the sword, with the blood-curdling cry of "Allah Akbar", do not know, or conveniently overlook, that only the immediate successors of Muhammad occupied themselves solely with temporal and religious conquest- , and even they were distinguished from the barbarian ravishers of humanity like Alaric, Attila, Genseric, Chengis or Tamerlane, by the nobility of character, purity of purpose and piety of spirit. Their devoutness might have been fortified by superstition, but was not stained by hypocrisy. Their fanaticism was softened by generosity and sound common-sense. Their ambition was remarkably free from selfishness- Godliness, for them, was not a veil for greediness.

There are few figures in history more romantic, more devout, more sincere and more modest than the first "Commander of the Faithful" Abu Bakr. His memorable injunction to the "Army of God " ran: "Be just; the unjust never prosper. Be valiant; die rather than yield. Be merciful; slay neither old men, nor women, nor children.

Destroy neither fruit trees, nor grains, nor cattle. Keep your word even to your enemy. Molest not those men who live retired from the world." The irresistible march of the "Army of God" bears testimony to that this remarkable injunction was uttered sincerely by the venerable chief, and obeyed strictly by the devout followers.

Everywhere the Saracen invaders were welcome as deliverers by peoples oppressed, tyrannised and tormented by Byzantine corruption, Persian despotism and Christian superstition. Fanatically faithful to the revolutionary teachings of the Prophet, and obediently acting according to the noble, wise and eminently practical injunctions of the Caliph, the Saracen invaders easily enlisted the sympathy and support of the peoples they conquered. No invader can establish an abiding domination over conquered peoples, except with their active support or tacit toleration.

The second Caliph, Umar, whose impetuous horsemen had pushed their victorious march through the Persian Empire, to the distant banks of the Oxus, on the one side, and were masters of the second metropolis of the Roman world Alexandria-on the other, made his triumphal entry into Jerusalem on a camel which also carried the entire royal provision and equipage—a small tent of coarse hair, a bag of corn, a bag of dates, a wooden bowl, and a leathern flask of water. Gibbon offers the following account of the simplicity, devoutness, equity, and righteousness of the conquerors of Persia, Mesopotamia, Syria, Palestine and Egypt "Wherever he halted, the company without distinction was invited to partake of his homely fare, and the repast was consecrated by the prayer and exhortation of the Commander of the Faithful. But in expedition or pilgrimage, his power was exercised in the administration of justice; he reformed the licentious polygamy of the Arabs; relieved the tributaries from extortion and cruelty; and chastised the luxury of the Saracens by despoiling them of their rich silk, and dragging them on their face in dirt."

Khaled, whom the Prophet called the " Sword of God", whose almost legendary valour had united Arabia, Mesopotamia and Syria under the banner of Islam, died in the possession only of his horse, his arms, and a single slave. The great hero is credited to have declared in his youth, "it is not the delicacies of Syria, or the fading delights of this world, that have prompted me to devote my life in the cause of religion, I only seek the favour of God, and his apostle".

The valiant conqueror of Egypt, Umar, was distinguished by poetic genius in addition to martial valour. The following remarkable passage occurs in his report to Caliph Umar : "The crowds of husband men who blacken the land may be compared to a swarm of industrious ants; and their native indolence is quickened by the lash of the taskmaster. But the riches they extract are unequally shared between those who labour and those who possess." That was a view far in advance of time. The idea of social equity was unknown in all the lands of ancient civilisation. The toilers, either as waves or as Sudras, were object of contempt and exploitation. They were hardly considered as human beings. The economic principle; primitively formulated in the memorable injunction of the first Caliph, evolved out of the interest of the Arab traders, revolutionised the old social idea. A part of the wealth produced by the toiling masses, when left with themselves, becomes a powerful impetus to trade. In his administration of the conquered kingdom of the Pharaos and the Ptolemies, the Arab warrior sought with success to mend the glaring inequities that had offended his poetic vision. Egypt, robbed and despoiled for centuries -by the' Greeks and the Romans, prospered under the Saracens.

There is no end of testimonies to prove that even in the predominantly martial period of their history, the Saracens were far from being barbaric bands of fanatical marauders, spreading pillage and raping, death and destruction in the name of religion. Then, the period of conquest was short, as compared to the long era of, learning and culture that flourished subsequently under the patronage of the Caliphs as well as of the tributary and independent Empire. The military period terminated with the establishment of the Abbassides at Baghdad the "City of Peace" -just about a hundred years after the ascendancy of the Prophet at Medina. Since then, the military activities of the Arabs were essentially of the nature of current defensive and offensive operations of a far-flung Empire.

The stern enthusiasm of the Saracen warriors was softened by time and prosperity. They began to seek riches no longer in war, but in trade and industry; fame, not on the field of battle, but in the pursuit of science and literature; and happiness, no longer in the fanatical worship of one God and his only Prophet, but in the harmless enjoyment of social and domestic life. War was no longer the passion anal proud profession of the Saracens, because they had found interest and delight in a peaceful world created by the prowess of their forefathers. The progeny of the intrepid heroes, who had flocked to the belligerent standard of Abu Bakr and Umar, with the hope of paradise and incidentally earthly spoils, found the modest occupation of trade and industry more profitable, and science and philosophy more gratifying.

Three hundred years of peace, prosperity and progress elapsed before the martial valour of the Saracens was rekindled by Christian aggression in the deceptive form of the crusades. Pillage and plunder, tyranny and oppression came to be associated with Muslim conquests only after the power of the Saracens had been overwhelmed by the Mongol barbarians from Central Asia; Arab learning and culture had been corrupted by the degenerating luxury of the court; and the proud standard of Islam, having lost its original revolutionary lustre, had been prostituted in the rapacious hands of the Turks and the Tartars.

It is a gross misreading of history to confound Islam with militarism. Muhammad was the Prophet not of the Saracen warriors, but of the Arab merchants. The very name with which he baptised his creed contradicts the current notion about its aim. Etymologically, Islam means to make peace, or the making of peace : to make peace with God by doing homage to his Oneness, repudiating the fraudulent divinity of idols which had usurped His sole claim to the devotion of man; and to make peace on earth through the union of the Arabian tribes. Peace on earth was of immediate importance, and greater consequence. The temporal interest of the Arabian merchants required it; for, trade thrives better under peaceful conditions. Since decayed states and degenerated religions bred the germs of continued wars and perennial revolts, their destruction was a condition for peace. The creed of Muhammad made peace at home, and the martial valour of the Saracens conferred the same blessing on the peoples inhabiting the vast territories from Samarkand to Spain.

As soon as a country came under the domination of the Arabs, its economic life was quickened by the encouragement of industry and agriculture. The spirit and interest of the Arab traders determined and directed the policy of the Islamic State. In the Roman world as well as in all the other lands of antique civilisation, the ruling classes detested all productive labour, looked down upon trade and industry. War and worship were their noble professions. With the Arabs it was different. Nomadic life in a desert had taught them to appreciate labour as the source of freedom. With them trade was an honourable as well as a lucrative occupation of the free man. Thus, the Islamic State was based upon social relations entirely different from those of the old. Religion extolled industry, and encouraged a normal indulgence of nature. Trade was free, and as noble a profession as statecraft, war, letters and science. The Caliphs of Baghdad were not only great traders; the earlier ones learned, and actually practised some craft to purchase their personal necessities with the proceeds of manual labour. Most of the great Arab philosophers and scholars came from opulent trading families. The culture and refinement of the courts of Bokhara and Samarkand, the munificence of the Fatemite rulers of Africa and the splendour of the Sultans of Andalusia were equally produced rather by the profits of prosperous trade than by taxes extorted by despotic measures.

Under certain conditions, trade is a potent instrument of spiritual revolution. The aspiration of the Arab merchant produced the monotheism of Muhammad. This, in its turn, inspired the nomads of a desert to establish one of the vastest and most flourishing empires of history. The laws of the Koran revolutionised social relations. Increased production, the result of this revolution, quickened trade which ushered in an era of cosmopolitanism and spiritual uplift. Trade broadens the vision of man. Visiting distant lands, getting used to the sight of strange customs, mixing with peoples of diverse races, the trader frees himself from the prejudices and limitations born of the local conditions of his native land. He develops the capacities of toleration, sympathy and understanding for the habits, views and faiths of others. Observation and inquisitiveness, which guide his voyage on the unknown sea, or direct his steps in strange lands, kill in him the comfort of credulity. The growth of critical faculty places him at the gate of knowledge. The essence of his occupation teaches the trader to think in abstraction. He is not interested in his merchandise as such. His mind is occupied with the idea of profit. It is all the same to him, whether his camels or ships are laden with wool or corn or spices. He is concerned with something which is neither these nor other concrete things he handles. These are simply the means to attain his end—to make profit, which is a category abstracted from the concrete commodity he buys or sells. He appreciates things, not in their intrinsic value, but according to their capacity to produce profit.

Toleration for strange things, the attempt to understand them, freedom from prejudice, faculty of observation, ability to think in abstract—all these qualities acquired by the trader, thanks to the nature of his occupation, go into the making of a philosophical outlook. Having seen different Peoples cherish diverse forms of superstitions as divine, practise equally absurd rites and rituals or expressing devotion, extol prejudices to the dignity of eternal truth. The cosmopolitan mind of the travelled trader indulgently smiles upon the credulity of all, deplores their depravity equally, and respects the common element of faith beneath the superficial diversities of theological dogmas and forms of worship.

The main arteries of international trade of the mediaeval world ran through the countries which embraced Islam and were united in the Saracen Empire. The northern routes of trade with China, which passed through Constantinople to Italy and other countries of Western Europe, had become extremely risky owing to the Scythian inroads and the ruinous fiscal policy of the Byzantine Empire. After their conquest of Syria, Mesopotamia, Persia and the territories across the Oxus, the Arabs captured the Chinese trade and diverted it to pass through their domain of North-Africa and Spain, ultimately to reach the markets of Western Europe. During the eighth to the eleventh centuries, practically the entire trade between India and China, on the one hand, and Europe, on the other, was done by the Arabs. Thousands of traders travelled with their Caravans, loaded with precious cargoes, from the remote frontiers of China and

India all the way to Morocco and Spain. They were not persecuted or detested as their kind had been in all the countries of antique civilisation with the honourable exception of Greece. In the Empire of the Saracens, they belonged to the ruling class. Consequently, the learning and culture that thrived so luxuriantly owing to the prosperity of the Saracen Empire bore the stamp of their native broad-mindedness, cosmopolitanism and incredulity. Under the leadership of a martial aristocracy and jealous priesthood, human ideology takes the form of dogmatic faith or misty mysticism. Philosophy -the search for a rational explanation of the Universe-originates in a society ruled by an aristocracy engaged in trade. The city states of the Ionian Greeks were therefore the birth-place of philosophy.

Islam was a necessary product of history-an instrument of human progress. It rose as the ideology of a new social relation which, in its turn, revolutionised the mind of man. But just as it had subverted and replaced older cultures, decayed in course of time, Islam, in its turn, was also overstepped by further social developments, and consequently had to hand over its spiritual leadership to other agencies born out of newer conditions. But it contributed to the forging of new ideological instruments which brought about the subsequent social revolution. The instruments were experimental science and rationalist philosophy. It stands to the credit of Islamic culture to have been instrumental in the promotion of the ideology of a new social revolution.

Capitalist mode of production rescued Europe from the chaos of mediaeval barbarism. It fought and in the long run vanquished Christian theology and the spiritual monopoly of the Catholic Church with the potent weapon of rationalist philosophy. This weapon, invented by the ancient sages of Greece, came to the possession of the founders of modern civilisation through the Arab scholars who had not only preserved the precious patrimony, but added to it handsomely. The historic battle, begun by the nomads of the Arabian desert under the religious flag of Islam, was fought step by step through a thousand years on fields scattered over the three continents, to be won finally in Europe under the profane standard of the eighteenth century enlightenment and bourgeois revolution.

Holy Prophet's Proclamations

The founder of Islam has been characterised as "the man who, of all men, has exercised the greatest influence upon the human race". There was, however, nothing very extraordinary about the man until he claimed the credit of divine revelation. The foundation of that dubious claim was no more or no less fictitious than in the case of the prophets, apostles and saints of all other religions. Christian arrogance called the Arabian Prophet an "Impostor". But it has been forgotten that he was given that name together with Moses and Jesus. The authorship of the famous book, anonymously published *Three Impostors* which created sensation in Europe towards the close of the middle-ages, was attributed to the Christian King Frederic Barbossa as well as to the Muslim philosopher Averroes.

If Muhammad (PBUH) was an " impostor ", he did not take up that role any more consciously than others who appeared as instruments through which the fiction of divine revelation became a reality and carried conviction with the ignorant and superstitious masses. Having conceived the ideal of national unity, Muhammad realised that it could not be made acceptable to the warring Arabian tribes unless it were backed up with a supernatural sanction. People enjoying the bliss of ignorance and thinking in terms of preconceived notions, could not be convinced with any other argument. The will of minor gods could be overwhelmed by the will of a greater and all-powerful God. The protection against the wrath of the former could be found in the mercy of the latter. The belief in the absolute sway of one supreme God can alone encourage people to revolt against the tyranny of a whole host of tribal deities. If the supreme God was not there he had to be invented.

That was the chain of Muhammad's thoughts. There was no imposture in it. Did not the rationalist Voltaire put forward the same argument more than a thousand years after it had found favour with the Arabian Prophet? But in the latter case, the argument was put forward in defence of reaction; Voltaire advocated the necessity of inventing a God because that would be the only guarantee for the preservation of the decayed system of feudal monarchistic society. At the time of Muhammad, and under the circumstances it was advanced, the argument served a positively revolutionary purpose.

When man's mind is dominated by the belief in the supernatural, every progressive idea should be formulated in the terms of those beliefs if it were to secure popular support. Besides, the idea of One God was not the invention of Muhammad. The idea had grown out of social conditions described in the last chapter. Muhammad's mission was to discover evidence for the existence of One God. And if you wish to convince people you must adduce only that kind of evidence which can carry conviction to them.

But Muhammad's (PBUH) search for God was not inspired by cynicism as in the case of Voltaire. It was an honest effort on the part of an ignorant man inspired by a zeal. In quest of the God who alone could save the Arabian nation, he retired to the desert and gave himself up to meditation, fasting and prayer—those familiar practices adopted by the prejudiced seeking divine inspiration even in these days of the twentieth century. And the result was as usual in all such cases. " He was visited by supernatural appearances, mysterious voices accosted him as the Prophet of God; even the stones and trees joined in the whispering." Such experiences always result from cerebral disorder which takes place whenever the prescribed practices are carried too far. Fixed ideas, however fantastic or imaginary, may appear to take concrete form if the mind is focused on them so as to exclude the consciousness of other sensations. A scientific study of the psychology of seers reveals the fact that " inspiration " or any other " religious experience " is the result of a pathological state brought about either accidentally or purposely through prescribed practices.

Muhammad (PBUH) acted as all those of his kind had done before him, or did after him. But in his case, there was a fact which must go to his credit. He was too shrewd a man to be deluded by those psycho-pathological symptoms which are taken for the evidence of spiritual elevation. He was afraid that he was going mad; and might have abandoned his mission if his sagacious wife had not come to his aid in the nick of time. It was the rich merchant Khadija, mature with worldly wisdom, who was quick to appreciate the spiritual value of the mental aberrations of her husband. She persuaded him that his visions were not signs of insanity, but were messengers of God. Taking advantage of his psycho-pathological state of suggestibility, she could easily make him "see" an angel entering the room to deliver to him the Message of God. Undoubtedly, the drama could be enacted only in the setting of ignorance, superstition and prejudice, main characters being played under delusion. But that is how all religions are born. There is no reason to think that Islam was an exception. It was an exception in the sense that, except for the invention of a divine sanction, it contained less of religious dogmas and metaphysical speculation than sound political sense, progressive social principles and admirable codes of personal behaviour. "He did not engage in vain metaphysics, but applied himself to improving the social condition of his people by regulations respecting personal cleanliness, sobriety, fasting, prayer. Above all other works he esteemed alms giving and charity. With a liberality to which the world had of late become a stranger, he admitted the salvation of men of any form of faith-provided they were virtuous."

The Quran was not the work of an intellectual, and hence contains some dude ideas and fantastic speculations. These obvious defects of the Koran easily overshadow its great merit even as the source of inspiration of a great religion. But Muhammad's religion was rigorously monotheistic; and as monotheism it was uncompromising, which outstanding characteristic won for it the distinction of the highest form of religion. The idea of God is the foundation of religion in the philosophical sense. That idea cannot be free of all fallacies unless it leads to the conception of creation out of nothing. The rationalism of ancient philosophers of Greece as well as of India excluded the fantastic conception. Consequently, religions growing out of the background of that primitive rationalism could not conclusively establish the fundamental idea of God. The result was that all the great religions—Hinduism, Judaism and Christianity—eventually ended in one or other form of pantheism which logically liquidates religion as such. For pantheism identifying the phenomenal world with God puts the very idea of God under doubt. It disposes of the idea of creation and, consequently, the idea of God must also go. If the world can exist itself, from eternity, it is not necessary to assume a creator. And, deprived of the function of creation, God becomes an unnecessary postulate.

Muhammad's (PBUH) religion cuts the Gordian knot. It frees the idea of God from the embarrassment of primitive rationalism by boldly asserting the highly irrational idea of creation out of nothing. The God stands out in all his glory. The ability to create not only the whole world but an endless series of worlds is the token of his all-powerfulness. To have thus established the idea of God, albeit in a dogmatic and primitive manner, was the credit of Muhammad. For that credit he has gone down in history as the founder of the purest form of religion. Because Islam as a religion is irrationalism par excellence, it so easily triumphed over all other religions which, with all their metaphysical accomplishments, theological subtleties and philosophical pretensions, were defective as religions being but pseudo-religions.

Monotheism, however, is a highly subversive theory. While being itself the highest form of religion, it strikes at the root of the religious mode of thought. Placing God above and beyond the world, it opens up the possibility of doing without him altogether. Islam as the most rigorous monotheistic religion closed the chapter of human history dominated by the religious mode of thought, and by its very nature was open to unorthodox interpretations which eventually liquidated the religious mode of thought and laid the foundation of modern rationalism." We may compare the working of Monotheism to a mighty lake, which gathers the floods of science together, until they suddenly begin to break through the dam ..... The third of the great monotheistic religions, Muhammadanism, is more favourable to Materialism. This, the youngest of them, was also the first to develop, in connection with the brilliant outburst of Arabian civilisation, a free philosophical spirit, which exercised a powerful influence primarily upon the Jews in the middle ages, and so indirectly upon the Christians of the West." Being the most perfected form of Monotheism, Islam played that role. The crudities of the Koran did not prevent its basic idea from flourishing into all its revolutionary consequences.

His severe Monotheism contradicted Muhammad's claim to the sole Prophecy of God. While the Koran recognised Moses, Jesus and other Hebrew Prophets as apostles of God, Muhammad's claim, if not openly disputed in the beginning, was secretly doubted even among his associates. Divinity of its founder is not the fundamental creed of Islam. And that distinction results from its strict Monotheism. Immediately upon the death of Muhammad, his followers were divided on that crucial question. When the news of the Prophet's death reached the camp of the army setting out for the conquest of Syria, the devout Umar refused to believe that the Prophet could die, and threatened to strike off the head of the messenger whom he suspected to be an infidel. Upon that the venerable Abu Bakr admonished the impetuous younger man with the following words: "Is it Muhammad (PBUH) or his God that you worship? The God of Muhammad liveth for ever; but the apostle was a mortal like ourselves, and according to his own prediction, he has experienced the common fate of mortality."

It should be noted that the immediate successor of Muhammad, at the moment of his disappearance, called him an apostle, instead of the Prophet. With the less ambitious designation of an apostle, Muhammad was placed by his followers on the level of other religious teachers and lawgivers. Denial of the divinity of the Prophet made Islam the purest doctrine of Monotheism. Once divinity is conceded to a Prophet, before long he assumes the attributes supposed to belong only to the Supreme Being. The unity of God or the absoluteness of the First Principle can no longer be maintained logically. Dubious theological devices endeavour to reconcile the contradiction. The original simplicity of faith is lost either in theological dogmatism or mystical self-deception. Without the severity of its theology, Islam could not claim the historic role as creditably as it did. When the Prophet is deprived of divinity, or his claim to it is not generally admitted, the scripture cannot command absolute and infallible authority. Consequently, some latitude is left for the mind of the faithful. The teaching of a mortal cannot have the majesty of eternal truth, and scriptural laws cannot claim immutability.

Until the twelfth century, Islam did not possess a homogeneous body of dogmas. Subject to the belief in one God, the Mussulman had a practically unlimited latitude for his spiritual life. And history shows that the Arabian thinkers made free and full use of that flexibility of the new faith. In order to refute the Christian doctrine of Trinity, which they considered to be a vulgarisation of the sublime idea of the Supreme God,

Muslim theologists developed the fundamental idea of religion to the most abstract form ever conceived by human mind. They could perform that unparalleled feat of theological ratio-cination because "the Monotheism of Muhammad was the most absolute, and comparatively the freest from mythical adulterations".

The same authority testifies to the fact that the fundamental principles of religion laid down crudely by the founder of Islam were pregnant with the possibility of great development. And 'because of their rigid monotheistic nature, the development inevitably transcended the narrow limits of religious thought and culminated into a spiritual afloresence which closed the age of faith. "Even before the communication of Greek philosophy to the Arabians, Islam had produced numerous sects and theological schools, some of which entertained so abstract a notion of God that no philosophical speculation could proceed farther in this direction, whilst others believed nothing but what could be understood and demonstrated; ..... In the high school at Basra, there arose, under the protection of the Abbassides, a school of rationalists which sought to reconcile religion and faith."!

During the first five or six hundred years of its history, Islam produced not only scholars who occupied themselves more with heavenly bodies than with heavenly beings, who quietly set aside the Koran and placed greater spiritual value on the study of profane books, but revolutionary thinkers who ruthlessly sacrificed faith on the altar of reason. Not a few "Commanders of the Faithful" themselves-those who reigned at Baghdad, Cairo or Cordova until the eleventh century-attached greater value to positive knowledge than to revealed wisdom. The independent Empire of Bokhara preferred poets to the priests, doctors of medicine to doctors of divinity, and encouraged scientific research rather than the propagation of faith.

When we bear in mind that this line of intellectual development was opened up not only by the socio-political conditions created by the triumph of Islam, but originated in the central dogma of Muhammad's religion, neither the curiosities of the Koran nor the primitiveness of the Islamic faith should permit us to underestimate the historical role of Islam.

Basic Ideology

The age of Arabian learning lasted about five hundred years, and coincided with the darkest period of European history. During the same period, India also was lying prostrate, under the triumphant Brahmanical reaction which had subverted or corrupted Buddhism. Eventually, it was thanks to the inglorious success of having overcome the Buddhist revolution that India fell such an easy prey to Muslim invaders.

Under the enlightened reign of the Abbassides, the Fatmids and the Omminades rulers, learning and culture prospered respectively in Asia, North Africa and Spain. From Samarkand and Bokhara to Fez and Cordova, numerous scholars studied and taught astronomy, mathematics, physics, chemistry, medicine and music. The invaluable treasure of Greek philosophy and learning had been buried under the intolerance and superstition of the Christian Church. Had it not been for the Arabs, it would have been irretrievably lost, and the dire consequence of such a mishap can be easily imagined.

Vain piety and hypocritical holiness induced the Christians to spurn the science of antiquity as profane. In consequence of that vanity of ignorance, the peoples of Europe were plunged into the mediaeval darkness which threatened to be bottomless and interminable. The happy resurrection of the divine light of knowledge, lit by the sages of ancient Greece, at long last dissipated the depressing darkness of ignorance and superstition, prejudice and intolerance, and showed the European peoples the way to material prosperity, intellectual redress and spiritual liberation. It was through the Arabian philosophers and scientists that the rich patrimony of Greek learning reached the fathers of modern rationalism and the pioneer of scientific research, Roger Bacon, was a disciple of the Arabs. In the opinion of Humboldt, the Arabians are to be considered "the proper founders of the physical sciences, in the signification of the term which we are now accustomed to give it". Experiment and measurement are the great instruments with the aid of which they made a path for progress, and raised themselves to a position of the connecting link between the scientific achievements of the Greek and those of the modern time.

Al Kindi, Al Hassan, Al Farabi, Avicena, Al Gazali, Abu Bakr, Avempace, Al Phetragius, — the Arabian names are so contracted in historical works written in European languages — these are names memorable in the annals of human culture; and the fame of the great Averroes has been immortalised as that of the man who made the forerunners of modern civilisation acquainted with the genius Aristotle, thereby giving an inestimable impetus to the struggle of European humanity to liberate itself from the paralysing influence of theological bigotry and sterile scholasticism. The epoch making role of the great Arab rationalist, who flourished in the first half of the twelfth century under the enlightened patronage of the Sultan of Andalusia, is eloquently depicted by the well known saying of Roger Bacon: "Nature was interpreted by Averroes."

The standard of spiritual revolt against the authority of the Christian Church and the domination of theology, was hoisted in the thirteenth and fourteenth centuries. The rationalist rebels drew their inspiration from the scientific teachings of the great philosophers of ancient Greece, and these they learned from the Arabian scholars, particularly Averroes.

The bigotry of the pious Justinian, in the beginning of the sixth century finally purged the holy world of Christian superstition of the remaining vestiges of pagan learning. The last Greek scholars were forced to leave the ancient seats of learning. They emigrated from the Roman Empire, and sought refuge in Persia; but there also sacerdotal intolerance proved equally hostile to profane learning. Eventually, the derelict science of Athenian culture found a hospitable home in the court of the Abbassides Caliphs of Baghdad, who were so impressed by the wisdom of those foreign infidels that neither Quran nor sword was offered to them. On the contrary, all the remaining votaries of ancient learning, whose knowledge ridiculed faith and indulgently smiled at all religion, were invited to accept the liberal hospitality of the Commander of the Faithful.

The Caliphs not only took the exiled Greek scholars under their protection. They dispatched competent men to different parts of the Roman Empire with the instruction and the means to collect all the available works of the sages of ancient Greece. The precious works of Aristotle, Hipparchus, Hyppocrates, Galen and other scientists were translated into the Arabian language, and the Caliphs gave every encouragement to the propagation of those irreligious teachings throughout the Muslim world. Schools established at State expense disseminated scientific knowledge to thousands of students belonging to all classes of society, "from the son of the noble to that of the mechanic" Poor students received education free and teachers were handsomely remunerated for their services which were held in the highest esteem. The Arab historian, Abul Faragius, records the following views of Caliph Al Marion regarding the men of learning : "They are the elect of God, his best and most useful servants, whose lives are devoted to the improvement of their rational faculties ..... The teachers of wisdom are the true luminaries and legislators of a world which without their aid would again sink into ignorance and barbarism."

The current notion of the bigotry and fanaticism of Islam loses all historical authenticity when it is known that the men of learning so highly appreciated by the successors of the Prophet, were mostly devoid of any religious fervour, not a few of them holding views frankly heretical; and the general burden of their teachings was the assertion of the reason of mark as the only standard of truth. History does not provide the critical student with many instances of the head of a religious order encouraging the "improvement of rational faculties", as Caliph Al Manon did. For, the cultivation of rational faculties is entirely incompatible with faith. Yet, Al Manon was but one of the illustrious line of Abbassides Caliphs who not only encouraged the propagation of scientific knowledge, but themselves participated in it. Nor were the enlightened Abbassides an exception.

The Fatemites of Africa and the Omminades of Spain rivalled them in political power, material prosperity as well as in the patronage and propagation of knowledge. The library of Cairo contained over one hundred thousand volumes; whereas Cordova boasted of six times as many. This fact gives the lie to another calumny which depicts the rise of Islam as an eruption of savage fanaticism, namely, the tale of the destruction of the famous library of Alexandria. One must have a pious mind or credulous disposition to believe that those who took delight in founding and supporting such noble seats of learning, would have callously set fire to the library of Alexandria; that those who command the gratitude of mankind for having saved its most precious patrimony, could have possibly begun by contributing to the destruction of that treasure. When dispassionate and scientific study of history dissipates legends and discredits malicious tales, the rise of Islam stands out not as a scourge but a blessing for mankind.

While books written in the eleventh and twelfth century indignantly detail the shocking tale of the burning of the library of Alexandria, the historians Eustichius and Elmacin, both Egyptian Christians, who wrote soon after the Saracen conquest of their country are significantly silent about the savage act. The former, a patriarch of Alexandria, could be hardly suspected of partiality to the enemies of Christianity. An order of Caliph Umar has been usually cited as evidence of the barbarous act ascribed to his general. It would have been much easier not to record that order than to suppress any historical work composed by Christian prelates who had endless possibilities of concealing their composition. A diligent examination of all relevant evidence enabled Gibbon to arrive at the following opinion on the matter: "The rigid sentence of Umar is repugnant to the sound and orthodox precept of the Muhammadan Casuist; they expressly declare that the religious books of the Jews and Christians, which are acquired by the right of war, should never be committed to the flames, and that the works of profane scientists., historians or poets, physicians or philosophers, may be lawfully applied to the use of the faithful."

Since history began to be written with impartial criticism, the tale of the destruction of the Alexandrian library has either been discredited or subjected to grave doubt. In any case, at the time of the Saracen conquest, the library of Alexandria had ceased to be the repository of the valuable records of Greek learning. Long before that time, Alexandria had enshrined Christian bigotry in the place of scientific knowledge and philosophical wisdom. The character of the contents of the library must have changed accordingly. The pagan scholars, driven by Christian intolerance away from the seat of ancient learning, must have carried away the treasures they valued more than all other things. If the flame was actually lit by the order of Umar, it consumed ponderous tomes of theological controversy which had done immensely more harm than good to mankind. The fire of Islam might have consumed the none too precious records of vain and futile theological disputations; but the admirable ardour of the freethinking Caliphs collected, preserved and improved the valuable records of ancient learning, which had left the Alexandrian library before its useless and pernicious contents were put to the flames.

Byzantine barbarism had undone the meritorious work of the Ptolemies. The real destruction of the Alexandrian seat of learning had been the work of St. Cyril who defiled the Goddess of learning in the famous fair of Hyparia. That was already in the beginning of the fifth century. The Christian Saint would not tolerate that philosophical lectures and mathematical discourses held by a young pagan woman should be patronised by the elite of Alexandrian society, while the pious but incomprehensible sermons of the Archbishop were attended only by the rebels. If he was no match intellectually, he possessed the power to eliminate competition once for all. Under his instigation, the rebels, led by a regiment of monks burning with religious frenzy, attacked the seat of Alexandrian learning and, in the name of religion, perpetrated crimes too painful to be recorded and too shameful to be remembered.

"Thus, in the four hundred and fourteenth year of our era, the position of philosophy in the intellectual metropolis of the world was determined; henceforth, science must sink into obscurity and subordination. Its public existence will no longer be tolerated. Indeed, it may be said that from this period for some centuries it altogether disappeared. The leaden mace of bigotry had struck and shivered the exquisitely tempered steel of Greek philosophy. Cyril's act passed unquestioned. It was now ascertained that throughout the Roman world, there must be no more liberty of thought ..... Such assertions might answer their purposes very well so long as the victors maintained their power in Alexandria, but they manifestly are of inconvenient application after the Saracens had captured the city ..... For the next two dreary and weary centuries, things remained, until oppression and force were ended by foreign invaders. It was well for the world that the Arabian conquerors avowed their true argument, the scimitar, and made no pretensions to superhuman wisdom. They were thus left free to pursue knowledge without involving themselves in theological contradictions, and were able to make Egypt once more illustrious among the nations of the earth, to snatch it from the hideous fanaticism, ignorance and barbarism into which it had been plunged."

The works of the sages of ancient Greece were not only rescued, collected and preserved by the Arabs, they were profusely commented and improved upon. Complete works of Plato, Aristotle, Euclid, Appolonius, Ptolemy, Hyppocrates and Galen were available to the fathers of modern Europe at first only in Arabic versions, accompanied by erudite commentaries. Modern Europe learned from the Arabs not only medicine and mathematics. The science of astronomy, which widens the vision of man and reveals before him the mechanical laws of nature, was zealously cultivated by the Arabs. With the aid of new instruments of observation, Arab philosophers acquired exact knowledge about the circumference of the earth, the position and number of planets. In their hands, astronomy began to outgrow its primitive form, (deviations of astrology), cultivated more or less by the priests of all Oriental countries, and to develop into an exact science. Although algebra had been invented by Diophantus of Alexandria, it did not become an object of common study until the age of Arabic learning. As a matter of fact, the name of the science has given currency to the theory of its Arabian origin. But the Arabs themselves modestly acknowledged their indebtedness to the Greek master. Botany was studied for medical purposes; yet the discovery of two thousand varieties of plants by Dioscorides represented the birth of a new science. Alchemy was a secret, jealously guarded by the priests of ancient Egypt. It was also practised at Babylon. In a much later period, rudiments of chemistry were also known to the physicians of India. But the science of chemistry owes its origin and initial developments to the industry of the Arabs. They first invented and named the alembic for the purposes of distillation analysed the substances of the three kingdoms of nature; tried the distinction and affinities of alkalis and acids; and converted the precious minerals into soft and salutary medicine.

It was in the science of medicine that the Arabs made the greatest progress. Masua and Geber were worthy disciples of Galen, and substantially added to what they had learned from the great master; Avicena, born in distant Bokhara, in the tenth century, reigned in Europe as the undisputed authority of the medical science for five hundred years. The school of Salermo, until the sixteenth century, was the centre of medical learning in Europe. It owed its origin to the Saracens and taught the lessons of Avicena.

The distinctive merit of the Arab scholars was the zeal to acquire knowledge through observation. They discarded the vanity of airy speculation, and stood firmly on the ground known to them. That great merit of Arabian learning is decisively evidenced in the following view of its doyen Averroes: "The religion peculiar to philosophers is the study of that which is; for no sublimer worship can be given to God than the knowledge of his works, which leads to the knowledge of him and his reality. That is the noblest action in his eyes; the vilest is taxing, as error and vain presumption, the efforts of those who practise this worship, and who in this religion have the purest of religions." A religion which permitted the propagation of such irreligious views, though garbed in a pious phraseology, could not have its origin in intolerance and fanaticism. For this heterodox view, the philosopher, of course, incurred the wrath of the priesthood; but much more of the Christian than the Muslim.

After a short banishment, Averroes was restituted in his position in the court of the Sultan of Andalusia, and his books survived proscription in the Islamic world. But from their Latin version, the above and similar passages were expunged. Yet, the heretic movements of Europe, Burin; the twelfth, thirteenth and fourteenth centuries drew their inspiration from the suppressed teachings of the Arab philosopher; and it was the heretic movement that shook the foundation of the Catholic Church which had held Europe in spiritual subordination throughout the middle-ages. From the twelfth century onwards, until the triumph of modern learning, Averroeism was analogous to heresy in the horrified eyes of Christian holiness.

And it was not for nothing that it was so. For, the passage quoted above indicated the surest point of departure for the quest of positive knowledge which eventually cleared away the debris of ignorance, sanctified as faith, and glorified as virtue on the authority of theological dogmas.

In this passage, Averroes stated the basic principle of the inductive method-the surest way to true knowledge. If the preconceived notion of a creator is set aside, and if man is made to know him (as distinct from the blind faith in his existence) in his reality through the empirical knowledge of his works, that is, nature, the divine object recedes farther and farther, until it vanishes into nothingness, — the only demonstrable reality about his existence; and a religion which promoted that singular quest for the knowledge of God certainly represented the greatest advance of human ideology under the garb of religion. The latest of Great Religions, Islam was the greatest and as such destroyed the basis of all religions. That is the essence of its historical significance.

The centre of Islam and Arabic learning was in those very historical regions where the older civilisations of the Egyptians, Assyrians, Jews; Persians and Greeks had arisen, clashed and fallen. The positive outcome of those earlier civilisations went into the making of the Arabian culture, and the remarkable monotheism of Muhammad made its own the cardinal principles of the religion of those ancient peoples. It stands to the credit of the Arabian philosophers that they, for the first time, conceived the sublime idea of a common origin of all religions. Not only did they hold the view, singularly broad for the epoch, that all religions were so many efforts of the human mind to solve the great mysteries of life and nature; they went so much farther as to make the bold suggestion that the effort more reconcilable with reason was the greater, nobler and sublimer. This rationalistic view of religion attained the highest clarity in the mind of Averroes.

Thus, together with the invaluable metaphysical and scientific teachings of the sages of Athens and Alexandria, the Arabs contributed something original to the foundation of modern civilisation. It was scepticism-that powerful solvent of all faith. As soon as criticism challenges credulity, a new light dawns on the perspective of human progress. A curious book, anonymously published with the title *Three Impostors*, occupies a prominent place in the early history of scepticism in Europe. The credit for that scandalous composition was attributed either to the heretical Christian Emperor Frederic Barbossa, or the Muslim philosopher Averroes. The impostors were Moses, Christ and Muhammad. One of the suspected authors was a Christian and the other was a Mussalman. Religion certainly had fallen in bad days.

There had been scepticism before the thirteenth century, but no real incredulity. This doctrine and that had been disputed or rejected; but the foundation of Christian faith had never been touched. It was this foundation which was allied when the idea was conceived that all religions have a common ground. If all religions are essentially the same, then the doctrine and dogmas peculiar to each should be discarded as pernicious obstacles to the realisation of the spiritual unity of mankind. But freed from doctrines and dogmas, religion has no leg to stand upon. Its rationalisation amounts to its destruction. The revolutionary idea of the common origin of all religions was conceived for the first time by the Arab thinkers.

Although Arabian learning reached its climax in Averroes, he was but the greatest and the latest of a long succession of great thinkers and scholars; who flourished from the ninth to the thirteenth century. A brief reference to the substance of the teachings of the more illustrious of them will give some idea of the revolutionary significance of the learning which owed its origin to the cardinal principle of the Mohammedan religion, and was promoted by the staggering achievements of the " Sword of God ".

Having established unity, as the terrestrial reflection of their spiritual unitarianism, and promoted economic prosperity in consequence thereof, the new Islamic nation devoted itself to the culture of the mind. For a hundred years, it modestly learned from others, particularly the ancient Greeks. Thus equipped, it began to produce independent and original thought in every branch of learning.

Al Kindi was the earliest of the great Arabian philosophers. He flourished in the capital of the free thinking Abbassides, and leaped into fame in the beginning of the ninth century for teaching that philosophy must be based on mathematics; that is, it should cease to be idle speculation abstract thought should be guided by precise reasoning, based on concrete facts and established laws, in order to produce positive results. The teacher of this doctrine deserves the great distinction of having anticipated Francis Bacon and Descarters by seven hundred years as a forerunner of modern philosophy. Even today there are many " philosophers " and scholars who could be profited by the wisdom taught by the Saracen sage a thousand years ago.

Next to be mentioned is Al Farabi who lived in the following century, and taught at Damascus as well as Baghdad. His commentary on Aristotle was studied for centuries as an authoritative work on the subject. He also excelled in the medical science. Roger Bacon learned mathematics from him.

In the latter half of the tenth century appeared Avicena. He belonged to a rich landowning family of Bokhara engaged in prosperous trade. He wrote on mathematics and physics, but went down in history for his 'contributions to the medical science. The famous medical school of Salermo was a monument to his memory, and his work was the text book of medicine throughout Europe until the sixteenth century. The great physician's philosophical views were so unorthodox that even the free-thinking Emir of Bokhara could not resist the pressure of the Imams who were scandalised by the profanity of Avicena. He had to leave the court of his patron, and travelled all over the Arabic Empire teaching medicine and preaching his philosophy at different seats of learning.

In the eleventh century lived Al Hassan who deserves a place among the greatest scientists of all ages. Optics was his special subject. Having learned it from the Greeks, he went farther than they, who corrected their mistaken notion that the rays of light issue from the eye. By anatomical and geometrical reasoning, Al Hassan proved that the rays of light came from the object seen, and impinged on the retina. There is ground for belief, held by many historians of science, that Keppler borrowed his optical views from his Arab predecessor.

In the same century also lived Al Gazali, son of an Andalusian merchant. He anticipated Descartes in reducing the standard of truth to self-consciousness. He stands out as the connecting link between the antique and modern scepticism. His memorable contribution to philosophy is better stated in his own words : "Having failed to get satisfaction from religion, I finally resolved to discard all authority, and detach myself from opinions which have been instilled in me during the unsuspecting years of childhood. My aim is simply to know the truth of things; consequently it is indispensable for me to ascertain what is knowledge. Now, it was evident to me that certain knowledge must be that which explains the object to be known in such a manner that no doubt can remain, so that in future all error and conjecture respecting it must be impossible. Thus, once I have acknowledged ten to be more than three, if any one were to say: 'On the contrary, three is more than ten, and to prove my assertion I will change this stick into a serpent'; and if he actually did the miracle, still my conviction of his error would remain unshaken. His manoeuvre would only produce in me admiration for his ability, but I should not doubt my own knowledge."

The principle of acquiring exact knowledge, stated nearly a thousand years ago, by the Muslim savant, still holds as good as then; and the scientific outlook which makes such knowledge possible, is still comparatively rare among Indians, who even in these days of the twentieth century allow themselves to be imposed by feats of magic and "spiritual" charlatanism, and credit these as serious challenge to the reliability of scientific knowledge.

Al Gazali held that knowledge could not possess such mathematical exactness, unless it were acquired empirically, and governed by irrefrangible laws established by experience. He was of the opinion that incontestable conviction could be acquired only through sense perception, and necessary truth, that is, causality. In reason (self-consciousness) he found the judge of the correctness of the perception of senses. One is amazed to find such unique boldness of thought in the atmosphere of a religion generally believed to be the most intolerant and fanatical. Yet, Al Gazali's scepticism was avidly studied throughout 'the Muslim world of his time. His place in the history of philosophy can be judged from the opinion of the famous French Orientalist Renan, who thought that the father of modern scepticism, Hume, did not say anything more than what had been said by the Arab philosopher who preceded him by seven hundred years. The immensity of the historical significance of Al Gazali's views is appreciated still more clearly when we remember that it was the scepticism of Hume which gave impetus to Kant's " all shattering critical philosophy " that laid a cruel axe at the root of all speculative thought. But Al Gazali's views were a long way ahead of time. Experimental science, as he visualised, was not yet possible. In the absence or infancy of technology, the nature of objects could not be so mathematically ascertained as the philosophers wished. Therefore, in his later years, Al Gazali fell into mysticism; but his fall was no more strikingly inglorious than that of Kant. Objective drawback clipped the intrepid wings of the soaring spirit of the Arab thinker; whereas subjective predilection overwhelmed the critical genius of Kant.

Abu Bakr, who lived in the twelfth century, was the first astronomer to reject the Ptolemic notion regarding the position of heavenly bodies. He conceived of a planetary system and celestial motion, which tended towards the epoch-making discoveries of Giordano Bruno, Galileo and Copernicus. It is recorded that " in his systems all movements were verified, and therefore no error resulted". Abu Bakr died before setting forth his theory in a complete treatise. His pupil, Al Phetragius, popularised his teaching that all planetary bodies moved regularly. Throughout the middle-ages, the hypothesis was valued as a great contribution to astronomical knowledge. The teachings of a Muslim philosopher, which upset the biblical view of the Universe, penetrated the Christian monasteries. Not only Roger Bacon, but his illustrious opponent, Albertus Magnus, also acknowledged the indebtedness to the astronomical work of Al Phetragius in which Abu Bakr's views on planetary movement were expounded.

The basic principle of the philosophy of Averroes, the greatest and the latest of the great Arabian thinkers, have already been outlined. He lived at the turning point of the history of the Islamic culture. By the twelfth century, the pinnacle had been reached, and the forces of reaction had gathered strength to overwhelm those of progress. Islamic culture was already on the decline.

The freedom of thought permitted by the simple faith of a nomadic people had attained such soaring heights of boldness as eventually clashed with .the temporal interests of the "Commanders of the Faithful". When the positive outcome of Islamic thought developed so marvellously during five hundred years, was summarised in the highly revolutionary dictum of Averroes, that reason is the only source of truth, Sultan Al Masur of Cordova, under the pressure of the priests, issued an edict condemning such heretical views to hellfire, on the authority of religion. The denunciation of the - noblest product of Islam naturally marked the beginning of its degeneration from a powerful lever of human progress to an instrument of reaction, intolerance, ignorance and prejudice. Having played out its historic role-to rescue the precious patrimony of ancient culture out of the engulfing ruins of two Empires and the blinding darkness of two religions-Islam turned traitor to its original self, and became the black banner of Turkish barbarism and of the depredations of the Mongolian hordes.

Islam disowned its own. Averroes was driven away from the court of Cordova—the home of free thought for centuries. His books were condemned to the flames, not actually of fire, but of the more merciless sacerdotal reaction. Rationalism came to be identified with heresy. The very names of Averroes and his master, Aristotle, became anathema. In course of time, reaction triumphed so completely that for an orthodox Mohammedan, philosophy stood for " infidelity, impiety, and immorality". But the standard of spiritual progress, admirably held high, and boldly carried forward by the Arabs during five hundred years, could not be lowered and trampled under the fury of vain religiosity any more successfully by Islamic intolerance than previously by Christian piety and superstition. Averroes was disowned by his own people, only to be enthroned by those to whom belonged the future. The fierce contest between faith and reason, between despotic ignorance and freedom of thought, which rocked Europe and shook the foundation of the Catholic Church from the twelfth century onwards, drew inspiration from the teachings of the Arab philosophers. Averroes and Averroeism dominated the scientific thought of Europe for four hundred years.

3

Basis of Belief

The Holy Book

The first source of Islamic law is the Holy Quran which is the revelation of Allah and the Book in which His Message to mankind is contained. It is the word of Allah revealed to Prophet Muhammad (PBUH) through the angel Jibbrail. It is the foundation of Islamic Law and a Book of exalted power.

The Quran contains a set of moral and juridical injunctions which are the basis of Islamic law and which concern the life of human beings in every detail.

The early revelations received in Mecca deal largely with questions of beliefs and morals. It was later, after the Prophet's (PBUH) migration to Medina when Muslims lived in an organised society that the principles regarding contracts, succession, crime, constitutional law and international law were revealed. Many of these revelations were very short. The principle contained in a simple sentence could be the foundation on which a whole structure of law could be built, for example:

> "Give full measure when you measure and weigh with a balance that is straight." (17: 35)

> "Those who unjustly eat up the property of orphans eat up afire into their own bodies." (4: 10)

The place of the Holy Quran as a source of law is due to its being a source of guidance not only to the spiritual good of the Hereafter but also towards the spiritual, physical and social good attainable in this world. It attends to minimum details for the refinement of the individual or for peaceful and congenial relations among human beings. It calls for lowering the voice when talking and modesty in walking. In order not to accumulate wealth in a few hands and to avoid disputes and quarrels, a fair plan is provided for the distribution of wealth left behind by a deceased person. Human dignity is to be respected, injustice even to an enemy is prohibited and the rights and properties of others are to be protected. Parents are instructed to inculcate in their children Islamic virtues and good manners. Children have to treat their parents with reverence, obedience and tenderness. A ruler is to be aware of his duties and responsibilities. He is to be obeyed for the smooth running of the State and for peace and tranquillity.

The Quranic law is everlasting and perpetual. It does not change with the passage of time. It should be studied with the object of acting in accordance with its teachings and moulding our lives accordingly.

The Quran is addressed to the entire humanity, above all barriers and limitations of race, religion and time. It contains directives for the head of the state as well as a common person, for the rich as well as the poor, for peace as well as for war, for spiritual as well as material prosperity. Its laws guide human beings to perfection. It appeals to the reason of man and invites him to exercise his purpose in life.

Compilation of Quran : The task of recording the revelations received by the Holy Prophet (PBUH) was undertaken during his lifetime. He entrusted the duty of recording the Quran in writing to a number of his companions particularly the four Caliphas and Zaid bin Sabit, Khalid bin Walid, Sabit bin Qais etc. Whenever a chapter or a verse was revealed, it was written down. The Holy Prophet (PBUH) also indicated the proper place of a verse in a relevant chapter. One of his companions had reported: One day I was sitting in the company of the Holy Prophet (PBUH). During my presence, the Holy Prophet (PBUH) raised his eyes to the sky and then lowering them said:

> "Jibbrail had come to inform me of the proper place of the verse. "

The arrangement of the chapters was done by the prophet himself, under Divine guidance. In this way the Quran was recorded in scriptural form and learnt by heart during the lifetime of the Holy Prophet (PBUH).

The Quran was written on thin and flat tablets of stone, wood, branches of palm trees, bones of camels and goats and on pieces of leather. It was not compiled in a book form during the lifetime of the Holy Prophet (PBUH). According to the scribe Zaid bin Sabit:

> "The Holy Prophet (PBUH) departed from this world and the Quran had not been collected and compiled on anything so far."

The work of recording the text of the Quran in writing was, therefore, completed during the Prophet's (PBUH) lifetime but not its compilation. After the death of the Holy Prophet (PBUH) his companions felt the necessity to collect and compile the text of the Quran. Hadrat Abu Bakr, the first Calipha in consultation with Hadrat Umar undertook this noble task, which was completed during his rule and under his supervision. A large number of people who had learnt the Quran by heart had died in the battle of Yamama. Hadrat Umar therefore pointed out to Hadrat Abu Bakr that if more people who had memorised Quran died in future battles, Muslims would be deprived of a great part of the Quran. He suggested that the Quran should be compiled. Hadrat Abu Bakr however, hesitated and said that he would not do the job left undone by the Holy Prophet (PBUH). Hadrat Umar argued that under the circumstances the compilation of the Quran had become an absolute necessity. According to Hadrat Abu Bakr:

> "Umar went on persuading me to accept his suggestion till I was convinced that he was right so I accepted his suggestion."

Hadrat Abu Bakr then directed Zaid bin Sabit to collect the Quranic verses from every part of the Islamic Empire and compile them into book form. Zaid expressed his feelings in these words:

> "By Allah, if I had been asked to uproot a mountain and put it in another place it would not have been so

> hard a task for me as the compilation of the Holy Quran. I objected why Abu Bakr and Umar wanted a thing done, which was left undone by the Holy Prophet (PBUH). But Abu Bakr insisted that getting the Quran compiled was necessary. He persuaded me every now and then till my opinion also changed and became identical with that of Abu Bakr and Umar. I started the work and traced out and collected the Quran from every corner and every person who was in possession of any part of it. I collected it from palm leaves, white stones, small pieces of wood and people who had committed it to memory."

Zaid bin Sabit was not content just finding a written piece of the Quran. He also verified it from those people who had heard it from the Holy Prophet (PBUH) and committed it to memory. Though Zaid himself was a Hafiz of the Quran, he always tried to find a verse in writing before including it in his manuscript, so that the version of the Quran he recorded was the one heard from and written under the supervision of the Holy Prophet (PBUH).

The script prepared by Zaid remained with the first Calipha and after his death was transferred to the custody of Hadrat Umar. After the death of Hadrat Umar, this script was transferred to Hadrat Hafsa.

Imam Bukhari has narrated on the authority of Anas that after the conquest of Syria and Iraq, the people of these countries recited the Quran in different ways. This disturbed Hadrat Anas who went to Hadrat Uthman and requested him to take immediate action for the removal of these differences, otherwise it might create rifts among the Muslims.

Accordingly, Hadrat Uthman acquired the copy of the Quran prepared by Hadrat Zaid bin Sabit, from Hadrat Hafsa and appointed scribes to make copies of it. Copies of the Quran were prepared and sent to the capital city of every province of the Muslim state. Hadrat Uthman also ordered that all existing copies of the Quran with the exception of the authentic ones be burnt. Thus, the Quran that is being read now is the same as in the time of Hadrat Abu Bakr. Nothing has been deleted or added to it. The arrangement of the chapters and verses is the same as ordered by the Holy

Prophet (PBUH), in accordance with instructions received from Hadrat Jibbrail.

The fact that the Holy Prophet (PBUH) used to recite the Quran by this very arrangement has been established by traditions reported from him through different people. It also stands established by the opinion of the companions that the present form of compilation and arrangement of the Quran is the same as that ordered by the Holy Prophet (PBUH) under Divine guidance.

The Guide

> It is no new tale of fiction, but a confirmation of previous scriptures, and an explanation of all things, and a guidance and mercy to those who believe.
>
> (Quran: Sura 12: III Joseph)

Three voices God Loves:

The voice of the cock

The voice of one reading the Quran

The voice of one seeking pardon in the early morning.

Tradition of the Prophet Muhammad

Quoted by Al-Ghazzali:

The guide on the road of life is the Holy Quran.

The revelations that came to the Prophet Muhammad were written down by his Companions, put in order under his instructions, and finally compiled by the third Caliph 'Uthman, less than ten years after the Prophet's death. The text is exactly the same now as it was then.

In one book it ranges the whole of life: the worship of God, the nature of man, and the way he should live. It gives both a portrait of creation and instructions by which the individual, the family and the community should conduct their affairs.

The western reader, faced with an English "interpretation", finds himself at a disadvantage. The transition from the original has stripped away its beauty. The unsurpassed music of its language is gone - and the Quran is meant to be *heard.* The vivid word pictures it paints raise no such response as they do in the mind of an Arab reader. Moreover, while it is divided into chapter *(sura)* and verse, it does not provide a sequence easy to read or to tabulate. It calls for an effort of imagination and study which is difficult to make. The orthodox view that the Quran cannot be translated becomes quickly understandable to anyone who tries to enter into the truth and the experience it conveys.

Nevertheless, from early times the effort at interpretation has been essential for Muslims whose language is other than Arabic. It is the duty of every Muslim to read, and to the best of his ability to understand, the Holy Book. For example, a manuscript centuries old, in the library of Aligarh Muslim University, shows a Persian commentary painstakingly written under the Arabic text in Mughal times. In Istambul, the "Book Market" has numbers of editions on sale - some of them having the original Arabic transliterated into the modern Turkish script, with a version in Turkish alongside. Translations are appearing in languages ranging from Swahili to Russian and Chinese, including the European languages, with the aim of bringing the Quran to believer and unbeliever alike.

Language of the Quran : The language of the Quran, with its dignity, its rhythm, its range and the depth of its meaning, is to the Muslim a part of the miracle of its revelation.

In the remote deserts and tribal communities of Arabia, a rich linguistic vehicle developed, ready to carry a prophetic message to millions and to become the means of expression of a great civilisation.

The Arabic language is built on simple three-letter "roots" which each convey a basic idea and which are developed into an intricate pattern of words covering many shades of meaning. There are only about a thousand of these roots. Human personality enters into each original concept: acting, demanding, cooperating, suffering, seeking and being sought, intense or relaxed. The result is a structure that gives infinite flexibility.

Many of these roots are common to all the Sematic languages. Before Muhammad's day they had already served mankind well, as the linguistic basis of the early Mesopotamian civilisation, and as the means of expressing the grandeur of Old Testament prophecy. In Arabia the development of language was far richer and more complex. Pre-Islamic poetry used words that convey heroism, joy and sorrow, deep feelings and high ideals — words that were there prepared and ready to carry the inspiration of the Prophet of Arabia to the world.

The dynamic of Arabic is still active. The same original roots are being used to serve the needs of modern science and technology. And while colloquial speech diverges, the classical Arabic - simplified, but in essence the language of the Quran - is heard and understood all over the Arab World. It is the vehicle of radio, television and cinema, and is read in newspapers that may be bought on the streets of any world capital.

What the Quran means to a practising Muslim is explained here by two scholars, one a political scientist and the other a sociologist.

Muslim Lives by the Quran : "The Muslim lives by the Quran," says Professor Yusuf K. Ibish, Professor of Islamic Political Theory and Institutions in the American University of Beirut. He comes from Damascus, has a Harvard Ph.D., and is a trusted authority on Sufism.

I have not yet come across a western man who understands what the Quran is. It is not a book in the ordinary sense, nor is it comparable to the Bible, either the Old or New Testaments. It is an expression of Divine Will. If you want to compare it with anything in Christianity, you must compare it with Christ Himself. Christ was the expression of the Divine among men, the revelation of the Divine Will. That is what the Quran is. If you want a comparison for the role of Muhammad, the better one in that particular respect would be Mary. Muhammad was the vehicle of the Divine, as she was the vehicle. His illiteracy was comparable with her virginity, symbolic of purity. There are western orientalists who have devoted their life to the study of the Quran, its text, the analysis of its words, discovering that this word is Abyssinian, that word is Greek by origin. The Bible and other literary works have also been subjected to this treatment. But all this is immaterial. The Quran was divinely inspired, then it was compiled, and what we have now is the expression of God's Will among men. That is the important point.

One has to make an effort to understand. Like the bride behind the veil the Holy Quran does not lend itself easily to the seeker. You can read it as you would read any book, and you will gather certain things from it. But to grasp its message truly, you have to penetrate from the external appearance to the inner reality, from the exoteric to the esoteric meaning. It is a two-level process, and of course one needs the guidance of those who know.

The Muslim lives by the Quran. From the first rituals of birth to the principal events of life and death, marriage, inheritance, business contracts: all are based on the Quran. A man can live and die decently if he seeks inspiration from the Quran. Most people from outside look on it as a small book containing limited instruction about conduct and life. This is not so. There are guiding principles, and you can unfold any number of valid interpretations.

Professor Yusuf Ibish, Beirut

Motivator of Thought : Dr. Ali Issa Uthman is one of a Palestinian family coming from a village near Jerusalem, one of those divided by the armistice-line of 1948. He was educated in Chicago, where he took a Doctorate in Sociology. He was for some years Adviser to UNRWA on Education, and in particular on social studies. His book, *The Concept of Man in Islam, in the writings of Al-Ghazzali,* was published in Cairo in 1960. He says:

> The Quran is organic in ideas - not in structure. Get away from the idea of a book that starts and develops. When you have read it all, then you have everything. You can pick it up and start reading it anywhere.

It appeals to common people as well as scholars. My mother is illiterate and she has an enjoyment of the Quran that I perhaps do not have the music of it. My understanding can get in the way. She and my father always used to pray. They were disturbed if they could not get their ablutions done in time to pray the evening prayer before the sun set, or if ever they slept after the sun had risen. As a child, I used to open my eyes every morning in our Palestine village and see them at prayer. The younger generation who have been to school know and understand the words, but miss the feeling my parents had.

We cannot see Muslim thought in the right perspective unless we appreciate and understand the Quran as a motivator of thought and an end of knowledge. Without such understanding, the student of Muslim thought must continue to work in the dark. It is in the direct impact of the Quran on the Muslim mind that we may discover those unwritten, but perhaps most important and fundamental, orientations towards truth and human ends. In these orientations lie the Muslims' general sense of history and change, their peculiar sense of time, and their peculiar sense of purpose in seeking knowledge.

Truth in itself and outside man's knowledge does not have a biography of development. Only the individual's understanding of it has. Thus there is permanence in truth and change in understanding. The history of Muslim thought in general cannot be fully understood by an "evolutionary" approach to the history of ideas. The truth which is essential for happiness is supposed by Muslims to be all there and complete - in the Quran and the *Sunna,* (the tradition and practice of the Prophet).

Dr. Ali Issa Uthman, Palestine and Beirut

Towards Understanding the Quran : One of the most influential Twentieth Century commentaries on the Quran is that by Sayyid Abul Ala Mawdudi (1903-1979). Written in Urdu, this massive work of scholarship was produced in the midst of the struggles for independence and the early years of Pakistan. It is entitled *Tafhim Al-Quran* (Towards Understanding the Quran). He undertook the task in 1941 and completed it in 1973, six volumes and thirty years later, strenuous years of leadership and controversy. A full English translation is appearing.

The following extracts from Mawdudi's Preface are taken from *Translations from The Quran,* made on the basis of Mawdudi's work by Altaf Gauhar, author and Editor-in-Chief of *South* magazine and *Third World Quarterly,* published from London. "These translations were undertaken at a time when the only book to which I had access was the Quran," he says.

Tafhim al-Quran is not a literal translation of the original text. It is an attempt to present the meanings of the Quran in plain language keeping the historical perspective in view. The Quran speaks to you in the language of life, vividly and melodiously: by comparison the language of translation is a poor echo of the glorious original one is left cold and begins to wonder whether this is indeed the Book which has no equal.

The Quran is great literature as it is great instruction. Its words go straight to the heart and it is this quality which, like a crack of lightning, shook the length and breadth of Arabia.

The Quran presents an arrangement which is completely contrary to our expectations. We find beliefs, precepts, orders, criticisms, warnings, promises, arguments, evidence, historical illustrations and references to natural phenomena following one another in rapid succession without any apparent regard for logic ... It talks of the origin of man, the structure of the earth and the heavens ... It recalls the beliefs and criticizes the conduct of different nations, analyses metaphysical problems and refers to many other things. The object however is not to give lessons in metaphysics, philosophy, history or any other science, but to remove misunderstandings about reality ... to acquaint (man) with the result of actions which conflict with its underlying principles.

Whether one is a believer or not, as a rational person one must read this book *by* taking into account the fundamental assumptions made in the book itself, and by the Prophet who presented it to the world.

Holy Quran and the Prophets : No less than eight chapter headings in the Quran recall figures in the Old and New Testaments. Moses and Jesus, founders of Judaism and Christianity, are prophets like Muhammad with the title of *Rasool* (apostle), greater than *nabi* (announcer).

In the course of the Quran, David and Solomon receive no less than thirty-three mentions, and Nuh appears some thirty times, as well as heading a chapter. The Sura of Joseph is the longest narrative given. Jonah, "the Man of the Fish", and Sheba, whose famous Queen visits Solomon, are both names of Suras.

Many of the stories are allusive rather than narratory. Evidently the facts were well known to the hearers, and the commentators fill in the details. Some of the information given is found in Jewish sources other than the Old Testament, and in the case of Jesus in the Apocryphal Gospels. The lives of the prophets were current knowledge in Muhammad's day, as they have continued to be throughout the Muslim world.

In one chapter of the Quran (Sura *6:* 83-86 *Cattle)* eighteen prophets are named. The authoritative modern commentary by Abdullah Yusuf Ali analyses these in four groups. They cover, he says, the great teachers accepted among the three religions based on Moses, Jesus and Muhammad. First come Ibrahim, Ishaq and Jacob. Then follow those who "led active lives and are called 'doers of good'." These are Nuh, David and Solomon, Job and Joseph, Moses and Aaron. In contrast, the next group were not men of action but preachers of truth who led solitary lives. They include Zachariah and his son John (the Baptist), Jesus and Elias (Elijah), and their designation is "the righteous". Finally come four who were concerned in the clash of nations, and who through conflict and personal misfortune kept to the path of God: Ismail, Elisha, Jonah and Lot.

The chapter headed *The Prophets* (Sura 21) has a similar passage. Elsewhere over and over again the historic sequence is repeated - a warning, followed by either repentance or destruction, as God sends His messengers to one nation after another. The view of history in the Muslim mind is a prophetic one.

According to the Quran, the succession of prophets has been completed — sealed — by the mission of Muhammad. The truth necessary for man to live by has been revealed. There is no need for more. But if men do not presume to claim the stature of the prophets, there is still plenty of scope for humbly following their example. Muhammad's own constant emphasis that he was only a man like other men lays stress on the responsibility carried by all believers.

Here is one of many passages which show the heritage of prophetic inspiration common to Muslim, Jew and Christian.

We inspire thee [Muhammad] as We inspired Nuh and the prophets after him, as We inspired Ibrahim and Ismail and Ishaq and Jacob and the tribes, and Jesus and Job and Jonah and Aaron and Solomon, and as We imparted unto David the Psalms; And messengers We have mentioned unto thee before, and messengers We have not mentioned unto thee; and Allah spake direct unto Moses;

> Messengers of good cheer and of warning, in order that mankind might have no argument against Allah after the messengers. Allah was ever Mighty, Wise.
> (Quran: Sura 4: 163-165)

Prophet's Traditions

The Prophet (PBUH) as the founder of Islam and the messenger of Allah's revelation to mankind is the best interpreter of the Book of Allah and his Hadith and the Sunnah; his sayings and actions are, after the Quran, the most important source of Islamic law.

The word *Sunnah* means literally a manner of acting, a rule of conduct, a mode of life. Applied to the life of the Prophet (PBUH), this meant, therefore, a rule deduced from the sayings or conduct of the Prophet. Such sayings and conduct could take the form of an utterance of the Prophet (PBUH) an action or practice of the Prophet (PBUH), or the approval by the Prophet (PBUH) of the action or practice of someone else.

The Holy Quran being the word of Allah, treats major issues and often deals with subjects in brief terms, leaving the details to be explained by the Holy Prophet (PBUH) of Allah. It says:

> "—-and We have sent down unto thee the Message: that thou mayest explain clearly to men what is sent for them." (16:44)

In the Quran we are commanded to pray and pay *Zakat,* but there is no explanation of the frequency of prayers or the number of Rakat in each prayer. Neither is there an explanation given as to the amount on which the duty of *Zakat* applies or the percentage which has to be paid. All these details were learnt either from the Prophet's deeds or words or from both. The Holy Quran commands that we should be good to our neighbour; a number of *Ahadith* further stress this duty. The same applies to many other situations; hence the vital connection between the Quran and the practice and sayings of the Prophet (PBUH).

Many verses of the Holy Quran deal with questions of law but not all the injunctions of the Shariah are clearly stated in it. There are many statements which needed further explanations before they could become guides for human actions. This explanation and clarification was provided by the Holy Prophet (PBUH) who himself participated in the formation of the Shariah.

When the Islamic commonwealth was founded in Medina in 622 A.D., the Prophet was not only the spiritual leader but also the supreme judge of the Islamic community. Cases would be referred by his followers to the Prophet (PBUH) for his judgement. The underlying principle applied was the word of Allah from the Quran; but if the Quran was silent, or needed interpretation, the Prophet (PBUH), as the messenger of Allah would be the authority for reaching a decision.

The Holy Quran itself commands that the Prophet's (PBUH) teachings should be obeyed. It says:

> "So take what the Messenger assigns to you, and deny yourselves that which he withholds from you."
> (59:7) .

It also says:

> "He who obeys the Messenger obeys Allah."(4: 80)

The Quran frequently commands:

> "O ye who believe ! obey Allah and obey the Messenger." (4: 59)
>
> "Obey Allah and obey His Messenger. "
> (3: 32, 5: 92, 64: 12)

Thus, after the Quran, the Prophet's (PBUH) *Sunnah* and *Hadith* are the most precious sources of guidance which Islamic society possesses and along with the Quran, they are the fountainhead of all Islamic laws and thought.

The Prophet (PBUH) was a *Nabi* and a *Rasool* who brought the cycle of Prophecy to an end. So, after him there will be no new *Shariah* or Divine Law brought into the world until the end of time.

Compilation of Hadith : Tradition in Arabic means Sunnah or Hadith. The difference between the two is that while Sunnah indicates the doings of the Holy Prophet (PBUH), Ahadith indicates his sayings.

The word *Hadith* is derived from 'Tahdis' which means to inform. There is another finding by the researchers of the word

Hadith. According to them, this word is derived from a root which means to be new or modern, the opposite of which is ancient. Thus, by ancient is meant the Holy Quran and by new or modern is meant the *Hadith* of the Holy Prophet (PBUH). It is reported by Abdullah bin Masud that the Holy Prophet (PBUH) had said:

> "Only two things carry importance, one is speech and the other is the method of action. So the words of Allah are the best of speech and the best method is the deeds of the Holy Prophet (PBUH)."

From the beginning of the birth of Islam, Muslims were interested in what the Holy Prophet (PBUH) said and did. After his death, when Islam had spread widely, new converts wanted to hear about him from his Companions and close associates. These people were the best authority for a knowledge of *Hadith* as they had listened to the Prophet (PBUH) and witnessed his actions. Thousands of Companions adhered to the Prophet's commandment:

> "Preach what you hear me say. Also let those who see and hear me, take upon themselves to communicate my words to others and preach to their children, relatives and friends."

The Companions therefore considered it their duty to preach the Traditions of the Prophet (PBUH) to those who had not seen and listened to him. After their death, Muslims had to rely on the communications of the successors, people of the first generation after Prophet Muhammad (PBUH) who had received their information from the Companions, and in the following generations, with the accounts of the "successors of the successors", that is, people of the second generation who had been associated with the successors and so on.

In those days, to recite and to memorize the Traditions was considered to be a great privilege. They were preserved in writing as well. In due course of time, a great amount of *Hadith* literature was collected.

Some writers headed by William Muir and Goldzhier put forth the argument that the collection and compilation *of Ahadith* was started some ninety years after the death of the Holy Prophet (PBUH). However, there is ample testimony to the fact that such records existed much earlier. During the time of the Holy Prophet (PBUH) and his Companions, more than ten thousand *Ahadith* were collected out of which 5,374 were attributed to Abu Hurrayrah. It has been verified from different sources that Abu Hurrayrah used to write down what he heard from the Holy Prophet (PBUH). Another Companion, Hadrat Abdullah bin Umar, on the order of the Holy Prophet (PBUH) used to write down every word of the Prophet's (PBUH) speech. This compilation was known as Sadiqa. These Companions persuaded their children and relatives to follow their instance. For example, Hadrat Anas used to stress upon his children:

> "O my children, write down the text of Hadith."

Hadrat Ali used to keep a booklet with him which contained many traditions mainly concerning the orders and instructions issued from time to time by the Holy Prophet (PBUH).

Imam Zohri, who was born in a Quraish family had preserved the Prophet's (PBUH) utterances in such detail that historians have remarked :

> "Zohri would go to any soul in Medina and record from him or her about the Prophet's life events."

Soon after the death of the Prophet (PBUH), the need for some authoritative guidance in Quranic interpretation was felt. The need was felt all the more because of the political and religious divisions. Also because of the expansion of Islam from a small community in Central Arabia to a mighty empire due to which Muslim rulers faced all kinds of political, economic, legal and social problems quite unknown during the days of the Prophet (PBUH). The problem was to apply the Prophet's (PBUH) teachings and way of life to conditions which were never thought of before. It was solved by recording and placing in the appropriate context a large number of sayings and practices of the Holy Prophet (PBUH).

Numerous collections of *Hadith* were prepared by many scholars from various angles, and different methods were adopted in the arrangement of the material. Two models were mainly adopted. In the first category, *Hadith* traced to each Companion was put together under his name, no matter what their theme might be. Such a collection is called Musnad. Therefore, the titles of the chapters are Musnad of Abu Bakr, Musnad of Abu Hurrayrah, Musnad of Aishah, etc.

The most famous compilation in this category is Musnad of Imam Ahmad bin Hanbal, founder of the fourth school of law. It contains 40,000 Ahadith of which 10,000 have occurred more than once.

The second category of *Ahadith* are grouped into chapters and sub-chapters according to their theme. For instance we find chapters on *purity, prayers, fasting, Zakat, pilgrimage, marriage,* so on. The best known work of this type is Al-Muwatta which contains 1,720 *Ahadith* compiled by Imam Malik bin Anas, founder of the Maliki school of law. Another compilation of this category is Al-Musannaf of Imam Abd Al-Razzaq Al-Sanani (126-211 A.H.) which has been published in eleven volumes. It contains 11,033 *Ahadith.*

Hadith compilers introduced each *Hadith* with its own Isnad which means the series of authorities who may be called narrators or transmitters or Muhaddis. These authorities can be as few as two. Imam Malik, for example, in some *Ahadith* related from his teacher Nafi, who related from his teacher Abdullah bin Umar, a distinguished Companion of the Holy Prophet (PBUH). Yet the number could be three, four, five and even six, depending on how far the compiler's time was from the time of the Prophet.

The early authorities of *Hadith* who scrutinized each *Hadith,* both the text and the *isnad,* included in their compilations only those which they believed to be genuine, and rejected those which they suspected as fabricated. Yet, they graded each Hadith in terms of the degree of reliability. A *Hadith* could be authentic, Sahih, or less than authentic, although it was not false or a fabrication but a weak or Zaeef Hadith which resulted from some weakness in the text or in the *Isnad.* The authorities on *Hadith* said that the text should have no conflict with the Quran or with a more reliable *Hadith.* The *Isnad* must be full and unbroken and each narrator mentioned in it must be known for his knowledge, piety and memory.

Upto the beginning of the third century of Islam, compilations of *Hadith* did not discriminate between authentic *Hadith* and others lesser than authentic so the *Ahadith* were mixed up.

Imam Muhammad ibn Ismail-al-Bukhari (194-256 A.H.), was

the first to conceive the idea of compiling the authentic *Ahadith* and therefore, he called his compilations as Sahih, "the authentic compilations". It took him sixteen years to compile this work which contains 7,397 *Ahadith* including four thousand repeated ones. He selected these *Ahadith* from amongst 600,000 *Ahadith* which he gathered in long and repeated journeys around the capitals of the world of Islam. On account of the strict conditions that he laid down for accepting a *Hadith* as *Sahih,* his work was acknowledged as one of the most authentic books on *Hadith* literature.

The example of Imam Bukhari was also followed by a number of other leading scholars. Eminent among them was Imam Muslim ibn Hajjaj (202-261 A.H.), whose compilation contains 12,000 *Ahadith* including 4,000 repetitions. The collections by *Bukhari* and *Muslim* are held in high esteem and are known as the two Sahihs i.e., the two collections recognized as authentic. Only those traditions which are recognized as absolutely correct are included in these works.

Among some others authors who followed them were Abu Daud (205-275 A.H.), author of *Al-Sunan; Al-Tirmidhi* (210-279 A.H.), author of *Al-Jami; Al-Nasai* (215-303 A.H.), author of *Kitab al-Sunnah;* and *Ibn Majah,* author of Kitab al-Sunnah. These four works along with those of *Bukhari* and *Muslim* became widely recognized in the Muslim world as the six leading Books *Al-Kutub al-Sitta* or *the six Sahihs,* i.e., *the sound, correct and reliable collections.*

At a later period, new collections were compiled by many scholars. In these works, contents were taken from the 'Six Books' and arranged in different ways until about the end of the fourth century of the age of Islam it was felt that all *Ahadith* circulating orally had been reduced to writing. Therefore, *Hadith* literature became exceedingly rich, and we as Muslims are very fortunate to have for our benefit such a great intellectual and religious wealth from which guidance can be derived.

The Reasoning Process : The Holy Quran is the fundamental source of the Shariah. It is the last and final revelation therefore its teachings shall always remains the source of Shariah for all times.

The Sunnah of the Holy Prophet (PBUH) comes next which sometimes elaborates and explains what has been mentioned in the Holy Quran and sometimes adds something to its commandments. In the latter case, it becomes the basis for legislation in Islam. The Quran and the Sunnah are thus the eternal sources of law for Muslims and the basic principles of legislation in Islam. However when sometimes the Quran and the Sunnah are silent about a matter, then it is a clear indication by the Supreme Law giver that the matter should be decided by the people concerned, in accordance with the needs of time and place. In all such matters, there is no alternative for a Muslim but to resort to Ijtihad which is the process of reasoning based on the Quran and the Sunnah. The Muslims are free to strive and endeavour to find solutions by using their own independent judgement Ijtihad in the light of the Quran and the Sunnah.

The main purpose of Ijtihad is to find ways and means to preserve and safeguard the principles of Islam in an ever changing and developing human society and to find solutions to new problems which have not been directly or clearly discussed or decided by the Quran and the Sunnah. The literal meaning of the word 'Ijtihad' is effort and it comes from a Hadith of the Prophet (PBUH) in which the Holy Prophet (PBUH) asked Muaz whom he had appointed governor of Yemen, by what criteria would he govern the regions assigned to him. 'According to the book of Allah', he answered. "And if you find nothing therein", the Prophet (PBUH) asked. Muaz answered, "According to the Sunnah of the Prophet (PBUH)." "And if you find nothing therein?" the Prophet (PBUH) asked again. "Then I will exert myself to form my own judgement", Muaz answered. And this the Prophet (PBUH) approved. Umar bin Aas was told by the Holy Prophet (PBUH) that if by exercising Ijtihad, he took a correct decision, he would get the reward of ten good deeds and if he took a wrong decision, he would get the reward of one good deed.

The most outstanding contributions in the field of Ijtihad have been made by Hadrat Umar. Less than twelve years after the Holy Prophet's (PBUH) death, he found it necessary to exercise Ijtihad. His first Ijtihad was with regard to the interpretation of the word 'thief in the Quranic verse:

> "As to the thief, male or female, cut off his or her hands. " (5:38)

He excluded from the definition of thief all those who stole because of hunger or during famine.

Hadrat Umar also exercised Ijtihad in awarding punishments for theft. For example, the hands of a slave who had stolen a mirror from his master's wife were not cut on the ground that he himself, being the property of the master, could not be considered to have stolen. Similarly, he acquitted a man who had stolen from Bait-ul-Mal. Once, during Ramadan, he broke his fast on a cloudy day in the mistaken belief that dusk had fallen. But soon the sun started shining. Hadrat Umar said:

> "It does not matter. We pondered over the matter according to our lights."

A well-known incident is his interpretation of verse 60 of Surah Taubah regarding charity. It says:

> "Alms are for those whose hearts have been (recently) reconciled (to the truth)." (9:60)

Among others, who received a share from both Zakat and war booty were the Quraish chiefs like Abu Sufyan and Safwan bin Umayyah. They used to get one hundred camels each. Hadrat Abu Bakr gave them additional authority for land grants. But Hadrat Abu Bakr passed away before the grants could be awarded. When the chiefs approached Hadrat Umar for implementation of the grants he not only tore those orders, but also stopped giving them the hundred camels which they used to get. His reason was that such a grant was a political necessity, when Islam was weak. But since Islam had become powerful during the time of Hadrat Umar, the old practice was no longer justified.

In the early centuries of Islam, there were jurists who developed and advocated Ijtihad. But in the later centuries, with the influence of different schools of law that had evolved and developed, this faculty of Ijtihad gave way to Taqlid that is, an acceptance of what the great scholars of fiqh have held in the past.

There are many problems facing Muslim society today in political, economic and social spheres - that can only be solved by Ijtihad, specially, in those matters where no distinct and direct command is found either in the Quran or the Sunnah. Some of these problems are, the current commercial transactions including insurance, the right of private ownership, nationalisation, tax system, the method of election to assemblies and election of the Head of the State, and the problems concerning international law particularly on the points of nationality and domicile, in different Muslim countries in the context of the concept of Dar-ul-Harb.

Ijtihad is concerned with matters, relating to human actions. It has no concern with one's faith, beliefs or religious convictions. The reason for this distinction is that in worldly matters we may ourselves discover the right way by using our intelligence. But intelligence alone cannot guide us in the field of religion.

Furthermore, Ijtihad should not be against any command or principle of the Holy Quran. People qualified for Ijtihad must not only possess vast religious knowledge, but must also be men of Taqwa that is, piety who can rise above their own personal ambitions and weaknesses. Although Islam does not believe in priesthood yet it does not give the right to everyone to undertake the difficult task of ijtihad. This right is limited to those only who fulfil all the basic and essential conditions of Ijtihad, in both religious knowledge and piety.

Ijtihad is meant to make the legal system of Islam dynamic and effective it should encourage a steady growth and development in Islam according to the needs and social circumstances of different times and places which will make Islam forceful and vigorous and prevent stagnation and decay.

It is only through the use of Ijtihad that we will be able to meet the challenges of modern civilization. It will contribute immensely to the intellectual revival of Islam in modern times and give a new force and vitality to Muslim society. It will also help to bring the Muslims all over the world close to one another.

The Analogy : The fourth source of Islamic law is Qiyas which, literally, means "judging or comparing with a thing." Qiyas means essentially to use human reasoning to compare an existing situation with one for which legislation already exists. If the Quran has banned wine, it means that by reasoning, it has also banned all forms of alcoholic drinks, whose effect is like wine or something that causes intoxication.

The death of Prophet Muhammad (PBUH) deprived the Muslim community of the means of obtaining revelation and at the same time of his guidance in political and religious matters. The expansion of the Muslim Empire and the spread of Islam outside Arabia raised questions previously unknown, the answers to which could not be found in the Quran or the *Sunnah.* Thus, they found themselves forced to take decisions or to regulate their conduct from their own opinion and reasoning.

Such resort to reasoning is often traced back to the conversation between the Prophet (PBUH) and Muaz ibn Jabal, the Governor of Yemen. When the Prophet (PBUH) appointed Muaz ibn Jabal as Governor and Judge in Yemen, the Prophet (PBUH) asked him:

> "According to what will you judge?"
>
> "According to the book of Allah."
>
> "And if you find nothing therein ? "
>
> "According to the Sunnah of the Prophet (PBUH)."
>
> "And if you find nothing therein?"
>
> "Then I will exert myself to form my own judgement." ibn Jabal replied.

According to another *Hadith,* the Prophet (PBUH) is reported to have told Abu Musa Ashari:

> "Judge upon the Book of Allah. If you do not find in it what you need, upon the Sunnah of the Prophet (PBUH) and if you do not find in that also, then use your personal opinion."

Imam Abu Hanifa, one of the four great Imams was the first to give prominence to the doctrine of *Qiyas,* although as a principle of law, it was in practice even before him.

The Consensus : Ijma is the third source of Islamic law. Literally, Ijma means agreeing upon or uniting in opinion. It means the consensus of the Islamic community on some point of law. It can operate only where the Quran and the *Hadith* have not clarified a certain aspect of the law. It is a gradual process through which the community over a period of time comes to a consensus over a question of law. The view of Muslims over the centuries has been that giving opinion on problems of law should be the function of Ulama who alone are well-versed in the science of law which is very complex and requires deep study before we can claim to be an authority over them.

The laws of the Quran and the *Sunnah* were, no doubt, supreme but there was no bar to making laws according to the needs of the people as long as they did not go against the spirit of the revealed law and the *Sunnah.* These laws were, however, to be made in consultation. It is reported from the Holy Prophet (PBUH):

> "If anything comes to you for decision, decide according to the Book of Allah. If anything comes to you which is not in the Book of Allah, then look to the Sunnah of the Prophet (PBUH). If anything comes to you which is not in the Sunnah of the Prophet (PBUH) then look to what people unanimously agree upon. "

In reply to Hadrat Ali as to how to proceed in cases where there was no definite direction in the Holy Quran or the *Sunnah,* the Prophet (PBUH) is reported to have said:

> "Gather together the righteous from among my community and decide the matter by their counsel and do not decide it by any man's opinion ."(Abu Daud).

And again:

> "My nation will not agree unanimously in error."

Counsel was freely resorted to by the Prophet (PBUH) himself in all important matters. Medina was attacked thrice by the Quraish, and every time the Prophet (PBUH) held consultations with his followers about the best way to repel the enemy. On one of these occasions, he acted upon the opinion of the majority and marched out of Medina to meet the enemy, although his own opinion was that the Muslim army should not leave the town.

The Holy Prophet (PBUH) has said:

> "Whatever the Muslims hold to be good is good before Allah. It is incumbent upon you to follow the most numerous body. Whoever separates himself from the

main body will go to Hell. If you yourselves do not know, then question those who do."

These traditions of the Holy Prophet (PBUH) are a sanction of *Ijma.*

Ijma is of three types:

1. *Ijma* or consensus of the Companions of the Holy Prophet (PBUH) which is also universally accepted and binding and is therefore, unchangeable.
2. *Ijma* of the jurists.
3. *Ijma of* the people, i.e., general body of the Muslim community.

As regards the last two, the jurists, particularly Imam Abu Hanifa, are of the view that they cannot be confined or limited to any particular age or country, and therefore, *Ijma* of one age can be modified by *Ijma* of the same or subsequent age.

4

The Preaching

Invitation to Faith

Man is endowed with a lot of talents and potentials some of which he gains naturally through his physical and mental make up like eating, walking, sleeping and talking. In the intellectual field, he can acquire knowledge through environment, books and teachers. In these physical and mental fields, no Dawa is required because human experience, make up and intuition take care of these areas.

There are certain other areas, which he cannot learn anything about through science and observation only. For example:

1. Is there a Creator of this universe?
2. Is there life after death?
3. Is there a higher aim of life?
4. What is the place of morality in human life?
5. Are there any laws that Allah has prescribed for mankind and to which He demands complete obedience?

These areas can be explained only through Dawa. So Dawa means inviting ourselves and all others to obey Allah and His laws which were given to the mankind through a long chain of messengers and prophets. For this the Holy Quran enjoins upon us:

> "Let there arise out of you, a band of people, inviting to all that is good, enjoining what is right and forbidding what is wrong: They are the ones to attain felicity." (3:104)

It is for this purpose that Allah also said:

> "You are the best of peoples evolved for mankind, enjoining what is right, for bidding what is wrong, and believing in Allah. " (3:110)

And also:

> "If a contingent from every expedition remained behind, they could devote themselves to studies in religion and admonish the people when they return to them that thus they (may learn) to guard themselves (against evil). (9:122)

Islam requires total surrender to Allah, in private as well as in public, inwardly as well as outwardly. This has two important and clear implications, one, as most of human life comprises of relationships with other people, living in surrender to Allah cannot be realized fully unless other people join us in our endeavour. Hence, inviting others to join in one venture, that is Dawa, is an essential part of being a Muslim. Two, Islam is a process, a life-long pursuit. Hence, we must continuously invite ourselves and everyone else to join in this pursuit: Thus, Dawa is integral to Islam. To be a Muslim means to continually strive to become a true Muslim, that means to do Dawa.

Dawa cannot be restricted to any race, colour, community or religion, Dawa has to be addressed to the 'self, to the individual and also to the society at large.

Dawa is the most important and significant Sunnah of the Prophet (PBUH) as the Holy Quran says:

> "O Messenger! proclaim the (message) which hath been sent to thee from thy Lord. If thou didst, not, thou wouldst not have fulfiled and proclaimed His mission." (5:67)

Allah has bestowed upon every human being the faculty to

recognize and differentiate between good and evil. He has also put a yearning in them to adopt good and shun evil. This fact is inherent in His laws that human beings who follow His laws will be rewarded while those who reject His laws will be punished.

On the other hand, man has also been given free will so that in this life of endeavour and achievement, he may be free to work for and achieve what he likes. In pursuit of his goals a man may adopt ways and means which hinder his intuitive faculties to recognize. However man has been given more than just instincts and intuition by Allah, to save him from blunders and pitfalls. He virtually made it fool proof by sending a chain of prophets to clearly and openly, indicate right and wrong conduct, and to make the laws given by Allah clear to man by prophets own example. The Quran says:

> "Although there came to them our messengers with clear signs, yet, even after that, many of them continued to commit excesses in the land." (5:32)

And also:

> "O people of the book! Now hath come unto you, making (things) clear unto you, Our messenger, after the break in (the series of) Our messengers, lest ye should say: "There came unto us no bringer of glad tidings and no warner (from evil)"; But now hath come unto you a bringer of glad tidings and a warner (from evil)." (5:19)

All these prophets were human beings and they themselves put into practice what they were preaching. With the advent of the Holy Prophet (PBUH), Muslims were given the responsibility of being the models of right conduct for all mankind. According to the Quran:

> "Thus have We made of you an Ummah justly balanced, that ye might be witnesses over the nations." (2:143)

In the order of Dawa, the first thing is the belief in the fundamental concepts of:

(1) Tauhid-Unity of Allah.

(2) Risalat - Prophethood.

(3) Akhirat - Day of Judgement.

Thus, the starting point and the basic core of Dawa should be as the Quran makes very clear: total surrender to one Allah, obeying His messengers and belief in accountability in life after death.

It is to these beliefs that everyone should be invited but we should not start our invitation by repudiating what is wrong with others, but in the way the Quran says:

> "Invite (all) to the way of thy Lord with wisdom and beautiful preaching and argue with them in ways that are best and most gracious." (16:125)

Dawa is the fulfilment of this command *"to invite all to the way of thy Lord."* Muslims should make the effort to invite other men to share and benefit from the religious truth which they have been given. Since this truth is not only theoretical, but also practical, the men of religion are urged to take it to others.

"Inviting" is not forcing; Allah has commanded:

> "Let there be no compulsion in religion." (2:256)

The object of this invitation can be fulfiled only with the free consent of the invities that is why the Holy Quran has specified the means of persuasion to be used. If the non-Muslim remains unconvinced, the Muslim is to rest his case with God: The Holy Prophet (PBUH) allowed those Christians who were not convinced by his presentation of Islam to keep their faith and return home in peace.

From this, it follows that the order desired by Islam is one where men are free to present and argue their religious beliefs with one another. It is a kind of seminar where he who knows better is free to speak and to convince, and the others are free to listen and be convinced. Islam puts its trust in man's rational power to discriminate between the true and the false.

> "He that receives guidance benefits his own soul: But he that strays injures his own soul." (39:41)

Islamic dawa is therefore, an invitation to think, to debate and to argue.

The Faithfuls

The Quran guides man with regard to his dealings with other individuals of the society. It lays emphasis on justice, trust, respect for life and property, patience, humility, thankfulness and forgiveness. The fundamental relations between a man and other individuals are those of parents and children, husband and wife. It also includes relations between relatives, neighbours, the poor and the needy, orphans and non-Muslims. The Quran says:

> "Treat with kindness your parents and kindred and orphans and those in need; Speak fair to the people."
> (2: 83)

Parents and Children : Among worldly relations, the relations between parents and children have the highest status. Islam has given great importance to this relationship placing respect and kindness to parents next only to belief in Allah and the command to be grateful to Allah is immediately followed by the command to be grateful to one's parents. The Quran says:

> "Show gratitude to Me and to thy parents."
> (31.-14)

It further says:

> "We have enjoined on man kindness to his parents."
> (46:15)

Allah says:

> "Be kind to parents. Whether one or both of them attain old age in thy life, say not to them a word of contempt, nor repel them, but address them in terms of honour.
>
> And out of kindness, lower to them the wing of humility, and say:
>
> "My Lord! Bestow on them Thy Mercy even as they cherished me in childhood." (17:23-24)

The Holy Prophet (PBUH) received very little of his mother's love and upbringing; yet whenever he visited her grave, he wept and prayed to Allah to have mercy on her soul.

Once a person came to the Holy Prophet (PBUH) and asked:

> "O messenger of Allah, what are the rights of parents on their children ? "

He replied:

> "For you, they can be heaven or hell."

It is clear from this that, kind and gentle treatment of parents leads to heaven and their ill-treatment to hell.

Among parents, the status of mother is higher, because she undergoes more sufferings for the sake of her children. The Quran says:

> "In travail upon travail did his mother bear him, and in years twain was his weaning:" (31:14)

The Holy Prophet (PBUH) said:

> "Heaven is beneath the feet of mothers."

The rights of children on their parents are that they should bring them up in the best possible manner, to cherish and nurture them, to protect them from all kinds of evil and to provide them with the best education and training.

The Holy Prophet (PBUH) said:

> "No father has given his child anything better than good manners."
>
> "He who is not affectionate to God's creatures and to his own children, Allah will not be affectionate to him."

Husband and Wife

> "And they (women) have rights similar to those (of men) over them." (2: 228)

This verse clearly shows that both husband and wife have equal rights over each other. In his Farewell Pilgrimage, the Holy Prophet (PBUH) declared:

> "O you people! You have rights over your wives and your wives have rights over you. Treat your wives with kindness and love; verily you have taken them on the security of Allah."

Both husband and wife are a source of support, comfort and protection to each other. They are, therefore, expected to live together in peace and love, as the Quran says:

> "He created for you mates from among yourselves that you may dwell in tranquility with them and He has put love and mercy between your hearts."
>
> (30: 21)

Husbands are required to provide sustenance to their wives, clothe them and house them. They are required to live with them (wives) on a footing of kindness and equity.

A virtuous wife is bound to love her husband and prove to be a source of comfort to him. The Quran says:

> "Therefore, the righteous women are devoutedly obedient and guard in (the husband's) absence what Allah would have them guard." (4:34)

According to Abdullah Yusuf Ali, the meaning of the verse is that "the good wife is obedient and harmonious in her husband's presence, and in his absence guards his reputation and property and her own virtue as ordained by God,"

In this regard, the Holy Prophet (PBUH) said:

> "The best wife is one who pleases her husband when he looks at her; carries out his orders when he orders them; and who guards his property and her sanctity in his absence from home."

Relatives : Islam lays great stress on the rights of relatives. Allah has commanded us to do good and show kindness to our relatives, and the command to do so comes immediately after the command to do good to our parents. The Quran says:

> "Worship none but Allah and treat with kindness your parents and kindred and orphans and those in need."
>
> (2:83)

The Holy Prophet (PBUH) is reported to have said:

> "Giving of alms to relatives carries two rewards: one the reward of alms and the other is the reward of helping relatives."

> "A person who does not respect the rights of his relatives will not enter Paradise. "
>
> "One who breaks off his relations with his relatives shall not enter Paradise."

Neighbours : Verse 36 of Surah Nisa enjoins the doing of good to *"neighbours who are near, neighbours who are strangers."*

Verse 7 of Surah Maun condemns those who refuse (to supply) neighbourly needs.

It is reported the Holy Prophet (PBUH) laid so much emphasis on the rights of neighbours that some of his companions thought that neighbours might be included in the list of heirs.

There are a number of sayings of the Holy Prophet (pbuh) in connection with the rights of neighbours. He is reported to have said:

> "If you wish to become a perfect believer, you should treat your neighbour generously. "
>
> "The most virtuous of you all is he who gives the best treatment to his neighbours."
>
> "That person is not a perfect Muslim who eats his fill and leaves his neighbour hungry."
>
> "He who believes in one Allah and the life beyond, let him not injure his neighbour."

Orphans and the Needy : In many verses of the Holy Quran, the commandment regarding the needy and the poor and orphans are linked with those regarding parents and relatives. It says:

> "And treat with kindness your parents and relatives and orphans and those in need." (2:83)
>
> "Spend of your substance, out of love for Him, for your kin, for orphans, for the needy, for wayfarer." (2: 177)
>
> "Say: Whatever you spend that is good is for parents and relatives and orphans and those in want." (2:215)

Apart from the command to do good and show kindness

to them, emphasis is laid on the feeding of the poor. The Quran says:

> "And they feed, for the love of Allah, the indigent, the orphan, and the captive." (76: 8)

> "Have you seen the one who denies the Day of Judgement? Then such is the one who repulses the orphan, (with harshness) and urges not the feeding of the poor." (107: 1-3)

One of Holy Prophet's (PBUH) sayings about giving something to one who asks for help is, *"O Aishah! Do not turn the poor away, without giving them, if but half a date."*

About good treatment to orphans, the Holy Prophet (PBUH) said:

> "The best Muslim house is that in which is an orphan who is well-treated and the worst Muslim house is that in which is an orphan ill-treated."

Law and Protocol

Islam imposes strict discipline of good behaviour and conduct upon its followers. The maintenance of one's dignity and self-respect is an essential quality in a man. It is needed in every aspect of life and at every turn; without it, a feeling of inferiority exists, no one pays any attention to what such a person says. Others never respect a person who neither respects himself nor maintains discipline.

Islam expects Muslims to present the highest example of good morality and manners. As long as Muslims maintained firm faith and discipline, they did not lose their sense of self-respect.

The Quran says:

> "You are the best of peoples, evolved for mankind, enjoining what is right, for bidding what is wrong...." (3:110)

Self-respect is different from vanity. It is the name given to the quality by which a person understands and learns to respect himself so that he does not stoop to anything low. When a self-respecting person comes across an evil, he passes by it untouched. The evil ones do not have the courage to even try to attract him.

To maintain one's self-respect, one has to be careful at all times and in every way. Such a person's behaviour must reflect his self-respect. Yet there must be no shadow of vanity or a sense of superiority about him. Dignified behaviour is the essence of self-respect. The Prophet (PBUH) said the following in the context of prayers:

> "When you hear the call for prayers, proceed calmly and with dignity and do not be in a hurry."

Beggary is strongly condemned in Islam as it is a negation of self-respect. It makes a man shameless. Even asking for help in everyday matters is not encouraged. The Prophet (PBUH) said that when a person must ask for help or assistance only the God-fearing should be approached. This command ensures that God-fearing persons will either comply, or if not in a position to help, will refuse politely. So the one who has asked for help will not lose his self-respect. A Muslim endowed with the values of Islam cares only for Allah; he does not bow down to anyone but Allah. As a Muslim, he knows that honour and respect are for Allah and His Prophet and through him for every Muslim. Thus, to maintain one's self-respect is to maintain the respect and honour of Islam.

Rules above All

The institution of law exists in human society from time immemorial. Every race, every religion and every group of men has made some contributions in this sphere.

Law, as defined in an English dictionary is a rule of actions established by an authority, such as the government in a country. A citizen has to abide by the law and show respect to it, otherwise there are prescribed penalties for actions contrary to the established laws.

According to the Holy Quran, the greatest of Ruler and the Supreme Law-Giver is Allah. All His creatures have to obey His commands and to follow His laws. No man can change Allah's law. Those who refuse to obey or judge according to His law as contained in the Quran are wrongdoers, unbelievers and rebels.

Islam is the greatest law-giving institution in the world and its laws are supreme in all matters. These laws are restricted within the limits prescribed by the Shariah. The commandments of Allah and His Prophet are unchangeable and cannot be amended. They are to be accepted and obeyed and no legislative body can make any alterations or modifications in them or make any law that is against their teachings.

In the eyes of Islam, every person is equal and everyone has equal rights to seek redress through a court of law. Everyone has equal rights to protection of life, property and honour. Islam proclaims equal treatment in law, irrespective of one's status or position in life. Even the ruler is not exempted. He has to appear before a court of law, if called. The teaching as well as the practice of Prophet Muhammad (PBUH) followed by that of his successors show that judges never hesitated to decide against the rulers in cases of default.

Calipha Hadrat Umar, in a case filed against him, appeared personally before the judge with the appellant, who was a Jew, and so did Hadrat Ali, the fourth Calipha of Islam, in yet another case.

An incident is noted in *Sahih Bukhari* that in Medina, a woman of the Banu Makhzum tribe committed a theft. She was likely to be subjected to the punishment of the cutting off her hand. The chiefs of this powerful tribe prevailed upon Usama bin Zaid, who was held in high esteem by the Holy Prophet (PBUH), to intercede for her. On Usama's intervention the Holy Prophet (PBUH) said angrily, "Would you intervene in the punishment prescribed by Allah?"

Then he turned to those who were present and said:

> "What has been the cause of the downfall of the previous nations is that when a thief of noble origin was caught, he was allowed to go without punishment, whereas a thief of humble origin was subjected to punishment. I swear, by Allah, that if Fatima, daughter of Muhammad, committed a theft, I would have her hand cut off."

This tradition is a significant example of the supremacy of law in Islam.

Another incident is that of Amr bin Aas, who was the Governor of Egypt. A man accused him of whipping him without any just cause. Khalifa Hadrat Umar, after making enquiries, ordered that the man should lash the Governor with an equal number of stripes. Some of the men present there persuaded the aggrieved man to forgive Amr bin Aas and accept monetary compensation for the injury caused to him by the Governor.

The third incident relates to Jabalah, a convert from Christianity to Islam and the chief of his tribe. During tawaf of the Kaaba, the edge of his shawl accidentally came under the foot of an Arab villager. Jabalah, in anger, slapped the man on his face and broke his tooth. Khalifa Hadrat Umar permitted the villager to take revenge from Jabalah by slapping him on the face and breaking his tooth. When Jabalah came to know about this, he fled from the Islamic territory. With all his tribe, he went back to his old religion.

In Islam, therefore, nobody is above law; the ruler and the ruled are subject to the same law and there can be no discrimination on the basis of power or position. If the ruler himself committed a prohibited act, he would not be able to reproach others for the same act. Therefore, Islam has struck at the root and source of this kind of evil by emphasizing the supremacy of law, it declared that nobody is above law, not even the Prophet and his family.

The Polity

Islam is a religion of peace and no Muslim State can follow a policy of territorial expansion and unprovoked aggression. The foreign policy of a Muslim state should be such as to advance the cause of Islam and the moral, cultural and political objectives of its society and to preserve and protect its territorial integrity. The Quran and the Holy Prophet's (PBUH) Sunnah provide sufficient guidance to enable a Muslim state to frame its foreign policy.

In pre-Islamic days, international law had no independent existence; it was dependent on the will and pleasure of the head of the state. The first Muslim State in Medina was established and governed by the Holy Prophet (PBUH). It was a confederacy of villages inhabited by Muslims, Jews, Christians and pagan Arabs.

The rules of international conduct comprise not only internal legislation, but also treaties, relations and agreements with other states. The ambassador is considered to be immune from all violation, even if he brings an unpleasant message. He enjoys all liberty of creed and security as long as he stays in a Muslim state. Like other aspects of life in Islam, international relations of a Muslim state are based on Divine guidance given in the Quran. They are based on the following principles:

(1) Belief in the unity of mankind, in origin, in human status and in aims.

(2) Respect for other people's interests and rights to life, honour and property, as long as they do not encroach upon the rights of Muslims.

(3) Maintaining peaceful relations with the exchange of goodwill missions,

(4) Intolerance of encroachment in international relations. The Islamic state must defend itself and suppress all attempts to violate or disturb its peace, or endanger its security or exploit its peaceful policies.

The law of war and peace in Islam does not allow an aggressive war nor makes the killing of people and animals or the destruction of crops, homes and places of worship its objective. It does not allow the killing of women, children and aged people nor the torture of war prisoners or the imposition of its teachings on the conquered people. It is only a defensive measure justified as long as wrong, injustice and aggression exist in the world.

(5) Fulfilling the obligations undertaken by the Muslim state and honouring the treaties concluded between the Islamic State and other states. This is binding as long as the other parties remain faithful to their obligations and honour their treaties.

This state does not exist only for itself and its own subjects. It has a wide scope and an important mission in the international field. It has not only to strive for the prosperity and advancement of its own citizens but also make valuable contributions to humanity on an international level in education, economics, industry, politics and other fields.

Islam seeks to establish a world community, with complete equality among people without distinction of race, class or country. It seeks to convert by persuasion, allowing no compulsion in religions beliefs. According to Islam, it is the duty of every individual to make constant efforts for spreading good and preventing evil.

Status of Minorities

Islam is a religion of love, mercy and tolerance and it preaches freedom of belief and faith. It recognizes the rights of non-Muslims living in an Islamic State. They were called protected people or *zimmies* because they lived in peace and tranquility under the protection of the Islamic State.

The messenger of Allah practiced religious tolerance towards non-Muslims and did not use force to compel people of other religions to embrace Islam as it would have been against the commands of the Quran:

"Let there be no compulsion in religion." (2: 256)

Muslims are commanded here not to force Islam on people of other religions, because belief in any religion depends on faith, and faith cannot be induced by force. In Islam, religious tolerance is so highly recommended that there is no room for any compulsion to accept Islam; only argument and logic can be used to show others the guidance of Islam. The Quran advocates a just and kind treatment for non-Muslims. The Holy Prophet (PBUH) was command by Allah to grant asylum to any unbeliever who asked for it.

Muslims believe in all previous messengers and all of them are held in equal esteem. For a Muslim, Allah is none other than the God of Hadrat Musa and Hadrat Isa. The followers of these messengers are called the *'People of the Book'* in the Quran. The Holy Prophet (PBUH), therefore, gave them special consideration and status in the Islamic State of Medina and freedom to practice their religions. He showed immense goodwill and understanding towards them. Their scriptures and places of worship were respected. They enjoyed complete security and protection of their lives, property and religion. No synagogue or church was destroyed. They were allowed to maintain and repair their places of worship and also to construct new ones. They were granted judicial antonomy. Their civil cases were decided according to their own laws and by their own courts. In addition, they were allowed to seek justice in a Muslim court, if they so desired. The Muslim authorities were not allowed to interfere with their personal laws.

In fact, in safeguarding the rights of non-Muslims, an Islamic state has gone to such extremes as to give them the liberty of maintaining even those practices which are entirely opposed to the teachings of Islam. For example, the consumption of alcohol is forbidden to Muslims, yet the non-Muslim inhabitants of the country have the liberty to use alcohol. They have special permission from the state to manufacture or import alcohol.

Islam insists on kind treatment of non-Muslims. The Holy Prophet (PBUH) said:

> "If anyone wrongs a man to whom, a treaty has been granted, or burdens him above his strength, I will advocate against him on the Day of Judgement,"

Hadrat Abu Bakr said:

> "If a province or people receive you, make an agreement with them and keep your promise. Let them be governed by their laws and established customs; and take tribute from them as is agreed between you. Leave them in their religion and their land."

Hadrat Umar treated non-Muslims very kindly and justly. While imposing taxes upon them, he was very careful that enough was left for their maintenance. Even on his deathbed, he left instructions that non-Muslims should be treated justly and not overburdened with taxes. Such were the injunctions of the Holy Prophet (PBUH) and his immediate successors about the rights of non-Muslims.

Law of Faith

Islamic law is based on submission to the Will of Allah. This is a fundamental principle of religion and since Islamic law is based upon Islam, it covers all aspects of life. It is a way or path guiding the Muslims. The law governing all matters is known as Shariah.

Islamic law or the *Shariah* is the law which binds Muslims into a single community. The word *Shariah* is derived from a root, meaning path or road. It is the path which leads to Allah, His law which guides Muslims to run their spiritual, moral, social and physical lives in accordance with Islamic principles. The purpose of this law is to chalk out a system of duties which would enable the believers to live a righteous life in this world and prepare themselves for the next.

A Muslim is expected to live according to this law, both in his private and social life. It is, therefore, the guide to all human actions and embraces all aspects of human life. It guides man as to how he should conduct his life, deal with his neighbours, how he should eat and sleep, buy and sell and how he should pray and perform other acts of worship. It is through this law that the value of human actions in the sight of Allah is made known to human beings so that they can distinguish between the straight road and that which will lead them astray. The *Shariah* or the Islamic law provides for him the knowledge of right and wrong. It is by his freewill that man must decide which path to follow.

In essence, all of the *Shariah* is contained in the Quran. It contains the principles of all the laws, further explained in the *Hadith* and *Sunnah* which together constitute the second source of Islamic law. This was further understood with the help of the consensus of the Islamic community-Ijma. Finally, these three sources of Islamic law were complemented by human reasoning-Qiyas, where necessary.

Thus the *Shariah,* the source of all laws for the Muslims is revelation manifested through the Quran and explained through the *Sunnah* and then interpreted through *Ijma,* the agreed opinion of the jurists and finally *Qiyas* or human reasoning.

These sources fall into two main categories; the primary sources which comprised the Quran and the *Sunnah* and the secondary or dependent sources which are *Ijma* or consensus and *Qiyas* or reasoning.

The supremacy of the Quran and Sunnah over the other sources can be illustrated from many incidents. For example, when the Holy Prophet (PBUH) appointed Muaz ibn Jabal as the Governor and judge in Yemen, he asked him:

> "According to what will you judge?"
>
> "According to the Book of Allah.
>
> "And if you find nothing therein?"
>
> "According to the Sunnah of the Prophet (PBUH)."
>
> "And if you find nothing therein?"
>
> "Then I will exert myself to form my own judgement."

The Holy Prophet's (PBUH) response was:

> "Praise be to Allah Who has guided the messenger of His Prophet to that which pleases His Prophet."

It follows from this tradition that the Quran and the Sunnah were the roots of the law, while the opinion of the jurists could be brought in by way of supplementation where the main sources were silent.

Fight for God

The Arabic word Jihad means to strive, to exert oneself. In religious terminology it expresses struggle against one's evil inclinations or exertion for the sake of Islam and the Muslim Ummah, for example, an armed struggle against the unbelievers if Islam is under threat, the spread of belief in Allah or to work for the moral betterment of the Islamic society.

Jurists have distinguished four different ways in which the believer may fulfil his Jihad obligation: by his heart, his tongue, his hands and by the sword. The first is concerned with defeating evil. This type of Jihad was so significant in the eyes of the Holy Prophet (PBUH) that he regarded it as the greater Jihad. The second and third are mainly fulfilled by supporting the right and correcting the wrong. The fourth is equivalent to the meaning of war and is concerned with fighting the unbelievers and the enemies of the faith. The believers are required to sacrifice their wealth and lives in the service of Allah.

Jihad is thus, the use of all our energies and resources to establish the Islamic system of life. In the first phase, a person learns to control his own bad desires and inclinations. This is Jihad or struggle within ourselves which is responsible for establishing

Maroof-right, and removing Munkar-evil from our lives and from society. It demands the use of all our material and mental resources. Finally, we may be required to give up our life for the cause of Islam.

Jihad does not necessarily mean war or fighting since exertion in Allah's path may be achieved by peaceful means as well. In the early Surahs revealed in Mecca, the emphasis was on persuasion. The Holy Prophet (PBUH) in the discharge of his prophetic mission warned his people against idol - worship and invited them to worship Allah; as is evident from the following verse:

> "if any strive (with might and main), they do so for their own souls:" (29:6)

Which expressed Jihad in terms of the salvation of soul rather than a struggle for conversion to Islam. In the later revelations, Jihad is often expressed in terms of strife and there is no doubt that in certain verses, the concept of Jihad is synonymous with the words war and fighting.

In Mecca, the Muslims suffered for several years under the worst kind of punishments, were denied religious freedom, persecuted for the sake of their religion and terrorized with regard to property and personal safety. For all these reasons, they were compelled to leave their homes and migrate to Medina, patiently submitting to Allah's orders. Whenever they felt the urge to resist the oppression or to take revenge from the oppressors, the Prophet (PBUH) held them back, telling them to be patient.

"I have not been ordered to fight," he would say.

Then Allah revealed the first verses permitting war:

> "To those against whom war is made, permission is given (to fight), because they are wronged - and verily Allah is most powerful for their aid.
>
> (They are) those who have been expelled from their homes in defiance of right - (for no cause) except that they say, "Our lord is Allah. " Did not Allah check one set of people by means of another there would surely have been pulled down monasteries, churches, synagogues and mosques, in which the name of Allah

> is commemorated in abundant measure Allah will certainly aid those who aid his (cause)."
> (22:39-40)

This permission was motivated by the fact that the Muslims suffered injustice, and were forced to leave their homes and migrate without justification. These verses point out that God helps only those who fear Him and therefore do not use war as an instrument for destruction, for subjugating the weak and satisfying their own desires. On the contrary they obey Allah's orders and summon people to do what is right and abstain from wrong.

These verses are very clear and do not contain even the slightest evidence of religious compulsion. They are not only concerned with Muslims, but deal with non-Muslims as well when it is said: "there would surely have been pulled down monasteries, churches, synagogues and mosques."

Fighting between Muslims and non-Muslims has been dealt with comprehensively in many verses of the Holy Quran. These verses describe the causes which may lead to it, its aim, upon the attainment of which fighting must stop, the preparations for it by the Muslims and the necessary caution against its unexpected outbreak.

The following verses caution Muslims against being the transgressors:

> "Fight in the cause of Allah those who fight you, but do not transgress limits. For Allah loveth not transgressors." (2:190)

> "And fight them on until there is no more tumult or oppression, and there prevail justice and faith in Allah; But if they cease, let there be no hostility except to those who practice oppression." (2:193)

These verses order the Muslims to fight in the way of Allah. They prohibit the provocation of hostility and this prohibition is reinforced by Allah's dislike of those who provoke hostility. They also define the aim upon the attainment of which war must end. This aim is achieved when there is no more persecution in matters of religion.

The principles explained in these verses can be found in the same or similar words, in many other Surahs for example, Surah Al-Nisa, Surah Al-Anfal and Surah Al-Taubah.

> "and fight the pagans all together as they fight you all together. But know that Allah is with those who restrain themselves." (9:36)

From these verses of the Holy Quran, it becomes clear that there is not a single verse in the Quran which could support the opinion that the aim of fighting in Islam is conversion. It also becomes clear that the reasons for fighting are: to stop aggression, to protect the mission of Islam and to defend religious freedom.

Poll-tax or Jizya is not a financial compensation for the granting of one's life or preservation of religion, but a symbol of submission and resistance from harmful acts and a contribution in carrying out the burdens of the state.

Although Jihad is considered to be very important, it is not included in the five pillars of Islam. The reason is that the five pillars are not necessarily to be enforced by the state; they must be observed by individuals. In other words, the basic articles are regarded as individual duties like prayer or fasting which each believer must perform and each is liable to punishment if he fails to perform the duty. Jihad, on the other hand, unless the Muslim community is subjected to a sudden attack and therefore all believers including women and children are under the obligation to fight, is regarded by all jurists as a collective obligation of the whole Muslim community. It is regarded as Farz-e-Kifaya which is binding upon the Muslims as a group not individually. If the duty is fulfiled by a part of the community, it ceases to be obligatory on others. The whole community, however, falls into error if the duty is not performed at all.

Jihad must be preceded by an invitation to Islam. The Prophet (PBUH) followed the rule, which he had himself laid down and his early successors seem to have followed their master's example. In the campaigns against the Byzantines and Persians, the Arab commanders addressed invitations to their enemies, inviting them first to accept Islam or pay the tribute, before they launched their offensive. In the early Muslim conquests, the commander often waited for three days after the invitation had been sent before actual fighting took place. During this period, the Muslims were ready to negotiate when the enemy demanded it. This often led to a peaceful settlement as in such cases as the surrender of a number of towns in Iraq and Syria.

In Islam, the objective of man is neither the achievement of victory nor the acquisition of the enemy's property; it is rather the fulfilment of a duty-Jihad in Allah's way. The Muslims were advised to refrain from shedding blood or destroying property for the achievement of their objective. This general rule is based on Hadrat Abu Bakr's address to the expedition sent to Syria as well as to other similar utterances by succeeding Khalifas.

It is repeatedly stressed in the Holy Quran that the object of any fighting forced upon Muslims should be to put down aggression and persecution, for persecution is worse than killing. When the enemy stops fighting the Muslims should do likewise; when freedom from persecution is secured, fighting should be brought to an end.

If war becomes unavoidable, every effort must be made to limit its mischief and horror. It must be waged in such a way so as to cause the least possible amount of damage to life and property. All hostilities must be brought to an end as early as possible. Savage practices like disfiguring the dead enemy or torturing prisoners of war are prohibited in Islam.

5

Religious Practices

Iman (the Belief)

Meaning and Importance : The basis of the Islamic teaching and way of life are various obligatory acts of worship, Ibadat which are often referred to as the Five Pillars of Islam. These consist of:

a. Declaration that there is no god but Allah.

b. The prescribed prayers, five times a day.

c. Fasting, once a year in the month of Ramadan.

d. Zakat, helping the needy by giving alms.

e. Hajj, pilgrimage to Mecca, if and when circumstances permit.

Just as the pillars bear the burden of a building, these principles, according to the teachings of the Prophet (PBUH) are the basis of piety and of a virtuous worldly life; as the Prophet (PBUH) has taught that the only difference between individuals is the extent of their piety and not their colour or the social status that they enjoy in this world.

The purpose of the Islamic worship is to strengthen the Muslim faith and sense of submission to Allah, to discipline a Muslim for his role as Allah's faithful servant and vicegerent on earth, and to reinforce the ties of brotherhood and affection among Muslims. These acts of worship require the participation of all aspects of man's nature — his soul, his mind, his feelings, his body, his time, his energy and his possessions. Thus, they demand the worship of Allah with all the faculties of an individual. For example, the declaration of faith is to be always present in the mind and heart of the Muslim and is to be uttered again and again with the tongue during his daily prayers. Prayers are to be performed five times daily, everyday of a man's life. Fasting is for a full month every year, while Zakat or "poor-due" is to be paid once yearly; and the pilgrimage is to be performed once in a lifetime, if possible.

These aspects of Islamic worship and the total involvement of human beings make them extremely unique. They are a complete expression of man's dependence and submission to His will, his humility before His Creator and his desire to serve and obey Him alone.

In these religious institutions, there is punctuality, regularity, orderliness, uniformity and an exhibition of complete equality.

Tauhid-Unity of Allah : The first part of the declaration that there is no god but Allah attests not only to the Oneness and Uniqueness of Allah, but it also signifies the Oneness of Lordship, the Sovereignty and the Authority in the universe and in this world. As there is no other Creator and Sustainer of the universe, there can likewise be no other Ruler, Law-giver and Supreme Authority for mankind. Allah is the Lord of all creation; He creates what He pleases, giving each of His creatures the nature, role and function which He desires for it; in this He is accountable to no one and all things are under His absolute control.

The primary emphasis of the Quran is upon the doctrine of Tauhid. There are numerous verses in the Quran which highlight the concept of *Tauhid* which is the cardinal principle of Islam. In the very opening chapter of the Holy Quran, Surah Fatiha, it is said:

"Thee do we worship and thine aid we seek." (1:5)

Similarly, verse 36, it is said:

"Serve Allah, and join not any partners with Him." (4:36)

The most concise expression of this principle is to be found in Surah Ikhlas. This Quranic Surah as translated by Abdullah Yusuf Ali says:

"Say: He is Allah,
The One and Only;
Allah the Eternal, Absolute,
He Begetteth not,
Nor is He begotten;
And there is none
Like unto Him. (112:1-4)

True unity of Allah means that Allah is:

(a) *Unique in Person:* This signifies that Allah is only One and there is no plurality of gods. The Quran says:

Allan has said:

"Take not (for worship) two gods: for He is just one God." (16:51)

(b) *Unique in Attributes:* This signifies that no other being can be equal to Allah in attributes. For example, man may attain a degree of perfection in the attribute of kindness, but only Allah possesses the perfection of the attribute of kindness.

(c) *Unique in Action:* No one can do the works which Allah has done or may do. All the messengers of Allah have conveyed the message of His unity:

"O my people, " said they, "Worship Allah. You have no other god but Him." (7: 59, 73, 85)

The role of the Prophet of Islam was to bring about the acceptance of this principle of religion by entire mankind. The Quran says:

"Not a messenger did We send before thee without this inspiration sent by US to him: that there is no god but I; therefore, worship and serve Me." (21: 25)

The doctrine of *Tauhid* confers dignity on man who is otherwise a slave to every manifestation of power. Only Allah becomes his refuge, security and stability.

Associating partners with Allah is called Shirk. *Shirk* is not only the worship of idols, but also offering prayers and supplications to anyone, dead or living, believing that they hold the same attributes in a lesser degree than Him. Thus, the belief that Allah is not Sovereign or Independent and Sole Dispenser of affairs of the world and that other deities can intercede with Him and that any attempt to implore any other being besides Allah for the grant of any wishes of the believer or to answer his prayers is *Shirk*. The Quran considers *Shirk* to be an unpardonable sin. It says:

> "Allah forgives not that partners should be set up with Him; but He forgives anything else to whom He pleases; to set up partners with Allah is to devise a sin most heinous indeed. " (4: 48)

Man has been created as lord of creation and everything in nature has been placed under his control. By worshipping other beings besides Allah man debases himself, the Quran says:

> "Shall I seek for you a god other than the (true) God, when it is Allah Who hath endowed you with gifts above the nations." (7:140)

In Surah Luqman, ascribing partners to Allah is regarded as a tremendous wrong.

The Holy Prophet (PBUH) is reported to have said:

> "Shirk is the greatest of all sins".

Meaning and Importance of Prophethood : The next basic requirement of Islam is belief and faith in all the prophets of Allah. This means that a Muslim believes that the prophets are devoted servants of Allah, selected and appointed by Him, to convey His Commands to mankind without any addition or deduction. Prophethood is a gift of Allah and only He can bestow this gift on whom He wishes.

Allah deputed prophets in different periods of time to communicate His guidance to human beings. They were raised from the nations to whom they were sent as messengers. They preached in the language of their nations, the Quran says:

> "We sent not a messenger except (to teach) in the language of his (own) people, in order to make (things) clear to them." (14:4)

And again:

> "And there never was a people without a warner having lived among them (in the past)." (35:24)

According to the Quran, all prophets sent by Allah were men, had human bodies and were mortal. At the same time, the Quran tells us that the prophets were Allah's chosen and selected. Allah chose them and guided them and gave them the Book and the prophethood. They all received revelation from Allah and were sent for the guidance of their people. They all did good deeds and were truthful. The Holy Quran insists that the prophets were raised to be obeyed and followed. They called their followers to profess and follow the Divine code of rules to regulate their life. There are numerous verses in the Quran in which emphasis is laid on obedience to the prophets and following their example.

It says:

> "We sent not a messenger, but to be obeyed, in accordance with the will of Allah." (4:64)
>
> "He who obeys the messenger obeys Allah. "(4:80)
>
> "Say, (O Muhammad!), if you do love Allah, follow me; Allah will love you and forgive you your sins." (3:31)

Many prophets came to this world. The last in the line of prophets is the Holy Prophet Muhammad (PBUH) who is termed as "the seal of the prophets."

The Quran says that the appearance of the Holy Prophet (PBUH) was foretold by previous prophets. His distinguishing feature was that he confirmed the truth of all the prophets that preceded him. He not only conveyed the message revealed to him, but also explained and acted upon it himself and after demonstration, urged the people to follow it for their own benefit.

The Prophethood of Hadrat Muhammad (PBUH) is distinguished in many ways:

1. It is universal which means that the Holy Prophet (PBUH) was not sent for any particular country or community but for the whole world and the entire mankind. Allah says in the Holy Quran:

"We have not sent thee but as a universal (Messenger) to rnen, giving them glad tidings and warning them (against sin)." (34:28)

And the Holy Prophet (PBUH) also confirmed this:

"Every prophet who preceded me was sent especially to his own people but I have been sent as a Prophet for all mankind. "

2. The Prophethood of the Holy Prophet (PBUH) is eternal. With him, the chain of revelation and Prophethood has come to an end. There will not be any other prophets.

   "But he is the messenger of Allah and the Seal of the Prophets. " (33:40)

   The Holy Prophet (PBUH) said:

   "With me the edifice of prophethood has been completed and with me the chain of prophethood has come to an end. "

   "No doubt, no prophet will come after me. "

   At another place, he said:

   "When a prophet died, another prophet took his place; but there will be no prophet after me."

3. The religion and the Divine law which the Holy Prophet (PBUH) brought is perfect in all respects. This distinction was not enjoyed by any other religion. The Quran says:

   "This day have I perfected your religion for you, completed my favour upon you, and have chosen for you Islam as your religion. " (5:3)

Through the Holy Prophet (PBUH) a perfect law was given to suit the requirements of all ages and for all countries and this law that is, the Holy Quran was guarded against all corruptions. The life of the Holy Prophet (PBUH) is an explanation of the Holy Quran as confirmed by his wife Hadrat Aishah:

"His morals are the Quran."

It means that while the Holy Quran was the command, the Prophet's (PBUH) life was an example of the teachings of the Quran.

The Quran compares his personality to the sun, while the previous prophets were like lamps. Just as the light of the sun cannot be substituted by any other light and is universal, similarly, after the advent of the Holy Prophet (PBUH), no necessity is felt of any other prophet to follow him.

Salat (the Prayer)

Meaning and Importance : The importance of prayer in Islam is great as it is the foremost duty of the Muslims and the chief of the pillars on which the structure of Islam stands. It is the distinguishing feature between a Muslim and a non-Muslim. The Holy Prophet (PBUH) said:

> "What stands between a man and disbelief is the abandonment of salat. "

And again:

> "Know that among your duties, prayer is the best. "

A unique service that the Prophet (PBUH) rendered to humanity was that he made prayer to Allah not only the foundation stone of the individual development of a man but also the basis of a vast brotherhood of humanity.

The first revelations were in the following order:

> To read and write; to warn the people and declare the Greatness of Allah; and to pray to Allah not only during the daytime but also during night.

The Quran says:

> "Establish regular prayers - at the Sun's decline till the darkness of the night —And pray in the small watches of the morning —" (17: 78-79)

The object of prayer is to remember Allah. It is, therefore, the chief reason why prayer was dearest to the Prophet (PBUH), he said:

> "Prayer has been made a coolness for my eyes."

He declared prayers to be the pillar of Islam and said:

> "He who gives up prayer has indeed disbelieved."

The Quran mentions prayer many times and has laid the greatest emphasis on it; therefore, the sin of giving up prayer is great as also praying carelessly or with an absent mind.

> "So woe to the worshippers who are neglectful of their prayers. " (107: 4-5)

Observance of prayer five times a day is compulsory. Basically, it consists of recitations from the Holy Quran and glorification of Allah accompanied by various bodily postures, such as standing, bowing, prostrating and sitting. Through these postures, Muslims express submission, adoration and humility to Allah. The self-discipline which is needed to perform salat regularly and at proper times, to perform the ablution which precedes prayer and to carry on these prayers in the early morning when sleep is so attractive, during the busy daylight hours when one is preoccupied with work and other activities, and at night when one is tired and wants to sleep reaffirms the human being's total dependence on his Creator and his position as His slave.

The Holy Prophet (PBUH) exhorted his followers to offer their prayers as if they were standing in front of Allah, looking at Him. In prayer, the Divine presence is to be felt as a reality:

> "You should worship Allah, as if you see Him; if you do not see Him, He surely sees you."

Prayer is further meant to seek help as well as guidance from Allah. This seeking of help and guidance is linked up in the daily prayer of the Muslims:

> "Thee do we worship and thine aid we seek. Show us the straight way." (1: 5-6)

In the Holy Quran, prayer is referred to as a sustenance for the human soul so that the man who does not pray to Allah must be regarded as spiritually dead.

Prayer protects one from sins and shameful deeds. Prayer purifies him and brings him closer to Allah. The Quran says:

> "Establish prayer, for prayer restrains from shameful and unjust deeds. "

This continuous reminder keeps the conscience alive,

functioning in a proper manner. Without the regular performance of prayer, it is likely to become inactive and easily corrupted. It will be obvious that prayer once a week or even once or twice a day, does not fulfil this purpose and is only a partial and insufficient expression of the human being's relationship with his Sustainer, who in the words of the Quran is *"nearer to him than his jugular vein."*

The three conditions of the believers as given in the Holy Book are:

> "Those who believe in the unseen, are steadfast in prayer and spend out of what we have provided for them." (2:3)

It will be seen that belief in Allah, the Great Unseen, is immediately followed by the keeping up of prayer, thus showing that by means of prayer, belief is turned into a certainty of the Divine existence. This is again followed by spending out of what Allah has given to man, for the benefit of others, in charity. Thus, faith in Allah is translated into practice by prayer, which in turn, leads to the service of humanity. According to the Holy Prophet (PBUH), self development of a man depends upon prayer:

> "The believers must (eventually) win through— those who humble themselves in their prayers." (23: 1-2)

The Holy Prophet (PBUH) further explained what the Holy Quran taught. On one occasion, he thus addressed his companions:

> "Tell me, if there is a stream at the door of one of you in which he washes himself five times a day, what do you say, will it leave any dirt on him?"

And on receiving the reply that it would not, he added,

> "This is the likeness of the five prayers with which Allah washes away all faults. "

> " When one of you ", said the Prophet (PBUH), "says his prayers, he holds confidential intercourse with his Lord."

A Muslim is required to pray at the prescribed times wherever he may be. But it is preferable and meritorious to pray in congregation with his fellow Muslims if possible. This gathering of all Muslims living in the same locality five times daily, is a step towards the establishment of healthy social relations. In the daily service, these relations are limited to a narrow circle i.e., to members of the same neighbourhood. The circle becomes wider in the weekly Friday service which gathers together all Muslim members of a particular locality, and still more extensive in the two annual gatherings of Muslim festivals of Eid-ul-Fitr. Thus, prayer promotes social relations between different sections of the Muslim community.

Salat is the central point of the life of a Muslim, without which he would not be able to maintain a strong and vital link with his Lord or continue his inner struggle against wrong doing or temptation. Because of all these aspects, Salat is the principal means whereby the Muslim keeps in mind the limited and temporary nature of this world's life and the certainty of death and life to come. Thus, he is able to maintain a sense of balance and proportion between the needs and claims of this world and the Hereafter.

Cleanliness : A true Muslim must be pure and clean in mind, body and heart. Islam enjoins strict cleanliness and purity on its followers. We are told in the Quran:

> "He loves those who keep themselves pure and clean."
> (2:222)

And again:

> "Allah loveth those who make themselves pure."
> (9:108)

The Holy Prophet (PBUH) is reported to have said:

> "Purification is the key to prayer," and also, 'Religion is built on cleanliness', and again, "Purification is one half of faith. "

In the light of the Quranic verses and traditions, it becomes clear that a person should be clean inwardly as well as outwardly at all times, especially at the time of saying prayers. Inward purification is to rid the mind of all corrupt ideas and evil thoughts. Outward purification is attained by taking a bath or performing ablution. If a man cleans himself five times a day, he would undoubtedly be in a constant state of physical purity.

There are certain conditions regarding cleanliness of body, clothes, place of worship, etc. that have to be fulfilled before a person can say his prayers. The Holy Prophet (PBUH) said:

> "Surely Allah does not accept prayers without purification."

Filth : Apart from waste products discharged from the body which are regarded as filth, other impurities recognized by Islam are semen, flowing blood, pus, swine and everything associated with it and wine. All these are included in the definition of Najasat Ghaleezah. If even the smallest quantity of Najasat Ghaleezah falls in any article of food or drink, the whole of it is polluted and becomes unclean and unfit for use by a Muslim. If some Najasat Ghaleezah falls on the clothes, they must be removed and washed thrice, squeezing the cloth each time.

Wudu or Ablution : Ablution or Wudu in the prescribed manner is necessary for a person who intends to say his prayers as the Quran says:

> "O you who believe! When you prepare for prayer, wash your faces and your hands to the elbows, rub your heads (with water) and (wash) your feet to the ankles." (5:6)

Ablution consists of some practices that are obligatory or Farz i.e., those specifically mentioned in the Quranic verses; others that are traditional i.e., the Holy Prophet's (PBUH) practice or sunnat, and others that are termed desirable or mustahab entitling a person to spiritual recompense or Sawab. The approved method of performing Wudu is as under:

> Making the intention or Niyyat, of Wudu, i.e. to say: 'I intend to perform the Wudu for securing Allah's good pleasure and in compliance with His command.' Then recite the following:
>
> In the name of Allah, the Beneficent, the Merciful.
>
> Allah! Forgive my sins."

If possible, one should sit facing the Qibla. The water to be used for Wudu should be absolutely clean.

First the right and then the left hand should be washed upto the wrists thrice. The wet fingers should be passed in between each other. If there are any bangles on the wrists or rings on the fingers, as in the case of females, they should be moved around so that the skin under them does not remain dry.

After this rinse the mouth thrice. Next, some water should be taken in the right hand and sniffed into the nostrils thrice and then blown out. The left hand should be used for cleaning the nose. Then the whole face should be washed with both hands, thrice from the forehead down to the lower portion of the chin and from the lobe of one ear to that of the other. No portion of the face should remain dry. For males, the wet fingers of the right hand should be passed through the hair of the beard. Thereafter, first the right arm and then the left arm upto the elbows should be washed thrice. After washing the arms wipe the head with wet hands from front to back, and pass the back of wet hands over the nape of the neck. Clear the inner side of ears with forefingers and outer with thumbs. Finally wash the feet, right and then left upto the ankles.

The Wudu should be a continuous process, each part being washed and cleaned in the prescribed order, without any break or interval. No part should be allowed to dry up before the other is washed. After the Wudu, the Kalima-e-Shahadat should be recited:

> "I bear witness that there is no god except Allah, who is One, Who has no partners, and I bear witness that there is no god except Allah, who is One, Who has no partners, and I bear witness that Muhammad is His servant and apostle.

And then the following prayer may be recited:

> "O Allah! Make me one of those who repent for their sins; and make me one of those who keep themselves pure; and make me one of Your righteous servants."

Wudu may be performed before every prayer. But the necessity for it arises only when a person has passed urine, stool or wind or if he has been fast asleep.

The items that are specifically mentioned in the Holy Quran i.e., Faraiz-e-Wudu are four in number. These are:

1. To wash the face from the top of the forehead to the chin and as far as each ear.
2. To wash the hands and the arms upto the elbow.
3. To wipe the head with wet hands.
4. To wash the feet upto the ankles.

The items established on the example of the Holy Prophet (PBUH) i.e., Sunan-e-Wudu are fourteen in number. They are:

1. To make the intention of Wudu.
2. To wash the hands upto the wrist.
3. To say one of the names of God at the commencement of the Wudu.
4. To brush the teeth.
5. To rinse the mouth three times.
6. To put water into the nostrils thrice.
7. To do all the above items in proper order.
8. To do all the above items without any delay between the various acts.
9. Each part is to be washed thrice.
10. The space between the fingers of one hand must be rubbed with the wet finger of the other.
11. The beard must be combed with the fingers.
12. The head must be wiped once.
13. The ears must be washed with the water remaining on the fingers after wiping the head.
14. To rub between the toes with the little finger of the left hand starting from the little toe of the right foot.

There are five Mustahab or desirable acts in Wudu. They are:

1. To begin from the right to the left.
2. To rub the neck.
3. To perform Wudu without the help of another person.
4. To face the Qiblah while performing Wudu.
5. To sit on a high and clean place while performing Wudu.

There are four Makruhat or undesirable acts in Wudu. They are:

1. To perform Wudu in an impure place.
2. To clean the nose with the right hand.
3. To talk about worldly affairs, while performing Wudu.
4. To perform against the rules and regulations laid down by the Holy Prophet (PBUH). A person's Wudu becomes ineffectual on becoming subject to the state of Hads-e-Asghar i.e., the state of impurity or uncleanliness which is brought about by answering the call of nature, by passing wind or by vomiting or Hads-e-Akbar i.e., the state of impurity or uncleanliness which is caused by sexual intercourse, menstruation or the period of childbirth. In addition to these, the following acts and circumstances also render the Wudu void:
    1. Discharge of intestinal worms or stone.
    2. Flowing of any impurity from any part of the body.
    3. Taking a nap, or going to sleep by resting the body against any object.
    4. Laughing loudly during prayers.
    5. Losing consciousness or fainting due to some illness.
    6. Becoming insane or mad.

Dry Ablution : Regarding Tayammum (Dry Ablution) the Holy Quran says:

> "If ye are ill or on a journey And ye find no water, then take for your selves clean sand or earth and rub therewith your faces and hands. Allah doth not wish to place you in a difficulty, but to make you clean...."
>
> (5: 6)

It will be seen from the above mentioned verse of the Holy Quran that permission for resorting to Tayammum is granted on the grounds of illness, travelling and the non-availability of water. It can be performed instead of Wudu or Ghusl (bath). If one is suffering from a disease in which the use of water would be injurious and there are chances that the use of water would aggravate the illness; or if one cannot find water for *Wudu* or *Ghusl;* or if one is travelling in a place where there is no one to indicate where water could be found; or if there is a danger that the enemy might attack while one is performing ablution or taking a bath, then one can perform *Tayammum* instead of *Wudu* or *Ghusl.*

The approved, traditional method of Tayammum is as under: First to recite and then to make the following Niyyat: "I intend to make tayammum with the object of removing impurity and acquiring purity."

After this, both hands should be struck on some clean and pure earth or sand, the excessive dust blown off and both the hands rubbed on the face is such a way that no part of the face which has to be washed with water in *Wudu* is left out. In the case of males, it is desirable to pass the fingers through the beard. Again, both hands should be struck on the clean earth or sand, the excess dust blown off and first the right arm and then the left arm be rubbed upto the elbows. This completes the *Tayammum. A* dry stone free of dust, brick or an earthen pot may also be used for the purpose.

As in the case of *Wudu,* several prayers can be said with one *Tayammum.* The acts and circumstances which nullify *Wudu* also nullify *Tayammum.* If *Tayammum* is done because of the non-availability of water, then it would become ineffectual as soon as water is available. Similarly, if *Tayammum* was done on account of illness, then as soon as the disability to use water ceases, *Tayammum* will become void.

The Bath : The Holy Quran says:

> "O you who believe! Do not approach prayers in a state of ceremonial impurity (except when travelling on the road) until after washing your whole body. "
>
> (4: 43)

The Arabic word for bath is *Ghusl* derived from *Ghasl* which means to wash. In religious terminology, it is the act of washing the whole body after Hads-e-Akbar or greater impurity which is caused by sexual intercourse, menstruation or the period of childbirth. Other occasions of taking a bath founded on the practice of the Holy Prophet (PBUH) are upon the admission of a convert to Islam; before Friday prayers and on festivals and after washing the dead.

The approved, traditional method of *Ghusl* is as follows:

1. Make the Niyyat i.e., to say: "I intend to take a bath for seeking purification;"
2. Both hands including the wrists should be washed;
3. Any impurity that there may be on any part of the body should be removed.
4. *Wudu* should be performed in the prescribed manner taking special care about gargling and ensuring that water reaches the throat; but if one is fasting, care must be taken to see that water does not enter the throat while cleaning the nose.
5. Water should be poured thrice on the entire body from the head to the feet, first on the right-hand side and then on the left, taking care to rub the body well.

No portion of the body should remain dry and water should reach even the roots of the hair. In case of females, care should be taken about bangles and rings. There are three faraiz in a bath. They are:

1. Gargling.
2. Putting the water into the nostrils.
3. Pouring of water over the entire body, at last once in such a way that not even a hair's breadth of the body remains dry.

The acts in a bath established on the example of the Holy Prophet (PBUH) are:

1. To wash both hands upto the wrists.
2. To wash those parts of the body where impurity is found.
3. To make the intention of removing the impurity.
4. To perform *Wudu*.
5. To wash the whole body thrice with water.

The *Wudu* performed while taking a bath is sufficient for saying prayers.

Call to Prayers : Every prayer with the exception of the two Eid prayers and funeral prayers is preceded by a call or Adaan. When it is time for a particular prayer, the *Adaan* is called out. *The Muazzin* i.e., the person who calls out *the Adaan* should be a Muslim, male, adult. It is preferred that he should perform the *Wudu* before calling the *Adaan* and stand on a raised platform with his face towards the Qibla. Inserting the tips of his forefingers in his ears, he should give the *Adaan* in a loud and clear voice pronouncing the words correctly and distinctly. The words of the *Adaan* are as under:

1. "Allah is Great." (4 times)
2. "I do bear witness that there is no god except Allah." (Twice)
3. "I do bear witness that Muhammad is the Apostle of Allah" (Twice)
4. "Come to prayer." (Twice; turning the face to the right)
5. "Come to success. " (Twice; turning face to the left)
6. "Allah is Great." (Twice)
7. "There is no god except Allah." (Once)

   In the Adaan for the Fajr prayers, after saying item no 5, the following words are included:

8. "Prayer is better than sleep." (Twice)

Except When : A person is saying his prayers; The Imam is delivering the Khutba; A person is answering the call of nature; it is compulsory on all those who hear the *Adaan,* to repeat in a low voice, the words of the *Muazzin.* When he hears and the listener should say:

> "The strength to shun evil and to do good deeds is only from Allah." When he hears he should say:
>
> "You have spoken the truth and said a good thing. "

When the Adaan is over, the listener should pray in the following words:

"O Allah! Lord of this perfect call and the prayer to be offered presently, grant Muhammad the way of approach unto Thee and also eminence and raise him unto the glorious station Thou hast promised him and bestow his intercession on us on the Day of Judgement. Verily Thou never go back on Thy word."

The words of the *Adaan* in the order in which they are pronounced have come down to us unchanged from A.H. I., when the *Adaan* was said for the first time in the presence of the Holy Prophet (PBUH).

Iqamat - Announcement for Congregational Service

When the congregational prayers are about to start, people stand up and form rows and the Muazzin recites the *Iqamat*. The words of the *Iqamat* are the same as those *of Adaan,* but the person reciting the *Iqamat* does not insert the tips of his fingers in his ears nor does he turn his face to the right or the left while reciting:

After which he says:

"Prayer has indeed begun." (Twice) after which the people present in the mosque say:

"May Allah make the prayer well-established and permanent."

Names and Times of Prayers : The names of the five obligatory prayers are:

1. *Fajr:* This is an early morning prayer.

   The time of this prayer commences after the break of dawn and ends just before sunrise. It is makruh or undesirable to say prayers when the sun is rising. No nafil prayer is to be said till the sun has risen well.

2. *Zuhr:* (Early afternoon)

   The time of this prayer commences when the sun begins to decline and the shadows of things cease to decrease. It ends when the shadow of everything becomes equal to twice the shadow of a thing at noon or mid-day.

No prayer is to be said or the Quran recited at the time of the decline of the sun.

3. *Asr:* (Late afternoon)

   The time of this prayer commences after the end of the time for Zuhr prayers and ends before sunset.

4. *Maghrib:* (Evening)

   The time of this prayer commences immediately after sunset and ends on the fading of twilight.

   No prayer is to be said or the Quran recited at the time of the setting of the sun.

5. *Isha:* (Early night)

The time of this prayer commences after the fading of twilight and ends before dawn but it is desirable to say this prayer before midnight.

Number of Rakat in the Five Daily Prayers The five daily prayers consist of:

(a) Farz or obligatory

(b) Sunnat (traditional) i.e., the Holy Prophet's (PBUH) practice.

(c) Wajib

(d) Nafal

The Sunnat is again divided into Sunnat Muakkadah and Sunnat Ghair Muakkadah.

By Sunnat Muakkadah is meant an act which the Holy Prophet (PBUH) always did except for some valid reason. The *Rakat* which are *Sunnat Muakkadah* must be offered.

By Sunnat Ghair Muakkadah is meant an act which the Holy Prophet (PBUH) did but which he sometimes did not do without any valid reason. The offering of *Rakat* which are *Sunnat Ghair Muakkadah* entitles a person to spiritual reward.

1. *Fajr:*	2	Pre-Farz Sunnat (Muakkadah)
	2	Farz
Total =	4	Rakat

2.	*Zuhr:*	4	Pre-Farz Sunnat (Muakkadah)
		4	Farz
		2	Post-Farz Sunnat (Muakkadah)
		2	Nafil
	Total =	12	Rakat
3.	*Asr:*	4	Pre-Farz Sunnat (Ghair Muakkadah)
		4	Farz
	Total =	8	Rakat
4.	*Maghrib:*	3	Farz
		2	Post-Farz Sunnat (Muakkadah)
		2	Nafil
	Total =	7	Rakat
5.	*Isha:*	4	Pre-Farz Sunnat (Ghair Muakkadah)
		4	Farz
		2	Post-Farz Sunnat (Muakkadah)
		2	Nafil
		3	Witr-Wajib
		2	Nafil
	Total =	17	Rakat

Components of Salat (Arkan) : Each Rakat consists of:

a. Six items which are Farz: (1) Takbir Tahrima, (2) Qiyam, (3) Qirat, (4) Ruku, (5) Sajda, (6) Qaada Akhira.

   If any item (Ruku) is left out, the Salat shall have to be repeated.

b. Thirteen items which are Wajib.

If any item is left out then Sajda Sahw (Prostration due to forgetfulness) becomes necessary and this shall remove the defect.

c. Twenty items which are *Sunnat.*

If any item classified as *Sunnat* is left out due to mistake, no *Sajda Sahw* is necessary and the *Salat* does not become void.

d. *Mustahab.*

Conditions of Salat : Before a person can say his regular prayers, the following conditions must be fulfilled; otherwise the prayers would be void:

a. The body of the person must be clean.
b. The clothes worn must be clean and free from all impurities.
c. The place where the prayers are to be said must be clean and free from all impurities.
d. The 'Satar' (those parts of the body which should be kept covered) must be properly covered. For a male, the *Satar* consists of the portion of the body from the navel to the knees. For a female, her entire body with the exception of her face, hands and feet is *Satar.*
e. It must be the time for the particular prayer to be offered.
f. The *Qiblah* must be faced while saying the prayers.
g. Intention or *Niyyat* must be declared for saying the kind of prayer i.e., *Farz, Sunnat* etc., of the particular prayer time i.e., Fajr, Zuhr etc. that one is offering.

Method of Salat : The approved traditional method of *Salat* is as follows:-

1. Standing erect with the face towards the *Qibla* i.e., the Kaaba in Mecca, with both hands hanging down the sides of the body and with feet nearly four inches apart. The Niyyat should be made in the following words:

   "I intend to offer two/three/four Rakat of prayer Farz/ Sunnat/Nafal of Fajr/ Maghrib/Isha (as the case may be) for Allah the Most High and I am facing the Holy Kaaba."

2. Eyes should be kept at the spot where the forehead will touch the ground while doing the *Sajda.* This is a *Mustahab.*

3. Raising both hands, with the palms and the fingers open and facing the *Qibla,* as far as the ears in such a way that the thumbs of both hands are in line with the lobes of the ears. Females may raise their hands upto the shoulders, but the hands

4. With hands still raised, *Takbir Tahrima* i.e." God *is Great"* is to be said once. If a person is Munfarid, i.e., praying alone, the Takbir may be said in a fairly loud voice; but if he is a Muqtadi, i.e. saying the farz prayer in congregation under the leadership of an Imam, who shall say all the Takbirs in a loud voice, the *Takbir Tahrima* should be said in a low voice inaudible to the other members of the congregation.

5. While saying the *Takbir Tahrima,* both hands should be brought down and folded on the navel in such a way that the palm of the right hand sets on the back of the palm of the left hand with the thumb and the little finger of the right hand making a circle and holding the wrist of the left hand, and the remaining three fingers of the right hand resting on the left forearm. Females are to fold their hands on their breasts. This is called Qiyam. The eyes should be kept at the spot where the forehead will touch the ground while doing the *Sajda,*

6. While standing in the position of *Qiyam* the *Sana* is to be recited which is as follows:-

   "Glory to Thee O Allah; and Thine is the Praise and Blessed is Thy name and Exalted is Thy Majesty; and there is no one worthy of worship except (Thee)."

7. Then the Tawwuz i.e..

   "I betake myself to Allah for refuge from the accursed Shaitan, is to be recited.

8. After the Tawwuz, the Tasmiyah i.e.,

   "In the name of Allah, the Beneficent, the Merciful" is to be recited.

Serial Numbers: 6, 7 and 8 are Sunnat.

If a person is Munfarid all three-Sana, Tawwuz and Tasmiyah are to be recited; but if he is a Muqtadi, only Sana should be recited. The Imam shall recite all the three in a low voice, not audible to the congregation.

9. After the Tasmiyah, Surah Fatiha is to be recited:-

   "Praise be to Allah, the Cherisher and Sustainer of the worlds. Most Gracious, Most Merciful. Master of the Day of Judgement. Thee do we worship and Thine aid we seek. Show us the straight way. The way of those on whom Thou hast bestowed Thy Grace, those whose (portion) is not wrath, and who go not astray. "

   After the last word of Surah Fatiha, (amen) is to be said in a low voice. This is *Sunnat.*

   If a person is *Muqtadi,* he is not to recite *Surah Fatiha.* The Imam shall recite it in a loud voice and the congregation should hear the recitation of the Imam with attention and shall only say at the end.

10. Immediately after the *Surah Fatiha,* some other *Surah* is recited. The voice should neither be too loud nor too low. If a person is *Muqtadi,* he is not to recite any Surah but should hear the Imam's recitation. This is called Qirat.

11. After the *Qirat* is over, *"God is Great"* is said. While doing so, hands are unfolded and the Ruku performed. *Ruku* is to bow down, hold the knees with the open fingers of the two hands, keeping the back straight and in line with the head. The arms should be kept away from the ribs and the legs should be kept straight. In this position, the Tasbih Ruku, viz.

    "Glory to my Lord, the Great " is said three times. This is Sunnat. The Imam, Muqtadi and Munfarid shall all say the Tasbih Ruku in a low voice.

12. After saying the *Tasbih Ruku,* and standing erect, the *Tasmiyah* is recited viz:

    "Allah listens to him who gives praise." This is Sunnat.

13. After the Tasmiyah, the Tahmid viz:

"O our Lord! All praise is due to Thee alone" is recited.

This is *Sunnat.*

If it is a congregational prayer, the Imam shall say the *Tasmiyah* in a loud voice and the members of the congregation - the *Muqtadis* shall say the *Tahmid,* in a low voice. But if a person is *Munfarid,* he should say both the *Tasmiyah* and the *Tahmid* while rising from the Ruku and standing straight. This is *Sunnat.* Standing straight for a short while after Ruku is called Qaumah.

This is *Wajib.*

14. After the *Tahmid,* the Takbir i.e., *"God is Great* " is said once. The Imam shall say the *Takbir* in a loud voice, and the *Muqtadis* in a low voice.
15. While saying the *Takbir,* the prostration or *Sajda* is performed. For this, both knees, then both hands, then the nose and lastly the forehead are placed on the ground. The face should be between both palms and the two thumbs should be in line with the two ears. The fingers of the hands should be kept close to one another, but not closed; the finger tips should face the *Qibla.* The elbows should be kept away from the ribs and the stomach away from the legs. The elbows should not be put on the ground. Females are to perform the *Sajda* in such a way that they do not raise the rear portion of their body, but rest it on their calves. They are allowed to put their elbows on the ground.
16. While doing the *Sajda,* the Tasbih Sajda i.e., *"Glory to my Lord, the Most High"* is to be recited thrice, in a low voice. This is *Sunnat.*
17. After the *Tasbih Sajda,* first the forehead, then the nose and finally the hands are to be raised and the *Takbir viz: "God is Great* " is to be recited once.

This is *Sunnat.*

Next is to sit straight by folding the left foot and sitting on it and keeping the right foot erect, with the toes of the right foot facing the *Qibla.* The hands should be kept on the thighs close to the knees. Females should keep both feet on the right side and sit on their buttocks. This short sitting between two Sajdas is called Jalsa.

This is *Wajib,*

The eyes should be kept on the back of the hands. This is mustahab.

18. Then the *Takbir "God is Great"* is to be said once and the second *Sajda* performed in the same manner as the first *Sajda* reciting the Tasbih Sajda again at least thrice.
19. The *Takbir* is to be recited while rising from the second *Sajda.*
20. Next is to stand straight and repeat the whole procedure from S. No. 5 till S. No. 19.
21. Then the next position is to sit erect as explained in S. No. 17. If *the Niyyat* was for two *Rakat,* this will be called Qaada Akhira which is Farz, but if the *Niyyat* was for three or four *Rakat,* this sitting will be called Qaada Ula.

This is *Wajib.*

22. In the Qaada Ula, first the Tahiyya

    "All prayers and worship rendered through words, actions and wealth are due to Allah alone. Peace be on you, O Prophet, and the mercy of Allah and His blessings. Peace be on us and the righteous servants of Allah." And then the Tashhaud viz:

    "I bear witness that none deserves to be worshipped except Allah; and I bear witness that Muhammad is His servant and apostle." —are to be recited.

Both these items are *Wajib.*

While reciting the *Tashhaud, a circle* with the thumb and the middle finger of the right hand should be made and the third and the little finger of the same hand should be closed. While uttering the words, the forefinger of the right hand should be raised and while saying, it should be lowered. The position of the circle should be retained till the end of the Qaada Ula or Qaada Akhira, as the case may be. The tips of the fingers of both hands should face the *Qibla.*

23. If the *Niyyat* was for three or four *Rakat,* after reciting the *Tashhaud, Takbir* viz *"God is Great"* is to be said once and the person is to rise from the Qaada Ula for the Qiyam of the third *Rakat.*

The third and fourth *Rakat* are to be completed in the same manner as the second *Rakat.*

After the second *Sajda* of the fourth *Rakat,* is the *Qaada Akhira,* in which first the *Tahiyya,* then *Tashhaud* and finally the Darood viz:-

> "O Allah! Exalt Muhammad and the true followers of Muhammad as Thou exalted Ibrahim and the true followers of Ibrahim, for surely Thou art praised and magnified. O Allah! Bless Muhammad and the true followers of Muhammad as Thou blessed Ibrahim and the true followers of Ibrahim, for surely Thou art praised and magnified "is to be recited. This is Sunnat.

24. After the *Darood,* the following prayer is to be recited:-

    "O my Lord! Make me one who establishes regular prayers and also among my progeny. O Our Lord! Accept my prayer. O One Lord! Cover (me) with your forgiveness - me, my parents and believers on the Day of Judgement."

25. After this prayer, the *Salat* is to be ended with *Salam.* For this the face is first turned to the right. Looking over the right shoulder

    "Peace be upon you and the mercy of Allah "- is to be said. Then turning the face to the left and looking over the left shoulder, the same words are to be repeated.

Delayed Prayer : The believers are enjoined to offer their prayers at the appointed times. Failing to do so is a sin unless there is a reasonable excuse for delay. With the exception of prayers missed by women in child birth or menstruation and any Muslim who is insane or is unconscious for some time, every Muslim must offer the delayed obligatory prayer. These prayers have to be offered as soon as possible except at times when prostration is forbidden. In the *Niyyat,* the word Qaza should be added.

If several prayers have been missed in a day, then the *Qaza* should be offered in proper order. For example if prayers have been missed beginning from Fajr then Fajr Qaza should be offered first, then Zuhr and Asr and so on. If the missed prayers are too numerous to remember or if the time available is not enough for both missed and present prayers, then the present prayer should be offered first. The missed prayer should be offered later.

Qaza can be offered for only the Farz and Witr prayers. Except for the pre-farz *Sunnats* of *Fajr* for which Qaza may be offered before sunset the same day, no Qaza of other Sunnats is to be offered.

If Zuhr, Asr or Isha prayers become Qaza while travelling, one should, when he returns home, offer the Qaza of these as if he was still a traveller that is, two Rakat each. If however, the prayers become Qaza before a journey and one offers the Qaza during the journey, he should offer the full four Rakat of the three prayers.

If a person is unable to offer his missed prayers before death, he should make a will to pay compensation which is 1¾ kilos of wheat per prayer out of the property he leaves behind. The compensation for the missed Farz of the five daily prayer and the Witr of Isha comes to 10½ kilos per day.

Friday Prayer : Friday is a day of special importance for Muslims. The following verses of the Holy Quran relate to congregational prayers on Friday:-

> "O ye who believe! When the call is proclaimed to prayer on Friday (The day of assembly) hasten earnestly to the remembrance of Allah, and leave off business (and traffic) that is best for you if ye but knew! And when the prayer is finished, then may ye disperse through the land and seek of bounty of Allah."
>
> (62: 9,10)

The Friday prayer is therefore of special importance for Muslims as established by the above verses of the Holy Quran and the sayings of the Holy Prophet (PBUH).

Friday prayers take the place of the Zuhr prayers on that day, and may not be offered qaza, therefore whoever misses it, cannot make up for it. Instead, he has to offer the Zuhr prayer. Friday prayer must be offered in congregation.

Friday prayer are obligatory on all adult males of sound mind, who are healthy and are residents. Those exempted from attending the mosque for Friday prayer are minors, slaves, the sick, travellers and women. These people are to offer Zuhr prayers in their homes. All normal work is allowed on Friday. The Muslims can carry on with their usual duties and activities provided they come to the congregational service on time. After the service is over, they may return to their business and other worldly activities. It is traditional to take a bath on Friday and to wear clean clothes. Muslims are required to leave their business and go to the mosque as soon as they hear the Adaan for Friday prayers. On reaching the mosque, one should first offer the Tahayyat-ul-Masjid prayers and then the four pre-farz *Sunnats.*

The second Adaan is called before the *Khutba.* After the Adaan the Imam stands up and facing the audience, delivers the Khutba or the sermon, which is an essential part of the Friday service. The Khutba is obligatory and listening to it is Wajib. While the Khutba is being delivered, no conversation is allowed. Even praying, reading the Quran or reciting durud is forbidden. Everyone should be seated and listen to the Khutba quietly till the end. The Khutba consists of two parts, each of which begins with praising Allah and asking blessings for the Holy Prophet (PBUH). In the first part, some Quranic passages are recited and explained. After this, the Imam sits down for a short rest and then stands up to deliver the second part of the sermon. In this part especially, the imam prays for the general welfare of the Muslims.

After the Khutba, *Iqamat* is called and people arrange themselves in rows. Two obligatory Rakat are offered under the leadership of the Imam who recites the *Sana, Tawwuz* and *Tasmiya* in the first Rakat in a low voice. Then the Imam recites *Surah Fatiha* and some other passages from the Quran in a loud voice in both Rakat. The *Muqtadis* should listen to the Imam's recitation and say Ameen in a low voice. When this is done, the prayer is complete.

The Muqtadis may now offer individually four sunnat, followed by two more sunnat and two *nafal.*

Eid Prayer : The two main festivals in Islam are Eid-ul-Fitr and Eid-ul-Adha. Eid means recurring happiness or festival. Eid-ul-Fitr is celebrated on the 1st of Shawwal which follows Ramadan or the month of Fasting. Eid-ul-Adha falls on the tenth day of Zil Hajja and follows the completion of Hajj.

Eid is a day of thanksgiving during which Muslims assemble in a brotherly and joyful atmosphere to offer their thanks to Allah for helping them to fulfil their spiritual obligations. The Eid days start with congregational prayers in the morning. During the prayer the Muslims remember and glorify Allah's name, offer thanks to Allah for Ramadan and ask for His forgiveness and for strength of faith.

The method of prayer for Eid-ul-Fitr and Eid-ul-Adha is the same. Eid prayers are Wajib on all those persons on whom Friday prayers are obligatory. These are congregational prayers and cannot be said individually. Eid prayers are not a substitute for the obligatory Fajr prayer and there is no Qaza for Eid prayer. The time for Eid prayer is anytime after sunrise but before noon. Usually, Eid-ul-Adha prayers are held a little earlier than the Eid-ul-Fitr prayers. No Adaan or Iqamat is required. The prayer consists of two Rakat with the Imam reciting in each Surah Fatiha and another passage from the Quran in an audible voice.

The intention for prayer is in these words:

> "I intend to offer two Rakat Wajib of Eid-ul-Fitr / Eid-ul-Adha (as the case may be) with six additional Takbirs, behind this Imam and I am facing the Holy Kaaba."

When the Imam recites Takbir-e-Tahrima, Allah-o- Akbar in a loud voice, the Muqtadis should also say the Takbir in a low voice, and fold their hands below their navel as in other prayers. Both the Imam and the Muqtadis now recite the Sana in a low voice. After reciting Sana, the Imam raises both hands upto the ears and says Allah-o- Akbar in a loud voice. The Muqtadis also raise their hands upto the ears and say the Takbir in a low voice. The Imam and the Muqtadis should then lower their hands and keep them hanging by their sides. They should repeat this, that is, saying of

Takbir and raising and lowering of hands twice. After the third Takbir, the hands are to be folded in the usual manner. The Imam shall now recite Tasmiyah, Surah Fatiha and some other Surah. The Muqtadis should listen attentively and not recite anything. They should only say 'Ameen' in a low voice after Surah Fatiha. After this, the first Rakat should be completed in the usual manner.

In the second Rakat, the Imam recites Tasmiyah, Surah Fatiha and some other Surah. The Muqtadis should only listen attentively and just say Ameen after Surah Fatiha. After this, the Imam raises his hands and recites the Takbir in a loud voice. The Muqtadis also raise their hands and say the Takbir in a low voice. They should now bring their hands down and keep them hanging by their sides. The hands should be raised and lowered and the Takbir said two more times. Both the Imam and the Muqtadis now say one more Takbir without raising their hands and bow down for Ruku. The second Rakat should be completed in the usual manner.

After the two Rakat of prayer are over, the Imam delivers the Khutba in two parts, with a short break in between. The Khutba is Sunnat and should be heard attentively.

In the sermon of Eid-ul-Fitr, the Imam must draw the attention of the audience to Sadaqat-ul-Fitr. This is a charity, which is obligatory on every Muslim who can afford it. This charity is more rewarding and preferable if it is distributed before the prayers, so that the poor may also be able to celebrate the day in a festive and cheerful spirit.

In the sermon of Eid-ul-Adha , the Imam should draw attention to the duty of sacrifice, which is to be observed by every Muslim with means. It is preferable to slaughter the animal of sacrifice on Eid day after prayers. The sacrifice of an animal on second on third day of Eid is also acceptable.

Private Prayer Dua : Allah created man to be His vicegerent on earth and bestowed upon him the ability to distinguish between right and wrong. He can achieve nothing but what he strives for. It is stated in the Holy Quran that with every difficulty, there is relief. According to Abdullah Yusuf Ali:

> "Whatever difficulties or troubles are encountered by men, God always provides a solution, a way out, a relief, a way to lead to ease and happiness, if we follow His path and show our faith by patience and well-doing."

Along with honest endeavour and effort man needs the help of his Creator in order to achieve his worldly goals. As such man turns to Allah, Who is the solver of all difficulties and asks for His help. Such supplication and invocation is called *Dua*. The Holy Prophet (PBUH) is reported to have called *Dua* the kernel of worship and the weapon of a believer. According to Tirmidhi, the Holy Prophet (PBUH) said that only Dua can change Allah's' decree.

> According to the Holy Quran, "And He (Allah) giveth you of that ye ask for." (14:34)

Abdullah Yusuf Ali says:

> "Sincere and true prayer in faith is answered by God. Thus He gives us everything which a wise and Benevolent Providence can give."

The Holy Prophet (PBUH) is reported to have said:

> "Verily your Lord is ashamed (i.e., shy) of His servants when they raise up their hand to Him in supplication to return them empty."

The Holy Quran, the final and complete revelation from Allah for the guidance of the whole of mankind and for all time, contains guidance for every stage of man's life. It teaches man how to pray and the way to ask for Allah's help, guidance, forgiveness and protection. The Holy Quran says:

> "When My servants ask thee (i.e., the Holy Prophet) concerning Me, I am indeed close (to them): I listen to the prayer of every suppliant when he calleth on Me: Let them also, with a will, listen to My call, and believe in Me, that they may walk in the right way."
>
> (2: 186)

A commentator of the Holy Quran says:

> "The God of Islam, never distant or remote, is the constant companion of His servants, their unfailing support, and infallible prop to those in need and distress. Prayer is the strongest and most visible acknowledgement of God's sovereignty and man's utter dependence on Him."

And also:

> " Prayer is the highest medium in Islam, whereby man can enter into communion with God."

In verse 60 of Surah Momin Allah says:

> "And your Lord says: Call on Me: I will answer (your prayer)." (40: 60)

The two verses of the Holy Quran quoted above teach us that Allah is close to us and listens to our prayers and answers them. Our prayers should, therefore, be made to Allah with the fullest faith. They should be addressed only to Allah Who alone is able to respond to all prayer and invocations.

The Quran says: "For Him (alone) is prayer. " (13: 14)

Invoking the assistance of angels, prophets or saints is strictly forbidden. We must call upon Allah with sincerity and humility. The Holy Prophet (PBUH) is reported to have urged his followers to pray to Allah with full confidence in the acceptance of their supplications. Allah undoubtedly accepts one's prayer and grants it in his own time in the manner or form that He considers best.

The Holy Quran says:

> "When We bestow favours on man, he turns away and gets himself remote on his side (instead of coming to us); and when evil seizes him (he comes) full of prolonged prayer. " (41: 51)

In explanation of this verse Abdullah Yusuf Ali has pointed out:

> "If they receive good they go further away from God, instead of coming nearer to Him. If they suffer ill, they call on God and offer prolonged prayers, but it is not sincere devotion and therefore worthless."

Allah is Samad that is, Independent and Absolute and as such does not need our prayers. It is we who stand in need of Allah's help, protection and guidance. The Holy Quran says:

> "My Lord is not uneasy because of you if ye call not on Him ..." (25; 77)

According to Abdullah Yusuf Ali:

> "God needs no praise, for He is above all praise; He needs no petition for He knows our needs better than we do ourselves; and His bounties are open without asking, to the righteous and the sinner alike. Prayer is for our own spiritual education, consolation and confirmation."

The best of all the prayers contained in the Holy Quran is its first Chapter- Surah Fatiha. Marmaduke Pickthall says: "This Surah has been called the Lord's prayer of the Muslims: It is an essential part of all Muslim worship, public and private."

The Holy Prophet (PBUH) is reported to have said:

> "No prayer is complete without the recitation of the Fatihatul Kitab (Surah Fatiha)."

Abdullah Yusuf Ali has observed:

> "It (Surah Fatiha) sums up our faith, our hope and our aspiration in things that matter. We think in devotion of God's name and His nature; we praise Him for His creation and His cherishing care; we call to mind the realities seen and unseen; we offer Him worship and ask for His guidance and we know the straight from the crooked path by the light of His grace that illumines the righteous."

According to Encyclopaedia Brittanica, Surah Fatiha is 'a vigorous hymn of praise to God... The thoughts are so simple as to need no explanation, and yet the prayer is full of meaning.'

Mosque (Masjid) : The objective of the Muslims, according to several verses of the Holy Quran is to establish prayer and to enjoin good upon the people and to refrain from committing wrong. These verses also sum up the duties and responsibilities of the believers. In order to fulfil these obligations, the Muslims are required to establish a state based on equality, liberty, brotherhood and justice. The institution of mosque played an important role in the practical realization of this state.

It is a characteristic of the Islamic state that religion and politics go together. In the early days of Islam the head of the state was the ruler and chief administrator as well as the religious head. The mosque, was the central place of worship and state administration.

The mosque may not be a consecrated institution as in other religions, yet the Quranic injunction is to establish prayers in a particular place called *Masjid* or Mosque. As such, prayers are offered in congregation, under the leadership of the head of the state or his representative in the various mosques of the state.

The congregational prayer serves as a strong force in uniting the believers. The gathering of all people living in a locality five times daily in the mosque, helps in the establishment of healthy social relations between different sections of the Muslim community. This gathering becomes larger in the weekly Friday service and still larger in the two Eid gatherings. The largest gathering of Muslims occurs on the occasion of the annual pilgrimage or Hajj when Muslims from all parts of the world assemble together.

Congregational prayer levels social differences and promotes an atmosphere of equality and brotherhood. In the mosque a king may stand shoulder to shoulder with his poorest subject and the white man will stand with the black. The congregation prayer leads to a realization among the worshippers that all men are equal before Allah. Differences of rank, wealth and colour vanish, and all bow before Allah.

The mosque is the religious as well as a cultural centre for the Muslim community. The Friday sermon addresses religious, moral and welfare issues of the community. In the time of the Holy Prophet (PBUH) and his successors all matters relating to war and peace, administration and community welfare were addressed and discussed in the mosques. All important announcements were also made from the mosques. In fact during the early years of Islam, mosque was the centre of Muslim activities.

The Holy Prophet's (PBUH) mosque and later many other mosques became centres of education. The Prophet's (PBUH) mosque had arrangements to house people who came there to acquire knowledge. These people were lodged in rooms call Suffa, attached to the mosque. People who were trained as missionaries for the spread of Islam, were also given lodgings at the mosque. In later times, libraries were established in mosques, some containing more than 100,000 books.

The mosque also served as the council hall of the Muslims. In the time of Hadrat Umar two councils were appointed to advise the Khalifa, these councils met in the mosques. The meetings of the Shura used to take place in the mosque and all the administrative affairs of the Khilafat used to be carried on from the mosque during the rule of the first four Khalifas. Deputations from Muslim as well as non- Muslim tribes were received in the mosque, and some of the more important deputations were also lodged there. Judicial affairs were also settled in the mosque. Thus, from the earliest times till today, the mosque has been serving not only as a religious and cultural centre for the Muslims but also as an educational, social and political centre.

The mosque is regarded as the house of Allah and therefore one should enter a mosque with respect. Clothes should be clean and footwear must be removed. Talking loudly, indulging in idle talk or gossip or reading worldly books in a mosque is forbidden. Buying or selling is also not allowed inside a mosque.

Saum (the Fast)

The Importance : Fasting is one of the five pillars on which the structure of Islam rests. Fasting was made obligatory for Muslims in 2 A.H. It is next in importance to prayers. It is prescribed for the Muslims in the form of a month long abstinence from food and drink accompanied by intense devotional activity.

The month of fasting is the month of Ramadan, the ninth month of the lunar calendar, in which the first revelation of the Quran came to the Holy Prophet (PBUH). In this connection Allah says:

> "Ramadan is the (month) in which was sent down the Quran as a guide to man kind .... So everyone of you

> who is present (at his home) during that month should spend it in fasting, but if any one is ill, or on a journey, the prescribed period (should be made up) by days later. " (2: 185)

Ramadan is the month of purity in which virtue flourishes and evil is suppressed. The Prophet (PBUH) is reported to have said:

> "When the month of Ramadan comes, the doors of Heavens are opened and the doors of Hell are closed."

and

> "If a person does not abstain from telling lies or doing wrong when he is observing fast, let it be known to him that Allah does not want that he should stop taking his food."

At another place, he said:

> "Allah says, fasting is for Me and I shall certainly compensate it. Fasting is a shield; so when the fasting of anyone of you come up, he shall not utter foul words. If then anyone rebukes him or fights with him, let him say, I am a man observing fast."

Fasting, like prayer, is a universal religious institution and has been a part of the law brought by previous prophets. All the religions of the world and all the great religious personalities adopted fasting as the principal method of controlling one's desires. The Jews observe an annual fast on the occasion of the descent of Hadrat Musa from mount Sinai. Jesus Christ fasted for forty days in the desert and commanded his followers to fast. Thus, the institution of fasting is universal and existed in some form or the other even before Islam. According to the Holy Quran:

> "O you who believe! Fasting is prescribed to you as it was prescribed to those before you so that you may (learn) self-restraint." (2: 183)

But the Muslim fast is different in all respects from the fasts observed by the followers of other religions. It is not meant as a punishment or self-torture. The verse quoted above informs us that by prescribing a month's fasts, Allah wishes to teach us self-restraint and to make us righteous and God-fearing.

The instincts of hunger and sex are strong in both animals and human beings. Temporary restraint from these directs attention to higher and spiritual things.

Islam developed a higher significance of fasting, 'that you may guard against evil'. The keynote of fasting is self-discipline and self-control. It is an institution for the improvement of the moral and spiritual condition of man. It makes a Muslim disciplined and steadfast in his habits. It also makes him capable of enduring hardships. It gives rise to a sense of compassion and humanism and removes barriers between the rich and the poor. By fasting, the rich undergo an experience which makes them aware of the condition of the poor and hungry and instills in them a desire to help the poor. It enables the rich to thank Allah for the bounties bestowed on them.

Thus, on the material side, fasting involves total abstinence from food, drink and sex and on the spiritual side abstinence from falsehood, speaking ill of others, quarrelling or wrong behaviour.

Method and Conditions : According to the Shariah, Saum or fasting means abstinence from food, drink and sex with the Niyyat or intention of worship from dawn till sunset. If a person does not eat or drink during the prescribed time, but he has not made the Niyyat for a fast, then in the terminology of Shariat or Islamic law, it will not be a fast.

Fasting during the month of Ramadan is obligatory on all Muslim adults, male and female. However, females who are in a state of menstruation or period of childbirth are not to keep the fast as long as such condition lasts; but they have to fast for an equal number of days after the purification bath has been taken.

A person who is ill may postpone the fast of Ramadan, if his physician fears that the illness would increase or be prolonged. Likewise, a woman who is pregnant or suckling her baby may also postpone it. Postponement of fast during a journey is also allowed. These fasts should be kept as soon as possible, after the end of Ramadan and in any case, before the next Ramadan. A person who is so old and weak that he is unable to fast is not obliged to fast. But such a person must feed a needy person twice a day for each missed fast, or give grain or cash equal to Sadaqah-e-Fitr.

Before keeping a fast, it is desirable to take Sehri which can be eaten till dawn. The intention for the fast should then be made for which the following words may be used:

"I intend to keep tomorrow's fast of Ramadan."

Now the person is subject to all restrictions and prohibitions associated with a fast till the setting of the sun. Eating, drinking, smoking, taking of medicine by mouth and sexual intercourse are forbidden during fast. Swallowing something which is not used as food or drink, or as a medicine, injecting liquid medicine, voluntary vomiting, smoking, the entering of water in the throat while gargling are things for which only a Qaza fast is necessary i.e., the person shall have to keep a fast after Ramadan instead of the one that was broken. But if the breaking of the fast through eating, drinking and sexual act was intentional, then in addition to the *Qaza* fast, the person shall have to pay the Kaffara that is, for every fast thus broken, he shall have to fast for continuous sixty days. Even if a single day's fast is missed, he shall have to start all over again to complete the number of sixty days at a stretch. If it is a female, then the period of her menstruation shall not be treated as a break. If the person cannot fast for continuous sixty days, he may, for each broken fast, feed sixty poor people twice a day; or he may give grain or cash equal to Sadaqah-e-Fitr to sixty persons.

While fasting, the use of toothbrush, hair oil and perfume is allowed. If paste or tooth-powder is used, care must be taken that it does not enter the throat. Injecting medicine directly into the stomach or the brain shall make the fast void. Eating or drinking by mistake does not break the fast and the fast should be completed in the prescribed manner. No *Qaza* or *Kaffara* is due in such a case.

If there is a fear that the person may die of thirst, or he has become so weak that there is a danger to his life, then the fast may be broken. In such cases, only *Qaza* is necessary.

Immediately, after the setting of the sun, the fast is to be broken, after reciting the following prayer:

"O Allah! I fasted for Thee and 1 believe in Thee and I put my trust in Thee and with the sustenance Thou hast given me, I now break the fast. "

Fasting is forbidden on the days of *Eid-ul-Fitr and Eid-ul-Adha* and on the 11th, 12th and 13th cf Zil Hajja.

Tarawih : Tarawih are those prayers which are performed in the nights of the month of Ramadan. These prayers are *Sunnat Muakkadah* for both men and women. Men should preferably offer them in congregation in a mosque.

The *Tarawih* prayers start after the four *Farz* and the two *Sunnat Muakkadah* of Isha prayers. Twenty Rakat are to be performed each evening; intention is to be made for two *Rakat* at a time. The *Muqtadis* recite only the *Sana* in the first *Rakat* of each two *Rakat* after which they have to listen to the Imam's recitation of *Tawwuz, Tasmiyah* and *Surah Fatiha.* The *Muqtadis* says the *Takbir, Tasbih Ruku, Tahmid, Tasbih Sajda, Tahiyya, Tashhaud, Durud* and the *Salam* after every two Rakat. There is a short pause in which the following *Tasbih Tarawih* is recited:-

"Glory to Him to Whom belongs all honour and all greatness; to Whom is due all respect and all awe; to Whom belongs all power and dignity; and Who is Irrestible. Glory to the Everliving Eternal, Sovereign; Who never sleeps and Who will never die. He is full of the greatest glory and is Most Holy; Who is our Lord and the Lord of the angels and the spirit. There is no other god except Allah. We pray for His forgiveness and for entry in the garden of paradise and for protection from the fire of hell."

Those who are unable to go to the mosque for the Tarawih prayers may offer them in their homes.

Zakat (the Alms)

Meaning : The Arabic word Zakat (Alms) has been derived from 'Zakat' which means, to purify. By giving charity, the giver's heart is purified from the love of wealth as Allah has said in Surah Taubah that those who prize gold and silver to the extent of hoarding and do not spend out of it in the name of Allah will be branded with fiery hot gold and silver. The Holy Quran contains severe warnings to those who pile up wealth and withhold *Zakat.* There are also several warnings of the Prophet (PBUH) to those who do not pay *Zakat,* about the penalty of the Hereafter and the destruction of the property on which *Zakat* has not been paid.

The Holy Prophet (PBUH) described *Zakat* as wealth taken from the rich and given to the poor. *Zakat,* also called poor rate or poor-tax is really a welfare tax. It is the backbone of the economic system of Islam. Its aim is to improve the condition of the poor and give them economic security and to prevent the accumulation of wealth in a few hands. *Zakat* is a blessing for the giver and a blessing for the receiver and it increases the wealth of the nation.

> "That which ye lay out for charity, seeking the Countenance of Allah, it is these who will get a recompense multiplied. " (30:39)
>
> "The parable of those who spend their substance in the way of Allah is that of a grain of corn: it grows seven ears and each ear has a hundred grains. Allah gives manifold increase to whom He pleases. ". (2:261)

Just as maintaining regular prayers is the sign of Iman that is, faith, the regular payment of Zakat is an attribute of a true believer. On the other hand, one of the signs of non-believers is that they deny the Hereafter and do not pay *Zakat.* Hadrat Abu Bakr, the first Khalifa said that there was no difference between *Salat* and *Zakat.* In fact, he sent an armed force against a group of people who refused to pay *Zakat* while observing *Salat* and professing to be Muslims.

Importance : Zakat was made compulsory in the second year of the Hijrat. It is the second of the two most important pillars of Islam, the first being *Salat* or prayer. By offering regular prayers, a Muslim discharges his obligation towards Allah. By regularly paying the obligatory *charity-Zakat,* he performs his duty and discharges his obligation towards poor Muslims.

The importance *of Zakat* may be judged from the fact that the word *Zakat* occurs thirty-two times in the Holy Quran. With the exception of a few verses, it is always mentioned with Salat. The Quran says:

> "Those who believe and do deeds of righteousness, and establish regular prayers and regular charity, will have their reward with their Lord. " (2:277)

> " So establish regular prayer give regular charity and holdfast to Allah. " (22:78)

The other three pillars of Islam - Prayers, Fasting and Hajj are acts of worship which benefit no one but the person who performs them, but *Zakat* which is an act of worship, performed through giving away of a portion of one's wealth as commanded by Allah, benefits mankind.

The Quran has ordered the payment of *Zakat* several times. It says:

> "Those who (in charity) spend of their goods by night and by day, in secret and in public, have their reward with their Lord: on them shall be no fear, Nor shall they grieve." (2:274)

> "O ye who believe! Give of the good things which ye have (honourably) earned, And of the fruits of the earth which we have produced for you." (2:267)

The Holy Quran speaks of charity as next to prayer and says that prayer without charity is useless:

> "So woe to the worshippers who are neglectful of their prayers, those who (want but) to be seen, (of men) but refuse (to supply even) neighbourly needs."
> (107: 4-7)

Apart from the verses regarding *Zakat,* the Holy Quran contains repeated instructions about spending in the way of Allah. In the definition of righteousness contained in the Quran, we are told that the righteous spend for the love of Allah. Verse 92 of Surah Imran tells us:

> "By no means shall you attain righteousness unless you give (freely) of that which you love."

The same Surah says:

> "They ask you (Holy Prophet), how much they are to spend. Say what is beyond your needs."

Rate of Zakat : The amount of payment and distribution of *Zakat* was defined at Medina in the second year of the *Hijrat.*

The payment of *Zakat* is compulsory on every adult, free Muslim who owns property to the extent of the prescribed rate called Nisab, provided such property has remained in his ownership and possession uninterruptedly for full one year. Zakat is payable not only on cash but also on gold and silver, jewelry, crops, animals, minerals, agricultural lands and all kinds of commercial goods.

1. *On Cash, Gold and Silver:* Zakat is paid at a rate of 2 ½%. A person who possesses 52½ tolas of silver or 7½ tolas of gold is liable to pay *Zakat.*
2. *Produce from Mines:* Owners of mines have to pay one-fifth of the produce of mines. This is called *Khums.*
3. *Land Tax:* The basis of this compulsory tax on the produce of agricultural lands called *Ushr* is to be found in the Quran. It is levied at the rate of one-tenth of the agricultural produce of land benefiting by rain or some natural spring; and one-twentieth of the produce of artificially irrigated lands.
4. On all articles of trade exceeding 200 dirhams.
5. *On Sheep and Goats:* For every forty sheep or goats- one goat; from 121 to 200 sheep or goats-two sheep or two goats; and over, that for every hundred sheep or goats, one sheep or goat is to be received by the state.
6. *Bulls, Cows and Buffaloes:* On thirty to forty cattle, one calf of one year; on every forty cattle, a two year old calf.
7. *On Camels:* On every five camels, one goat or sheep; from ten to fourteen camels, three goats; and from twenty-five to thirty-five camels, a female camel and so on.

Sadaqatul-Fitr : This obligatory charity is an act of worship on the completion of the month of Ramadan. It is obligatory on all Muslims on whom *Zakat* is compulsory.

Distribution of Zakat : The Holy Quran tell us how the *Zakat* money is to be distributed. It says:

> "Alms are for the poor and the needy and those employed to administer the (funds); for those whose hearts have been (recently) reconciled (to Truth); for those in bondage and in debt; in the cause of Allah; and for the wayfarer..." (9:60)

1. People who are poor and do not possess wealth equal to Nisab.
2. People who are extremely needy to the extent that they are forced to beg for their daily food.
3. Those people who are appointed by an Islamic Head of State or government to collect Zakat. It is not necessary that they be needy persons.
4. Those people who have recently accepted Islam and are in need of basic necessities of life.
5. Slaves who work for remuneration and who have an agreement with their masters to purchase their freedom on payment of fixed amount.
6. People in debt who do not possess wealth with which to repay loans. It is conditional that the debt is not due to any un-Islamic purpose.
7. Those people who have to fulfil an obligation, but are unable to do so due to poverty.
8. Those travellers who maybe well-to-do at home, but during their journey do not possess basic necessities, can be given *Zakat* in order to fulfil their travel needs and to return home.

It is unlawful to give *Zakat* to the descendants of the Holy Prophet (PBUH), to one's parents or to one's children, It cannot be given to non-Muslims neither can it be given to a person as remuneration for services.

Hajj (the Pilgrimage)

The pilgrimage to Mecca in Saudi Arabia constitutes the fifth and last of the acts of worship prescribed by Islam. The Quran says:

> "Pilgrimage thereto is a duty men owe to Allah - those who can afford the journey." (3: 97)

To make the meaning of this verse clear, it is necessary to read the previous verse also:

> "The first house of worship appointed for men was that at Mecca; full of blessing and of guidance, For all kinds of beings: In it are signs evident whoever enters it attains security; pilgrimage thereto is a duty men owe to Allah-those who can afford the journey."
>
> (3: 96-97)

The literal meaning of the word Hajj is the will and desire to visit, but in the terminology of the Shariah, it means the will to visit the Holy Kaaba which was the first structure built by Hadrat Adam for the worship of Allah. Then, about 4,500 years ago, Hadrat Ibrahim and Hadrat Ismail rebuilt it at the command of Allah. The story of the rebuilding of the Kaaba is thus related in the Holy Quran:

> "And remember, Ibrahim and Ismail raised the foundations of the House (with this prayer):
>
> "Our Lord, Accept (this service) from us:
>
> Our Lord! make of us Muslims, bowing to thy (will) and of our progeny a people Muslim, bowing to thy (will); And show us our places for the celebration of (due) rites." (2: 127-128)

From the words of this prayer, the purpose for which the Kaaba was built, becomes clear and we come to know that its completion was ordained at the hands of the children of Hadrat Ismail who settled at this spot and from them, the Holy Prophet (PBUH) was raised for the perfection of this purpose.

Pilgrimage to the Sacred House is not an obligation. It is compulsory only on those who are sound of mind, adults and have the provisions of travel. All those persons who fulfil these obligations and yet abstain from performing Hajj once in their lifetime give a lie to their being Muslims. A *Hadith* of the Holy Prophet (PBUH) states:

> "If a person is not hampered by any disease, real necessities or a tyrannical ruler and yet does not perform Hajj, his death and the death of a Jew or a Christian are the same."

Hajj constitutes a form of worship with the entire being of a Muslim, with his mind, body and soul, with his time, money and the sacrifice of all comforts of life to assume for a few days, the condition of a pilgrim totally at Allah's disposal.

Hajj is the only pillar among the fundamental pillars of Islam which requires both physical and financial sacrifices. Prayer and fasting are only physical worships and nothing is spent in their performance. *Zakat* is only financial worship, it does not require any physical labour. But in performing *Hajj* both physical and financial sacrifices are required.

The rites of Hajj centre on complete submission and devotion to Allah. At the same time, they serve as an example of total submission and obedience of Prophet Ibrahim, especially his willingness to sacrifice what he loved most in the world, his son Ismail, at Allah's Command.

Pilgrims come for Hajj from all parts of the globe. As they approach Mecca, they enter into the state of *Ihram,* which means divesting oneself of all marks of status to assume the humble dress and conditions of a pilgrim devoted wholly to Allah. The pilgrims are to abstain from marital relations, quarrelling or from using bad language. They are also prohibited to harm any living thing in the boundary of Mecca.

Hajj is one of the fundamental religious institutions of Islam. It is the greatest of all acts of worship; it is in fact, the culmination of worship. It is an exhibition of brotherhood, equality, punctuality and discipline. It affords an opportunity to Muslims from various countries of the world to become acquainted with one another and of discussing common problems facing the Muslim community.

According to Abu Hurrayrah, the Holy Prophet (PBUH) said that anyone who visits the House of Allah, does not indulge in foul language and avoids the disobedience of Allah, will become as pure and free from sins as a child.

At another place, the Holy Prophet (PBUH) said:

> "Hajj which is free from sins and defects is rewarded with Paradise. "

The importance of *Hajj* has been well described by Imam Abu Hanifa who said that *Hajj* is the greatest of all worship, Ibadat, enjoined in Islam. Its chief importance lies in the fact that it strengthens one's faith in Islam.

Method : Hajj is an annual congregational worship which is performed in the twelfth month of the Muslim calendar, that is Zil-Hajja. The main stages of *Hajj* are as follows:

Ihram : The pilgrim puts on the Ihram, two white sheets of unsewn cloth. One sheet is used for covering the lower portion of the body (from the navel downwards) and the other is to be used for covering the upper portion of the body. The head remains uncovered.

The *Ihram* for women is their everyday ordinary clothes. It is compulsory for women to cover their heads, but no cloth should touch their faces.

Before putting on the *Ihram,* the intending pilgrim should first take a full bath, and clean the body thoroughly. He may now put on the *Ihram,* and cover his head with some unsewn piece of cloth and offer two Rakats of *Nafal* prayers.

Immediately afterwards, he should remove the cloth from his head and with his face towards the Kaaba, make the *Niyyat* of offering the *Hajj.* After this, he should recite the Talbiah in a loud voice:

> "Here I am at Thy service, O Allah! Here I am at Thy service. There is no partner with Thee. Here I am at Thy Service. All praise and all blessings and favours belong to Thee, and all sovereignty is Thine. Thou hast no partner."

The pilgrim has now formally entered the state or condition of *Ihram* and is subject to all the prohibitions and restrictions *of Ihram* which are as follows:

1. Wearing sewn clothes (by males).

2. Wearing of shoes which cover the raised bone of the feet.
3. Putting on a bandage on the head or face.
4. Covering the head or face. Women are required to cover their heads only.
5. Shaving, cutting or trimming of hair.
6. Cutting of nails.
7. Using perfumed hair oil, or any kind of perfume.
8. Using abusive or foul language, or quarrelling.

The following are the undesirable acts *of Ihram:*

1. Rubbing the body for removing dirt or dust.
2. Using perfumed soap for washing the body or face. Bathing with water is permitted.
3. Combing the hair, or passing the fingers through the hair or scratching the head, as these acts may cause the hair to fall, or may kill the lice in the hair.
4. Smelling perfume or some sweet-smelling grass.
5. Using a pin or needle for holding the sheets of the *Ihram.*
6. Using spices in food such as cardamom, clove or cinnamon or using perfumed tobacco.

The following are the permitted acts of *Ihram:*

1. Use of tooth brush or miswak.
2. Harmful insects may be killed.
3. Halal animals, but not hunted, may be eaten.
4. The use of blanket for covering the body, but not the head or face is allowed.

Ihram is the first and foremost *Farz* of *Hajj* and *Umrah.* It is a declaration of one's intention *or Niyyat to* perform *Hajj* or *Umrah. Ihram* is the visible indication or symbol of the pilgrim's renouncing all the vanities of the world to devote himself to the worship of Allah. *Ihram* is a time of forbearance and patience. It symbolises purity, renunciation and the equality and brotherhood of all believers.

After completing Ihram the pilgrim enters Haram, the sacred area around Mecca. Kaaba, the holiest and most sacred place for

Muslims is in Mecca and there are strict rules for the preservation of its sanctity. For this purpose, several circles have been drawn around the Kaaba. The first and innermost circle is called Masjid-e-Haram. The second circle is called Mecca Mukaramma, the city of Mecca, forbidden to non-Muslims, within which living things are protected from violence. It is a place of peace and security. If anyone seeks an asylum in Mecca, he cannot be captured or killed; the hunting or killing of any bird or animal is prohibited, even the cutting of its trees is forbidden.

Haram : The third circle is called *Haram,* the boundaries of which were fixed by Allah's command first by Adam and then by Ibrahim. The Holy Prophet (PBUH) got pillars erected to indicate the boundaries *of Haram.*

Mawaqit : The fourth circle is called Mawaqit. These are the places beyond which no one proceeding to Mecca for *Hajj* and *Umra* can advance without putting on the *Ihram,* otherwise he shall have to offer a sacrifice as penalty.

Kaaba or the House of Allah, according to old tradition, was constructed on the earth by angels nearly two thousand years before the creation of Adam. When Adam was sent down on earth, the angels indicated to him the exact location where this House had been constructed by them and Adam built the Kaaba. The House of Allah disappeared on account of the Flood during Hadrat Nuh's time. It was then re-constructed by Ibrahim and his son Ismail. At one place in the Holy Quran, Allah has called it 'My House' and at another place He has called himself Rabb of this House. There are twenty-four gates through which this House may be entered, but it is best for the pilgrim to enter through the Bab-as-Salam.

Mounted in silver and set in the south-eastern corner of the Kaaba is the sacred Black Stone, Hajr-e-Aswad received by Hadrat Ismail from the angel Jibbrail during the re-building of the Ancient House. According to tradition, this stone was milky white; it has become black because of the sins of people. This holy stone was touched or kissed by Hadrat Ibrahim and by the Holy Prophet (PBUH). Its kissing is symbolic of pure love of Allah and our resolve to obey Him in all matters.

Standing apart from the Kaaba but within the area which encompasses the ancient House are:

a. *Well of Zam Zam:* This well is in the south-eastern side of Masjid-e-Haram. The spring that feeds this well sprang up from under the feet of Ismail, when his mother Hajra, was searching for water for her infant son between the Safa and Marwa hills. From that time till the present day, millions of people have drunk the water of this well.

b. *Maqam-e-Ibrahim:* The place of Ibrahim. This is a stone on which Hadrat Ibrahim stood while constructing the Kaaba.

c. *Hatim:* This is a small area, between Rukn-e-Shami, the corner facing Syria and Rukn-e-Yamani, the south-western corner of the Kaaba but was not included in the covered enclosure. The offering of prayers in the *Hatim* is held to be like offering prayers inside the Kaaba.

Tawaf: The pilgrim enters the Great Mosque and walks seven times around the Kaaba. This is called Tawaf. Each of the seven circuits is called Shaut. Traditionally, *Tawaf is* begun by touching or kissing the Black Stone.

There are several kinds of *Tawaf:*

a. *Tawaf-e-Ziyrat also called Tawaf-e-Ifadah or Tawaf-e-Rukn:* It is a Rukn or obligatory component of Hajj and must be performed between the dawn of 10th and 12th of Zil-Hajj.

b. *Tawaf-e-Qudum:* It is *Sunnat* and is performed on entering Masjid-e-Haram.

c. *Tawaf-e-Sadr or Tawaf-e-Wida:* This is performed at the time of departure and is Wajib for all those living outside the Mawaqit.

d. *Tawaf-e-Umra:* It is obligatory or *Farz* for those performing *Umra.*

e. *Tawaf-e-Nafal:* Any *Tawaf* other than the preceding four categories is called Tawaf-e-Nafal. There is no restriction as to the time or number of such Tawaf, but they must be performed after wudu and Niyyat and in the prescribed manner.

After completing the seven circuits, the pilgrim goes to the Al-Multazim or the place of Holding and prays to Allah for forgiveness. This is a portion of the wall of the Kaaba between its door and the Hajr-e-Aswad.

Sayi : The pilgrim then performs the Sayi which is running seven times between the Safa and Marwah hills. These two hills are close to the well of Zam Zam. Safa is to the south-east, from which the *Sayi* is commenced and Marwa is to the north-east where the *Sayi* ends. It was between these two hills that Hadrat Hajra, wife of Hadrat Ibrahim, ran several times in search of water for her infant son, Ismail. It is in memory of this that *Sayi* is performed. This ritual expresses respect for maternal love and gratitude to Allah, who made the sacred spring of Zam Zam appear for Hadrat Hajra's relief.

The commandment about *Sayi* is contained in the Quran:

> "Behold! Safa and Marwa are among the symbols of Allah. So if those who visit the House in the season or at other times, should compass them round."
>
> (2: 158)

The pilgrim should first climb on the Safa hill. It is not necessary to climb the hill fully. He should climb to such a height only as would afford a view of the Kaaba. After descending from Safa, the pilgrim should move towards Marwa and thereafter; walk briskly between the two hills.

Journey to Mina: After the *Sayi,* on the morning of 8th Zil-Hajja, the pilgrim journeys to Mina, a plain which lies between Arafat and Mecca, about four miles east of Mecca. The pathway into this plain passes through a hill called Aqaba which is famous in the history of Islam as the place where the Holy Prophet (PBUH) took the two pledges from the Ansars of Medina. The pilgrims must reach this place before noon, so that the Zuhr prayers may be performed there. On the way to Mina and in Mina, the pilgrim should continue to recite Talbiah, Darood and Kalma Tauhid.

It is desirable to offer the *Zuhr, Asr, Maghrib,* and *Isha* prayers of the 8th Zil-Hajja and the *Fajr* prayers of the 9th Zil-Hajja in Mina.

Wuquf-e-Arafat: On the next day, that is, on the 9th of Zil-Hajja which is called Yaum-e-Arafat, the pilgrim should leave Mina after the *Fajr prayers* and move on to the plain of Arafat.

This plain is situated at a distance of nine miles from Mecca and about six miles from Mina. According to tradition, it was in this plain that Adam and his wife were reunited after years of wanderings. It was in this plain that the Holy Prophet (PBUH) delivered his Khutba Hajjat-ul-Wida and where he received the final revelation about the completion of Islam:

> "This day have I perfected your religion for you, completed My favour upon you and have chosen for you Islam as your religion." (5: 3)

The stay in the plain of Arafat is called Wuquf-e-Arafat. The best form of Wuquf, deserving the highest spiritual reward is to remain standing, facing the Qibla, while reciting *Talbiah, Istighfar, Kalma Tauhid* and praying to Allah. The assembly at Arafat is the most important part of the *Hajj,* without which *Hajj* would be incomplete. The stay at Arafat is the supreme experience of *Hajj.*

The Zuhr and Asr prayers on the 9th of Zil-Hajja are to be offered together in this plain.

Journey to Muzdalifah: Immediately after sunset, without offering Maghrib prayers, the pilgrim should leave Arafat for Muzdalifah, a plain between Mina and Arafat about six miles from Mecca and three miles from Mina. In the Holy Quran, this place is called the Sacred Monument and the Muslims are especially asked to remember Allah at this place:

> "Then when you hasten from. Arafat remember Allah near the Holy Monument." (2: 198)

At *Muzdalifah* the Maghrib and Isha prayers are offered together at one time. The whole night at *Muzdalifah* is to be spent in prayer and remembrance of Allah. After saying the Fajr prayer on the 10th of Zil-Hajja before sunrise, the pilgrim should leave for Mina. Pebbles for throwing at the devil (shaitan) are picked up from here.

Rami of Jamarat-ul-Uqba: The pilgrim now proceeds to Mina just before daybreak. Here he spends three nights stoning the three stone pillars called Jamarat, That which is nearest to Mecca is called Jamarat al-Uqba, the second which is near the mosque of Mina is called Jamarat-ul-Wusta. At a little distance from this place is the Jamarat-al-Sughra or the smallest Jamarat.

It is reported that Satan (shaitan) tried to deceive and mislead Hadrat Ibrahim at these three places and Hadrat Ibrahim stoned the devil. It is in memory of this, that Rami the symbolic ceremony of stoning the devil (shaitan) is held at Mina. It is to show that we reject the devil and obey no one but Allah.

On the 10th of Zil-Hajja, the pilgrim must cast seven of the forty-nine pebbles collected at Muzdalifah at *Jamarat-al-Uqba* only. The approved method of doing Rami is to stand about five or six feet from the stone pillar, hold the pebble with the thumb and forefinger of the right hand and throw each pebble, one after the other and while doing so, the following is to be recited:

> The pebbles should fall as close to the pillar as possible. Immediately after the Rami on the 10th, the Talbiah is to be stopped.

Sacrifice: Returning from the site of Jamarat-al-Uqba, the pilgrims offer a sacrifice in memory of Hadrat Ibrahim who was willing to sacrifice his son Hadrat Ismail at the Command of Allah. This sacrifice is also part of world wide celebration which unites Muslims everywhere in the common rite of Eid-ul-Adha. Both the sacrifice and the throwing of stones are only outward acts. The real thing is the spirit of piety and submission to Allah which these acts express.

After the sacrifice, the male pilgrim should shave his head. The female pilgrim may clip a lock of hair only. Now the pilgrim is no longer in *Ihram* and the robes can be put off. The pilgrim may now cut nails, take a bath and wear ordinary clothes. However the prohibitions of *Tawaf* are not yet lifted.

Tawaf-e-Ziyarat: The pilgrim should now try to reach Mecca as quickly as possible for the *Tawaf-e-Ziyarat* which is the second most important item of Hajj, the first being Wuquf-e-Arafat. If *Tawaf-e-Ziyarat* is not performed, the Hajj shall be void. If *Tawaf-e-Ziyarat* is performed after the 12th of Zil-Hajja of the year in which the Hajj is performed, sacrifice shall have to be offered as penalty.

After *Tawaf-e-Ziyarat,* the pilgrim should return to Mina to pass the night there.

Rami on 11th and 12th: On 11th and 12th of Zil-Hajja the prescribed time for Rami is after declining of the sun before the *Maghrib.* On both these days, the seven pebbles shall have to be thrown, one after the other, in the prescribed manner, at each of the three stone pillars in this order:

1. Jamarat-ul-Sughra, which is the first of the three pillars while proceeding from Mina to Mecca;
2. Jamrat-ul-Wusta, which comes next; and
3. Jamarat-ul-Uqba which comes last.

Tawaf-e-Wida: On his return to Mecca from Mina, the pilgrim should per form the *Tawaf-e-wida.* This *Tawaf* should be performed before leaving Mecca.

Before departure from Mecca, the pilgrim should go to Al-Multazim, offer two Rakat prayers at Maqam-e-Ibrahim, kiss the *Black Stone* and drink water from the *Zam Zam.*

Faraiz or Obligatory Acts of Hajj:

1. Putting on the *Ihram* and making the *Niyyat* of *Hajj* and reciting the Talbiah.
2. Wuquf-e-Arafat i.e. staying in the plain of Arafat between the declining of the sun on the 9th of Zil-Hajja upto the dawn of the 10th Zil-Hajja.
3. Tawaf-e-Ziyarat on the 10th, 11th or 12th of Zil-Hajja after the shaving of the head or the shortening of the hair.

These three obligatory duties are to be performed in the prescribed order and in the prescribed manner. If any of these three *faraiz* is left out, there can be no *Hajj* and the mistake cannot be set right by sacrifice.

Secondary Imperatives or Wajibat of Hajj:

1. Stay at Muzdalifah,
2. Sayi between Safa and Marwah,
3. Stoning the devil,
4. Sacrifice,
5. Shaving the head (males) or shortening the hair (females),
6. Tawaf-e-Wida.

If any of these items is left out, the *Hajj* shall not become void; but the pilgrim shall have to pay the penalty either in the form of sacrifice or sadaqah.

Sunnats of Hajj:

1. Tawaf-e-Qudum;
2. Spending the night of the 9th Zil-Hajja in Mina;
3. Leaving Mina after sunrise on the 9th for Arafat;
4. Leaving Arafat after the departure of Imam;
5. Staying the night at *Muzdalifah* on the return from Arafat;
6. Taking a bath in Arafat.

If any of these *sunnats* cannot be performed, there is no penalty.

Umra : The word *Umra is* usually translated as minor pilgrimage and it is commonly translated as *Hajj-e-Asghar.* Although many acts of worship performed in *Umra* are the same as those performed during *Hajj,* there are certain fundamental differences between the two. While *Hajj* is obligatory, *Umra* is not. *Hajj* can only be performed on the prescribed dates, but no date or time has been fixed for *Umra.* There is no *Wuquf-e-Arafat,* no *Wuquf-e-Muzdalifah,* no stoning of the devil, no combining of prayers, no *Tawaf-e-Qudum,* no *Tawaf-e-Wida* and no sacrifice of animals in *Umra.*

The *Ihram* is an essential condition for *Umra. Tawaf, Sayi,* shaving of the head or shortening of the hair are components or *Arkan of Umra.*

In *Umra,* the *Talbiah* is stopped at the beginning of the *Tawaf.* It is undesirable to perform *Umra* between the 9th and the 13th of Zil-Hajja.

Pilgrim Road

> In the Name of God be the course and the mooring.
>
> Prayer of Nuh as he launched the ark,
>
> and of pilgrims as they set out for Mecca.
>
> Quran: Sura II: 41 *Hud*
>
> I come with many sins
>
> From a far land ...

O God ! this Sanctuary is Thy Sacred Place.

Prayer on entering the gates of Mecca

Once at least in a lifetime, every Muslim capable of doing so is supposed to pack his bag, leave his home and take the road for Mecca; Mecca, to which his thoughts have turned every day since in childhood he learned to pray.

Over a million people go there each year, most of them during the month of pilgrimage. In 1980, the total had risen to 1,900,000 and about half of these came from outside Saudi Arabia. The Saudi government keeps a register of pilgrims from other countries. In 1968 these were 318,507; in 1969, 406,895. In 1974, out of a total of 1,484,975, the number from outside Arabia was 918,777.

Much of this human torrent flows through Jadda, with its modern airport and deep-water harbour. More and more come by air: 5 3 2,000 in 1979, 571,000 in 1980. This involves handling up to 50,000 arrivals a day during the short and hectic period just before the Hajj. To meet this challenge Jadda's immense airport, dedicated in April 1981, includes a special Hajj Terminal, imaginatively constructed like a huge tent. Here the pilgrims can enter, wait to meet their guides, and find transport by road on the final stage of their journey to Mecca.

Every contrast of colour and costume, class and race is to be seen, but to enter Mecca all are dressed alike in two sheets of unsewn white cloth. External trappings and all things superficial are laid aside. King and peasant, descendant of the Prophet and newest African convert, all are equal in this demonstration of brotherhood — and sisterhood. Women, never veiled on pilgrimage, take full part.

The King moves from Riyadh to lead the pilgrimage and entertain rulers and ambassadors of Muslim states. Informal discussions on policy and action are an important element. The Saudi Arabian government moves its headquarters to Mecca, and a considerable part of the oil wealth of the country has gone into modernising the arrangements for the reception of so vast a crowd.

Health precautions have turned what used to be a hazardous

journey into a still rigorous but comparatively safe undertaking. Strict quarantine regulations, hospitals and mobile clinics, water supplies, drinking taps by roads along which almost a million must walk in a day: all these help the health record, and there have been no serious epidemics in recent years.

In the 1970's, a programme of building completed the expansion of the Great Mosque itself, so that 300,000 pilgrims can gather in its court at one time, each with a clear view of the square-built, black-draped building at its centre, the Kaaba. Tradition dates the worship of God here back to the days of Ibrahim.

No non-Muslim may enter Mecca. Soon after the day when the Prophet re-entered the city and cleansed the sanctuary of its idols -and before his own Pilgrimage of Farewell - it was closed to any but followers of Islam.

Father Ibrahim : The pilgrimage rites recall two events: the story of Ibrahim and the Farewell Pilgrimage made by the Prophet shortly before his death.

The Patriarch and Prophet Ibrahim travelled the desert caravan routes linking the centres of early civilisation: the same routes along which, through the past fourteen centuries, millions of pilgrims have passed - destination Mecca. More important, he travelled the road from the worship of many gods to that of the One Creator. The stories of his family, of his break with idols and his finding faith in the God, Allah, are told in the Quran.

Muhammad regarded himself as the restorer of the pure faith in One God first pioneered by Ibrahim, the spiritual father of the three great monotheistic faiths, as well as the ancestor of the Jews and of many Arabs; cousins whose destiny has been closely linked in history ever since.

According to Meccan tradition, the sanctuary there was first built by Ibrahim and his son Ismail. To reach Mecca from Damascus took later pilgrim caravans forty days. Hebron, where Ibrahim settled and where his tomb is venerated by Muslim, Jew and Christian alike, is nearer still. The journey to Mecca would not be a long one for such a traveller.

There, it is said, he took Hagar when she was turned out by

Sarah. Her frenzied search for water was rewarded by the bubbling up of a spring, Zam Zam, from which every pilgrim drinks. Her desperate wanderings are recalled in the running to and fro of pilgrims between the two hillsides of Marwa and Safa. The climax of the Pilgrimage is the Feast of Sacrifice *(Eid-ul-Adha).* This is in honour of Ibrahim's willingness to sacrifice his son. If they can afford it, Muslim families all over the world kill a sheep or other animal at this time, and give part of the meat to the poor.

Significance of Hajj : The Arabic word *Hajj* means "to set out for a definite purpose". Specifically, it refers to the pilgrimage to the city of Mecca. A *Haji* is one who has performed the Pilgrimage. An Islamic Correspondence Course, edited by Haji Riadh El-Drouble and issued by Minaret House, London, devotes one unit to the Hajj. The story of Ibrahim and his readiness to sacrifice his son is quoted from the Quran. Many, but not all, Muslim commentators think that the son in the story is Ismail, but the text might refer either to him or to Ishaq.

The spirit of Hajj is the spirit of total sacrifice: sacrifice of personal comforts, worldly pleasures, acquisition of wealth, companionship of relatives and friends, vanities of dress and personal appearance, pride relating to birth, national origin, accomplishments, work or social status.

This sacrifice of self was attained to the highest degree by the Prophet Ibrahim (peace be on him) who is known as "The Friend of God" *(Khalil Allah).* The story of his sacrifice is narrated in the Quran in the following manner:

(Ibrahim said) "O my Lord! Grant me a righteous (son)." So We gave him the good news of a boy ready to suffer and forbear.

Then, when the son reached (the age of serious) work with him, he said, "O my son! I see in vision that I offer you in sacrifice: now see what is your view."

The son said: "O my father! Do as you are commanded. You will find me, if God so wills, one practising patience and constancy."

So when they had both submitted their wills (to God), and he (Ibrahim) had laid him (Ismail) prostrate on his forehead (for sacrifice), We called out to him: "O Ibrahim! You have already fulfilled the vision."

> Thus indeed do We reward those who do right. For this was obviously a trial. And We ransomed him with a great sacrifice. And We left (this blessing) for him among generations (to come) in later times: "Peace and salutation to Ibrahim!"
>
> Quran: Sura 37: 100-109 *The Ranks*

Although the events to which this narrative refers occurred many centuries ago ... the spirit of submission to God cannot be illustrated for us in any clearer manner.

"Hajj" also signifies the brotherhood of all Muslims, demonstrated in this greatest of all international assemblies ... (It) reminds Muslims of the forthcoming assembly on the Day of Judgement ... and also of the birth, rise and expansion of Islam, the overthrow of idolatry, the establishment of the worship of one God, and the difficulties and accomplishments of the Prophet Muhammad (peace be on him) and the early Muslims.

Motives for the Pilgrimage : Since 1960 the number of pilgrims from outside Arabia has more than trebled. Modern means of transport facilitate but cannot fully explain this increase.

What draws the pilgrims? Here are answers from a number of Muslims.

The leader of twenty thousand Iranian pilgrims: Abul Fazl Hazeghi, educator and parliamentarian:

> The purpose of the Pilgrimage is to clean the heart. A pilgrim has to set right anything wrong between him and another person, to make his will and to pay his debts. When he leaves home he should be free of debt, hate, bitterness, resentment, impurity.

Personally, I had three times the honour to take about twenty thousand pilgrims from Iran to Mecca. I have seen many people getting a new direction of life - completely different; some of them paying a large part of their wealth to be used for people's welfare, for the building of mosques, hospitals, clinics, etc. I was witness to many restorations between man and man, sect and sect, removing all kinds of misunderstanding and creating new friendships.

A professor:

> I have been several times to Mecca. I went with one idea, and came back with another. I looked forward to seeing the places where the Prophet lived and worked. I found more than that: the vast concourse of people from many lands, all the same, all equal; and their yearning for God, as all move round the Kaaba, hundreds of thousands of us together.

A former prime minister:

> I have been three times - twice for the Hajj. The simplicity of it is inspiring. But Muslims miss something of what it could be. It could be a conference at which everything of importance to Muslims is dealt with. The Prophet used it in this way. At his last pilgrimage, he made a great speech which is a charter for all Muslims.

An Egyptian lady:

> It is like a rehearsal for Resurrection Day - everybody equal, all kinds of people together, the whole of humanity before God.

An article addressed to London students faces the difficulties encountered by pilgrims. Mecca has its dust and flies, its colds and coughs, its taxi-drivers and water sellers who are cynics. "Hajj does need preparation and training," says the writer. He urges an imaginative use of television and radio to introduce different groups of Muslims to each other — in place of the sometimes incongruous mingling of sermons and western dance music. He concludes:

> Hajj has maintained the capacity to lift man from the jumble of his preoccupations and out of the mechanical framework within which he lives. Never is prayer offered with a greater feeling. In the unending flow of worshippers around the Kaaba throughout the day and throughout the night, there is satisfaction to the heart, joy to the eye, and mystery to the soul...

The scorched and barren landscape synchronises perfectly with these feelings of the pilgrim and even helps to produce them. It could never have done so were it cool and green and luscious. Yet there is no debasement, but ardour and grandeur.

The days of the Hajj are indeed unique days. Would that its great possibilities are realised!

Mecca Airlift : During the pilgrimage season hundreds of planes are chartered to bring pilgrims from every continent. Typical is one that started from Britain, in February 1968.

In the bitter cold of London's wintry dockland, the party gathers at the East London Mosque. It is an illustration both of the breadth of the Muslim world, and of the variety of Britain's multiracial society. Pakistanis and Indians are in the majority. A number of Iranians move together. Somali land, Zanzibar, Kenya and Nigeria are represented among the Africans.

Gayest note on a grey day is the emerald head-scarf of a Nigerian woman. She is one of a party of Nigerian students. Her husband says:

> Few months ago nothing was farther from my mind than the Hajj.

I had lost all faith and grip on life. But my brother's son never stopped coming to see me, and in the end he helped me to make a fresh start.

I am going home in a few months. I began to think, "I cannot take home the bad ways I have learned here," and I decided to clean up my life. Now my mother is coming from Lagos, and we shall meet in Mecca and make the pilgrimage together.

Among the party is an exiled ruler. An old man from Guyana is seen off by his son and daughter-in-law, immigrants to Britain. He has stayed with them for two weeks on his way. It is his first journey and he is nervous, as is an elderly Turk whose womenfolk are comforting him.

The wife of the caretaker of the mosque encourages the lonely, and sees that everyone has the necessary documents. She is Welsh. She became a Muslim twenty-seven years ago and has, she says, prayed the regular five times a day ever since. Her warm heart, common sense, box of medicines and knowledge of Mecca will stand the others in good stead. Youngest of the party is a fifteen-year-old schoolgirl, travelling with her mother and her father, who has a business in Lancashire.

The women wait in a room above the mosque. Five coaches are at the door. Before they leave, the Call to Prayer is sounded, sheets are rapidly laid on the floor, and all pray. One woman starts to sing -reciting the verses of the Quran which her Urdu pilgrimage book recommends.

Bags and people are piled into the coaches, and they are away. Tomorrow morning they will be in Jadda, the next day in Mecca.

Discipline of Hajj : In a talk to would-be pilgrims in London, it was said, "There is no beauty in the Holy Land. You go to please God, not yourself." While the hardship is now lessened, the Pilgrimage remains a severe physical ordeal. The lunar months of the Muslim calendar come round at different seasons of the year, and the Hajj often takes place in intense summer heat. Any loss of temper or any altercation destroys its value.

There are many books designed to help pilgrims find their way through the month they spend in Arabia. A recent one comes from Dr. Hassan Hathout, Egyptian doctor. It is a commonsense document, combining advice on health and diet with spiritual background. Dr. Hathout stresses the permanent gain in tolerance and self-restraint.

The journey of Hajj is not easy. It is a taxing process and I do not speak in terms of the distance you cover from Home to Hajj. Coming together with a few hundred thousand people within a limited span of time and space, having to perform the same rites, entailing mass movements in a limited time from one place to another, is an ordeal. Yet the main cause of difficulty is the human one. These people have many different backgrounds and customs, do not speak the same language, and yet they are gathered into this colossal human mass. One can imagine that endless situations would arise all loaded with nervous tension and intolerance. Yet strong "brakes" are placed on any tendency to nervousness or intolerance - it is a criterion of pilgrimage to be pure and tolerant. The Quran says: "The Hajj season comprises the specified months.

He who proposes to do Hajj in them must abstain from obscenity, wickedness and ill-tempered disputes during Hajj."

However provoked, you should remain gentle and tolerant. This attitude of peace and forgiveness is imposed by your own self - and you do not pretend to be tolerant, but you feel you really are. This is indeed a great exercise in self-restraint and self-exploration - for you will sometimes be surprised to discover your tremendous faculties for love and patience, thus unearthing treasures you can count on in your future life.

Some of us who are highly sophisticated, especially those with western upbringing, do time and again ... voice many complaints ... (but) it seems to me that one of the aims of Hajj is to put the one Nation together in the one pot and make them mix and mingle ... The privileged cast away their arrogance and pride because they know it is a sin to be harsh to your brother or be scornful of him ... It is democracy in practice - and it is democracy in love - under God . It is true that some Muslims live in circumstances precluding them from attaining the standard that would please. Instead of being angry with them we should be angry for them.

Prophet's Farewell Pilgrimage : One of the great events of Islamic history took place during Muhammad's last pilgrimage, shortly before his death. He addressed his followers in a speech that was the climax of his mission. This speech, made in dialogue with his hearers, has come down as a summary of his message. Every biographer of the Prophet describes the event, and every pilgrim recalls it as he follows the course of the Hajj in the Prophet's footsteps.

The crowd, an estimated one hundred thousand, gathered at Arafat, a few miles outside Mecca, as it does today. Muhammad rode the same favourite camel, Al Kaswa, that had carried him as a fugitive from Mecca to Medina ten years earlier. By his side was Bilal, the negro ex-slave whose great voice had won the honour of giving the first call to prayer on behalf of the Prophet. His voice, picked up by others through the crowd, was the relay-system by which the words of Muhammad reached the whole assembly.

Then came the last verse of the Quran to be revealed:

> This day have I perfected your religion for you, completed My favour upon you, and have chosen for you Islam as your religion.
>
> Quran: Sura 5: 4 *The Table*
>
> In the course of this address, the Prophet called for the wiping out of vendettas- starting with a blood-feud in his own family as an example. This may be compared with Moses' farewell speech to the men and women of the Exodus, when he said, "Vengeance is mine, saith the Lord, I will repay." (Deuteronomy 32:35)

Among many summaries of this speech, here is one designed for teaching children and students. It comes from *An Easy History of the Prophet of Islam,* published in Lahore.

1. All the customs and practices of the pagan age are abolished.
2. All compensation for bloodshed of the old days is abolished: and on behalf of my family I declare illegal the indemnity for the blood of Ibn Rabia ibn Harith [murdered cousin of the Prophet].
3. All usuries of the past are wiped out.
4. Fear God in respect of women. You, men, have your rights over your wives and they have their rights over you.
5. As regards your slaves, be fair to them. Give them to eat what you eat and to wear what you wear.
6. Your blood and your properties are as sacred for one another as are this day, this month and this place.
7. Each Muslim is a brother of another. All Muslims form one brotherhood.
8. An Arab has no superiority over a non-Arab, nor has a non-Arab over an Arab. You are all born of Adam, and Adam was made out of clay.
9. Whoever is entrusted with a thing belonging to another must deliver his trust to its owner.
10. The debtors must pay their debts.
11. I leave behind one thing, and you will never go astray if you hold it fast, and that is the Book of God.

Three Holy Cities: Mecca, Medina and Al-Quds (Jerusalem): Mecca, Medina and Jerusalem are all holy places to the Muslim. Almost every pilgrim to Mecca also visits Medina (2,25 miles northwest of Mecca), where the Prophet Muhammad lived for ten years and was buried.

Through the centuries, pilgrims to Mecca have regarded a visit to Jerusalem as a completion of their pilgrimage. The city is known in Arabic as Baitul-Maqdis (the Holy House), or Al-Quds.

There Muslim and Christian pilgrims have sought the same holy places. When the end of the Hajj has coincided with Easter, large numbers of pilgrims of both faiths have often mingled in the streets. The writer was among them in 1966, the year before the Six Day War.

The Christian shrines were visited by the Muslim pilgrims. One party from Iraq were heard in disappointed argument because a service prevented them from entering the cave in the Church of the Nativity in Baitulaham where by tradition Jesus was born. They had just been to Hebron, to the ancient mosque which marks the tomb of Ibrahim. From some countries, there were pilgrim parties of both faiths: from Nigeria, for instance, and Yugoslavia. The parked coaches from the latter country might carry either Christians or Muslims.

The streets of the Old City were brightly lit, the shops open all night. Many homes had been opened to house the thousands from Syria and Egypt who, with the Cypriots, formed the mass of Christian .pilgrims. Alongside these Christian homes were those with gay pictures chalked on the doors to welcome home Hajis. *Hajj mabrur wa dhanab maghfur.* "Pilgrimage made and sins forgiven." Less edifying were the second-hand clothes markets outside Herod's Gate and at the coach park, where Europe's old coats were finding their way to remote villages and Bedouin camps.

For the Muslims, all these things were incidental to the visit to Al-Masjid al-Aqsa, the Farthest Mosque, revered by the Prophet; the place towards which his prayers were first directed, and the starting point of his great mystical experience, the journey into heaven, during which he received the revelation about the five daily times of prayer. This event is known as the "Night of Ascent", and is said to have inspired Dante.

About one fifth of the area of the Old City is taken up with the courts of the Noble Sanctuary, Al-Haram al-Sharif, with its large congregational Mosque, Al-Aqsa, to the south, and in the centre the marvel of the Dome of the Rock. In 1966, repairs and restoration had just been completed. The fresh gold on the dome dominated the landscape and the city. A tall crane still stood by its side, and the little Dome of the Chain awaited repair, its condition a measure of the extent of the work done on the larger structure.

Every Muslim child knows the story of the Arab capture of Jerusalem. In AD 638 the Patriarch in the beleaguered city offered to surrender it, but only to the Caliph 'Umar in person. 'Umar, simply dressed, entered the city and said his prayers not in, but near, the Church of the Holy Sepulchre, so that his followers might not be tempted to take it over. The treaty he made is regarded as a model of tolerance. This and the parallel story of the reconquest of the city by Saladin (Salah ad-din) after a century of Christian occupation are viewed in sharp contrast with the bloodshed and slaughter associated with the Frankish armies in 1099 when the Crusaders took the city.

The Dome of the Rock, first of the great architectural achievements of Islam, was finished by the ninth caliph, Abdul Malik, in the year AD 691. In its thirteen centuries of life, it has been fortunate in its restorations. Each, including the most recent, has kept to the character of the building and has enhanced its beauty. As with other great works of art, it has a perfection which is, in its own sphere, unsurpassed.

The care of Al-Aqsa and the Noble Sanctuary is the trust of a group of families whose tenure goes back eight hundred years, though many were exiled after 1967. They were installed by Saladin after he recaptured Jerusalem from the Crusaders in AD 1189. Khatibs, Hussainis and Nashashibis have lived in the houses overlooking the Noble Sanctuary ever since, and generation has followed generation in its service. Some have been there longer still. Khalidis - the family of the great general Khalid ibn Walid have resided in the city since AD 638. More recent comers are Shihabis, who arrived from Lebanon three centuries ago. To them are entrusted the Prophet's cloak and pen, precious relics which are shown to the faithful each year on the Night of Ascent, Muhammad's mystical journey to heaven.

In the Dome of the Rock, human skill and artistry surround something unique in its rugged simplicity. The stretch of bare rock beneath the dome is a stark reminder of a Greatness no image can evoke, which commands the total submission of man's every gift and talent.

The rock is linked with Ibrahim. Centuries after his time, David bought it, and Solomon built his temple here. In these courts Jesus walked and taught. No place on earth has been the focus of so much faith and so much hope. It is central to all three of the great monotheistic faiths. They have a basic kinship stemming from Father Ibrahim. Cooperation between Jews, Christians and Muslims was the hope of the Prophet Muhammad. He was disappointed, but his respect for others who believe and obey God is deeply rooted in the Muslim mind.

6

Philosophical Basis

The God Almighty (Allah) had created man (and woman) in his own image by giving him three deform faculties, which he had given to no one else in his creation in the same proportion or combination. These three deform faculties are transcendent intelligence, free will and gift of speech.

Fundamental Ideology

There is no blind faith in Islam. In the Quran, Allah invites us to either accept or reject Islam, but with reason. However, while the Quran lays a great emphasis on reason, it does not consider it as a sole means of gaining knowledge and the only criterion for judging truth. Thus, while Islam is a great proponent of reason, it is against rationalism.

The intellect, through which divine knowledge is received, must not be mistaken for reason alone (al-aql-al-juzi). In Islám, the combined faculty of reason and intuition (al-aql al-kuli) serves as an instrument for reaching the divine truths, which are super-rational but not irrational. The Quranic term for the seat of knowledge is "fuad" which means both heart and mind. But if this faculty is obscured by the worldly passions, it can become the veil that hides man from the divine and leads him astray. We should therefore be worry of the two-edged nature of the "sword of reason".

Paradoxical as it may seem, while the Quran lays great

emphasis on reason, it also requires us to believe in the unseen (Al-ghayb). It will indeed by presumptuous on our part if we tried to comprehend the whole of the Quran strictly in the context of the current framework of the scientific method, which is constrained by a number of severe limitations. At a lower level, these limitations pertain to the direct verification of an occurrence (Null hypothesis) and at a higher level to the fragility of human observation (the Hisenburg principle of uncertainty) and the relativity of observation (Einstein). It is indeed in the recognition of human limitations that the Islamic faith also extends to things which are beyond the reach of human perception.

The faith in Islam (Al-Iman) is connected with transcendent intelligence, which must lead a believer to certainty—certainty of Absolute and attachment of all things to the Absolute. In this context the Quran describes three distinct stages of knowledge. First, "ilm-al-yaqin" (Knowledge of certainty) knowledge through information, second, "ayn-al-yaqin" (eye of certainty) knowledge through experience and third and the highest "haqq-al-yaqin" (truth of certainty) knowledge through being.

Free Will : Man is free to choose his destiny. Without such a freedom, he could not be the pride of God's creation. God knows how a particular individual will behave in a particular situation because He is God. But this in no way contradicts man's inherent freedom. Islam literally means submission (to the Will of God) and it is submission with free will which alone is acceptable to Him, thus, Al-Islam which represents an equilibrium in terms of the Absolute and with the Absolute, is based on the free will and submission with free will to the divine law, which includes ritual prayers, fasting, alms giving, correct conduct, etc.

Gift of Speech : Man has been given the gift of speech for the beneficial communication. The Quran enjoins people to speak well to each other. But, above all, the gift of speech has been given to man so that he may praise his Creator. The remembrance of God (dhikr-Allah) is based on Al-Ihsan (the way: virtue) which reflects excellence and implies that you should worship God as if you see Him and if you do not see Him, He sees you. Al-Ihsan also implies special compensations over and above justice (Adil) for individuals who may be suffering from any deficiencies, whether physical, economic, or spiritual.

The remembrance of God is the quintessential prayer in Islam, which in the Quran is rated higher than other religious obligations. This is because it is the remembrance of God, which by purifying our minds and hearts, will lead us to the "ayn-al-yaqin" (eye of certainty), enabling us to discern the things or creatures of the unseen and thus augment our faith layer upon layer.

Central Framework : To summarize, the central framework of Islam is based on Al-iman, Al-Islam, and Al-ihsan. Al-Iman (faith), which reflects certainly (yaqin) is based on transcendent intelligence; Al-Islam (the law: submission) which reflects equilibrium is based on the free will and Al-Ihsan (the way: virtue) which reflects excellence is based on the gift of speech. Thus, Islam is a religion of certainty, equilibrium and remembrance and is based on three deform faculties of transcendent intelligence, free will, and gift of speech. Equilibrium implies maintenance of a balance between Allah and His creation and between His transcendence (the law) and immanence (spirituality). Also, it implies an attitude of moderation both in speech and actions.

Another fundamental percept of Islam is that of orientation, which implies that not only our thinking should be correct on purely religious questions, but also on broad social and political issues. The central theme of Islam is welfare and not salvation. Therefore, for Islam the main objective is to attain the state of felicity by following the laws of God and not merely to observe these laws for their own sake. The Islamic law is there to serve man and not the other way around. Also, we should make a distinction between the Islam as such and the cultural practices of various Muslim countries.

Heavenly Knowledge

Allah wishes all mankind to lead a happy and a useful life on earth. To attain a state of felicity man needs both an orientation and a set of rules and regulations. The logical conclusion of any laws made by man, based on these are of self-interest, conflict and oppression. Only One God's laws could be attuned to the welfare of all mankind. The central theme of Islam is welfare and not salvation. Therefore, for Islam the main objective is to attain the state of felicity by following God's laws and not merely to observe these laws for their own sake. The Islamic law is there to serve the man and not other way round.

The final source of Islam's laws is the Quran. The life example of the Prophet (PBUH) had illuminated God's laws for us. The Prophet was, so to speak, a living Quran. However, as Quran is the final message of God to man, continuing Ijtihad (independent thinking) on it is necessary in order; to frame Islamic laws for all times to come. The legal interpretations of the Great Imams of the past can serve as a point of reference rather than as an iron-clad framework. It should be remembered that finality belongs to Allah and His Word (the Quran) alone, to ascribe finality to anyone else would tantamount to committing a grave Shirk. No doubt, while the truth of this statement would be self- evident to all true followers of Islam most of them would resist opening the gates of Ijtihad in the fear that once these gates are opened, these will also be opened to the enemies of Islam. However, they should have no such fears. In fact, this may bring the hidden enemies of Islam out into the open. Any way, we should not allow our fears of today to kill our hopes of tomorrow.

Moreover, the Quran is not mere a book of the sources of law. It is the God's all-embracing message to mankind, which give firm guidelines for the spiritual orientation of man. Without a correct spiritual orientation, any code of law would remain but an empty shell. Without the spiritual spring of Islam erupting in the hearts of men and women, no true Islamic order could be established and any attempted outward observance of Islamic laws would amount to no more than an exercise in futility.

Academic Standards

Islam has insisted that life is to be lived in a positive, gainful and effective manner and that an individual has deep obligations towards the collective welfare of the community. To achieve this objective it is essential to maintain a constant flow of fresh knowledge into the society so that its members can be saved from ignorance and stagnation.

The pre-Islamic Arabia was not entirely denuded of learning, but whatever evidence has been preserved shows that knowledge as something higher, nobler and truer did not exist at that time. The Prophet of Islam for the first time in the history of Arabian peninsula made knowledge an essential tool for understanding realities of life. Under his inspiring guidance, learning acquired respect and reverence which remained the hallmark of Islamic civilization for centuries afterwards.

The Quran itself in lucid and self-explanatory terms has laid great emphasis on the acquisition of knowledge. In the chapter entitled *Al-Adaq* (The Clot) which is considered by commentators to be among the earlier, if not the earliest revelations, the Quran in unmistakable terms points out God's desire to educate men in arts and sciences which are difficult for them to comprehend.

1. Read : In the name of thy Lord who createth,
2. Createth man from a clot,
3. Read: And thy Lord is the Most Bounteous,
4. Who teacheth by the pen.
5. Teacheth man that which he knew not.

There is ample evidence in Quran that knowledge was essential even for the prophets.

And unto Solomon (we subdued) the wind in its raging. It set by his command toward the land which We had blessed. *And of everything We are aware.*

And about the Prophet Lot the Quran says:

> And unto Lot we gave judgement and knowledge, and We delivered him from the community that did abominations. Lo ! they were folk of evil, lewd.

The importance which the Quran attaches to knowledge can further be explained by the frequency with which it has used the word *ilm* (knowledge).

According to one estimate it has been used 750 times in the Holy Book.

The Traditions of the Prophet have also emphasized in unequivocal terms that life without knowledge is hollow and barren.

Knowledge is a great fertilizer of the human mind, and to have the maximum harvest out of human existence it is essential to enrich one's life with continuous learning. Al-Bukhari in his monumental work attributes a tradition to the Prophet which says that disappearance of knowledge and absence of scholars from society would spell the demise of human civilization. Abu Daud (202-275/817-889) also makes several statements to illustrate the basic fact that knowledge alone could make life radiant with spiritual, material and moral richness. The position of the scholar among people, in his opinion, is the same as that of the moon among stars. He copies numerous traditions of the Prophet which accord a very prestigious and reverent position to scholars in a Muslim community. He also emphasizes that knowledge, particularly religious knowledge, should not be sold for worldly gains.

The entire Hadith literature is replete with references from Quran and the sayings of the Prophet which abundantly prove that religion and knowledge are the two main pillars of human life.

Some historians have attributed the following two traditions to the Prophet :

> Acquire knowledge, because he who acquires it in the way of the Lord performs an act of piety; who speaks of it, praises the Lord, who seeks it adores God, who dispenses instruction in it, bestows alms, and who imparts it to its fitting objects, performs an act of devotion to God. Knowledge enables its possessor to distinguish what its forbidden from what is not; it lights the way to Heaven; it is our friend in the desert, our society in solitude, our companion when bereft of friends; it guides us to happiness; it sustains us in misery; it is our ornament in the company of friends it serves as an armour against enemies. With knowledge the servant of God rises to the height of goodness and to a noble position, associates with sovereigns in this world and attains to the perfection of happiness in the next.

There has never been any doubt in Islamic history that knowledge is a benediction of God and it is fully integrated into Iman (Belief). A verse in the Quran reads as follows :

> God will lift up by degrees those among you who have come to believe and those who have been given knowledge.

And those who come to believe know.

And we have set out signs for people who know —for people who understand—for people who have come to believe.

Sayed Hussain Nasr has summed up the significance of knowledge in Islam in the following words:

> Many of the verses of the Quran that were to follow affirmed the sacred nature of knowledge and science (ilm) one of the God's name being 'He who knows (Al-alim). The Prophet himself though unlettered from the stand-point of human knowledge was at the same time the channel of the revelation of the Book which is considered by all Muslims to be the quintessential sum of all knowledge both human and divine. Moreover, he reaffirmed the teachings of the Quran by stressing that the acquisition of knowledge to the limits of one's abilities is incumbent upon every believer, as a part of his religious duties. His sayings such as 'Seek knowledge from cradle to the grave,' 'Seek knowledge even in China' were echoed through the later centuries as the most authoritative arguments for teaching and propagating knowledge (ilm) even though debates also arose as to exactly what the knowledge to which the Prophet alluded, and whose attainment he considered so essential, encompassed.

Islam has insisted that reason and revelations are the two wheels of the vehicle of life, ana in order to reach one's destination, both wheels have to be equal in size, strength and lubrication. In other words, search for knowledge is an act of piety ; it is equivalent to prayer. To make search for fresh knowledge easier, Islam has kept its principles and precepts flexible, and left an ample room for individual interpretation, so that growing complexities of human problems could be resolved in the light of increasing knowledge. Grunebaum says, "There is an element of sober reasonableness in Islam which works toward a human application of its precepts.

The Prophet was sent not to make life more difficult but to facilitate it." The emphasis, however, was on the usefulness of knowledge, so that the believer could shape the affairs of his life strictly according to the ethical ideals of Islam.

In short, the role of knowledge in the religio-political life of the Muslim community is decisive and all-pervading. It is considered to be a source of strength for human character. It enlightens the soul, dispels ignorance, enriches the mind, produces excellencies in intellect, saves men from omissions and excesses, cures passions and impulses of their waywardness and solidifies faith and belief in the revealed word of God.

The Perception

It is very difficult to formulate a concrete and operational definition for an elusive and eternally ambiguous term like knowledge. Difficulties multiply manifold in the case of Islam, because in it secular and religious knowledge are completely intermingled. In the mind of a Muslim, knowledge includes every thing which reason and revelation can unearth for the spiritual and material betterment of mankind. Since the Quran and the Prophet had emphasized the importance of knowledge in unmistakable terms, Muslim scholars in every period of Islamic history took special pains to explain the scope and subject matter of knowledge. The result of all these endeavours, however, has been that Islamic literature is crowded with bewildering variety of definitions.

Franz Rosenthal in his valuable work listed 107 definitions from various source books.

Philip K. Hitti defines ilm (Islamic knowledge) in the following words :

> The Arabic word for science (ilm) like its English correspondent, etymologically means "knowledge" or "learning." It may be used in the broad sense to mean knowledge systematized with reference to general truths and laws, or more specifically, to refer to knowledge as it relates to physical world in which case it is known as physical or natural science.

The term ilm (knowledge) as originally used was a universal blanket for all kinds of intellectual, philosophical and scientific pursuits, which enabled human beings to explore the mysteries of nature, and highlighted the true meanings of the revelation. But at a very early stage of the growth of Muslim scholarship, knowledge was categorized into different areas and instead of ilm (knowledge) singular, ulum (plural) became a common term for scholarship. The general opinion among the historians of Islam is that as territories which had advanced civilization were conquered outside Arabia, realization dawned upon Muslims that knowledge was extremely diverse in nature, and that each branch constituted a distinct area of specialization, requiring specific kind of intellect and a particular kind of education and training.

According to Franz Rosenthal there reached a stage when the number of various branches of knowledge had risen to 150 and according to one account in the sixteenth century, the number possibly could be as high as 316. In spite of this bewildering diversity, however, a belief that knowledge in essence is one, continued to persist in the world of Muslim scholarship. All branches of knowledge were interconnected and in order to understand the realities of life, and resolve baffling complexities which hampered the solutions of problems it was essential to use maximum amount of information from all branches of knowledge.

The Muslim scholars, however, never gave any definitive view on how to relate the original Quranic concept of Ilm to the later developments which produced countless fields of intellectual specialization. The study of the landmark figures in the history of Muslim scholarship clearly demonstrates that compartmentalization of knowledge did not deter them from mastering several branches of knowledge at the same time, pleading that division of human learning into different subjects was only an effort to systematize knowledge and facilitate its assimilation, otherwise knowledge was one compact whole.

In Arabic and Persian the term Hakeem which meant wise was used for physician as well as for philosopher. Very rarely a distinction was made between natural sciences, humanities, and other related subjects. As a general rule the reputation of a scholar depended on the number of subjects on which he could claim mastery, and the amount of light that he could shed on an issue through various interdisciplinary approaches.

Practical Aspects

Knowledge is the guardian of soul, architect of morality, and custodian of values and ideals which are the major determinants of human destiny both here and hereafter. Intellect, which is the unique characteristic of human beings, is meant to be utilized for the cultivation of divine attributes. It is the only instrument, which is properly cultivated and effectively used, could narrow the gap between God and man. Ignorant and untutored mind can never hope to develop the ability which uncovers the inscrutable secrets of the universe. Scholars of all shades of opinion in Islam agree that pure reason alone is an insufficient guide. Reason in their opinion needs always to be supplemented with the revealed word of God. Ideal conditions for human thought and action are possible only when a believer uses both the secular and spiritual knowledge in resolving the problems of life. Revelation does not put any serious constraint on the freedom of thought. Except for some fundamental principles relating to the sovereignty of God, the mission of the Prophet, and sanctity of the word of the Quran, all the rest of the fields of human activity are subject to independent judgement, and rational interpretation. Outside the boundaries laid down by Shariah, the entire world of knowledge is a fit subject for research. As a matter of fact such an investigation through reason and logic, it is said, would strengthen the faith of the believer.

In Islam knowledge is not the monopoly of the learned few. Every Muslim according to his needs and means is under religious obligation to accept learning as a continuous process in his life. Reason and debate are considered to be competent instruments for the spread of enlightenment, and independent judgement based on righteous niyat (intention) is a very powerful instrument to overcome difficulties of life. It is due to this insistence on research and inquiry as a religious duty, that the early Muslims produced some of the greatest early heralds of scientific knowledge. Between the ninth and twelfth centuries when the rest of the world was intellectually stagnant, Muslim scholars wrote some immortal works in every branch of scientific knowledge. Schools and academies in the Muslim empire were throbbing with creativity and innovation. A careful examination of some of the fundamental duties of the Islamic faith showed that without scientific knowledge their performance was impossible. Fasting, pilgrimage and numerous other religious ceremonies required careful and scientific understanding of the lunar calendar. Five daily prayers needed precision regarding the movement of the sun. It was essential to devise instruments by which the increasing and decreasing shadows between dawn and dusk could be measured with exactness. Prayers in Islam were congregational, and thus there was all the more reason for finding a universally accepted standard by which everyone could be in time in the mosque. Similarly, the numerous details regarding many other aspects of the sacred law could only be assured by specialized knowledge. For instance, the laws of inheritance, Zakat (Poor Relief) and Waqf (religious endowments) required considerable knowledge of various sciences.

Some Western scholars have tried to minimize the role of Islam in the sudden upsurge of scientific inquiry in the Muslim lands which followed its advent. Grunebaum says :

> No matter how important the contribution of Muslim scholars were able to make to the natural sciences, and no matter how great the interest with which, at certain periods, the leading classes and the government itself followed and supported their researches, those sciences (and their technological application) had no root in the fundamental needs and aspirations of their civilization.

This statement by a learned orientalist, however, smacks of prejudice. Islam's broad but firm injunctions in favour of knowledge and reason, played a decisive role in unleashing the spirit of inquiry, which led to the sudden upsurge of scientific learning in lands which for centuries had been intellectually barren.

Western View : Western scholars have been critical of Islamic civilization, pointing out that except for one powerful thrust during the 4th and 5th centuries of Hijra it has been intellectually sterile and stagnant. Muslim writers in their opinion were trapped in dogma, and their mind and thought revolved with few exceptions around unalterable stereotypes. Their capacity to widen the horizons was limited by the inflexible and insurmountable theological barriers. These impressions could be the result of prejudice or misunderstanding or may be both. It is not our intention to make another apologetic plea in defence of Muslim scholarship. The approaches of the Muslim scholars were far from being perfect. They had numerous faults of methodology, and many of them were patently careless in the collection of data. It is, however, unfair to think that Islam in any way was hostile to independent intellectual inquiry and that it was a religion which ultimately led to permanent stagnation in Islamic thought.

In order to make an objective estimate, it would be essential to list certain cardinal features of Muslim scholarship which distinguish it from the rest of the world of scholarship.

It was inherent in the thinking of Muslim scholars to believe that the revealed word of God was the main source of knowledge. All other knowledge derived through scientific experimentation, observation or reflection was meant to support or substantiate the instructions given in the Quran. The only purpose the knowledge has is to strengthen the faith of the believer. Such an approach is diametrically different from the Western views on knowledge, which insist that all scientific learning is meant to refute religious dogma, and find ways of interpreting and understanding the realities of life, which have no spiritual connotations. Judging strictly from Western standards knowledge is an end in itself and not a means to an end. In Islam on the other hand, knowledge is only a means to an end. D. B. MacDonald in his estimate of the contributions of Al-Ghazzali has made the following remarks regarding this fundamental aspect of the Muslim scholarship.

Unfortunately, he was beset by the utilitarianism of Islam, and so could not be content to let his book stand for itself as a human document, nor even as an *apologia pro vita sua.* He must needs make out of it a manual of apologetics suited to his time, and thus, undoubtedly, has dulled the personal touch. In so doing he has furnished perhaps the most striking example of the fatal Muslim didacticism which does not permit an artist, conscious or unconscious, to set a living figure before the reader and leave it to do its work, but must systematize and explain everything. In this, the Muslim writers differ markedly from the poets of heathen Arabia who had a frank delight in the simple expression of themselves without thought of their audience. Al-Ghazzali in his *Ayyuh al-Walad* has in unequivocal terms emphasized the knowledge which cannot be operationalized is only a monumental wastage. Unless research findings are helpful in resolving problems of life, in his opinion, they are a futile intellectual exercise. Tehsil-i-Ilm (search for knowledge) he points out, must have some meaning, a purpose and a denned goal. The above treatise was written in response to a young scholar who was encountering certain difficulties in streamlining his thoughts regarding the wisdom of striving and struggling for the accumulation of knowledge and incessant.reading of various sciences. Al-Ghazzali says :

> O youth, do not be bankrupt of works, nor empty of states, be assured that knowledge alone does not strengthen the hand—just so though a man reads a hundred thousand scientific questions and understood them or learned them, they do not benefit him except by working.

Without implementation, the tree of knowledge will not bear any fruit, and one would never be able to attain the nearness to God which is the ultimate objective of all learning. He says:

> Knowledge is the tree and the working is its fruit, and though you studied a hundred years and collected a thousand books, you would not be prepared for the mercy of Allah the Exalted except by working.

In advocating such a course Al-Ghazzali was only trying to portray the true and essential character of knowledge in Quranic terms. In Islam, religion is not merely a spiritual embellishment of human soul; it provides full guidance to the believers in resolving multifarious problems which they encounter in their search for the Straight Path. According to the Islamic view, religious and secular knowledge are two facets of the same reality. Both complement each other.

In 'Mizan al Amal' Al-Ghazzali says, "whoever thinks faith alone will suffice him is ignorant of the meaning of faith." In other words to make life more gainful faith based on revealed knowledge, and understanding derived from secular learning must go hand in hand. He sums up his thesis with a warning to his correspondent that "O youth, knowledge without work is insanity and work without knowledge is vanity."

The essence of devotion in Islam is to work ceaselessly for the glory of Almighty God and to abide with His commands in shaping human destiny on this earth. Ibada (prayer) is the only instrument by which this obligation can be fulfilled. But prayer without knowledge remains hollow, and knowledge by itself would be meaningless unless it is translated into action. Both ilm (knowledge) and amal (action) are needed to give enrichment and meaning to life.

Reward in its Own : In Islam knowledge is its own reward. It cannot be sold or bought as a marketable commodity in pursuit of worldly gains or reputation. Search for material rewards and ambition to win widespread fame are the common frailties of human nature, but to acquire knowledge simply for their sake is intellectually sacrilegious.

From the strictly Islamic point of view knowledge is only meant to uncover the truth and strengthen the faith of a believer. Knowledge used for any other purpose is against Quranic principles whose supreme ideal is to make scientific research an additional support for the dissemination of God's message on earth. It is meant to illustrate and substantiate the wisdom of the Holy Prophet as depicted in his words and deeds. In the books of Hadith the following tradition of the Prophet is narrated through Abu Hurrayrah :

> The second (person to receive sentence on the day of resurrection) a man who shall have obtained knowledge and instructed others, and read the Quran, he will be brought into the presence of God, and will be given to understand the benefits he had received which he will be sensible of and confess and God will say 'What didst thou do in gratitude thereof? He will reply, 'I learned knowledge and taught others and I read the Quran to please thee.' Then God will say

> 'Thou liest, but thou studiest that people might call thee learned.' Then God will order him to be dragged upon his face and precipitated into hell. The prophet said, 'He who desires knowledge in order to be honoured in the world or dispute with the ignorant and attract the notice of mankind, God will throw him into hell fire.'

Al-Ghazzali has administered the following warning to scholars who use scholarship for material acquisition, official position and popular recognition. O youth, how many nights you have remained awake repeating science and poring over books and have denied yourself sleep. I do not know what the purpose of it was. If it was attaining worldly ends and securing its vanities and acquiring its dignities and surpassing your contemporaries and such like, woe to you and again woe.

Ignorance is the malady of the human heart and soul, which can only be cured with knowledge. Learned doctors in Islam are the physicians who through insight and knowledge diagnose the ailments of mind and then write prescriptions for their ultimate elimination. It would be extremely unbecoming of a physician to have any other objective except to cure the disease.

Almighty's Kindness

The idea that knowledge is divine, and that scholars are accountable to God for it, inculcated among Muslim scholars a deep sense of responsibility and objectivity both in the collection of facts and their interpretation. They did not like search for truth to be contaminated with prejudices or selfish interests. In order to arrive at the right conclusions they very often used comparative method of study. Abu Nasr-al-Farabe (258/870-339/950) who ranks among the greatest philosophers of Islam has listed his views on research in natural and social sciences as follows:

> There he should set out next upon the science of man and investigate the *what* and the *how* of the purpose for which man is made what is the perfection that man must achieve. Then he should investigate all things by which man achieves this perfection or that are useful to him in achieving it. These are the good, virtuous,

> and noble things. He should distinguish them for things that obstruct his achieving this perfection. These are the evils, the vices and the base things. He should make known what and how every one of them is, and from what and for what it is, until all of them become known, intelligible and distinguished from each other.

Abu Raihan-al-Beruni (362/973-442/1051) whose examination of Indian history, geography and society is considered a spectacular piece of scientific inquiry, also laid down certain rigorous rules for genuine scholarship. E. G. Sachau who translated Al-Beruni's monumental work, *Kitab-ul-Hind,* made the following observations on his method and approach to social studies:

> He is a stern judge both of himself and of others. Himself perfectly sincere, it is sincerity which he demands from others. Whenever he does not fully understand a subject or only knows part of it, he will at once tell the readers so, either asking the reader's pardon—He is not a friend of those who hate to avow their ignorance by a frank 'I do not know' and he is roused to strong indignation whenever he meets with want of sincerity.

In his preface to *Kitab-ul-Hind,* Al-Beruni himself made the following remarks on scientific reporting and observation in research.

No one will deny that in questions of historic authenticity *hearsay* does not equal *eye-witness,* for in the latter the eye of the observer apprehends the substance of that which is observed, both in the time when and in the place where it exists, whilst hearsay has its peculiar drawbacks. But for these, it would even be preferable to eye-witness; for the object of eyewitness can only be *actual* momentary existence, whilst hearsay comprehends alike the present, the past, and the future, so as to apply in a certain sense both to that which is and to that which is not (i.e., which wither has ceased to exist or has not yet come into existence). Written tradition is one of the species of hearsay we might almost say, the most preferable. How could we know the history of nations but for the everlasting monuments of the pen ? The tradition regarding an event which in itself does not contradict either logical or physical laws will invariably depend for its character as true or false upon the character of the reporters, who are moved by the divergency of interests and all kinds of animosities and antipathies between the various nations. We must distinguish different classes of reporters. One of them tells a lie, as intending to further an interest of his own, either *by lauding* his family or nation, because he is one of them, or *by attacking* the family or nation on the opposite side, thinking that thereby he can gain his ends. In both cases he acts from motives of objectionable cupidity and animosity. Another one tells a lie regarding a class of people whom he likes, as being under obligation to them, or whom he hates, because something disagreeable has happened between them. Such a reporter is near akin to the first-mentioned one, as he too acts from motives of personal predilection and enmity.

Another tells a lie because he is of such a base nature as to aim thereby at some profit, or because he is such a coward as to be afraid of telling the truth.

Another tells a lie because it is his nature to lie, and he cannot do otherwise, which proceeds from the essential meanness of his character and the depravity of his innermost being.

Lastly, a man may tell a lie from ignorance, blindly following others who told him.

If, now, reporters of this kind become so numerous as to represent a certain body of tradition, or if in the course of time they even come to form a consecutive series of communities or nations, both the first reporter and his followers form the connecting links between the hearer and the inventor of the lie; and if the connecting links are eliminated, there remains the originator of the story, one of the various kinds of liars we have enumerated, as the only person with whom we have to deal.

That man only is praiseworthy who shrinks from a lie and always adheres to the truth, enjoying credit even among liars, not to mention others.

Value of Truth : It has been said in the Quran, 'Speak the truth, even if it were against yourselves' and the Messiah expresses himself in the Gospel to this effect: 'Do not mind the fury of kings in speaking the truth before them. They only possess your body, but they have no power over your soul.' (cf. St. Matt. X, 18, 19, 28; St. Luke, xii, 4). In these words the Messiah orders us to exercise *moral courage.* For what the crowd calls courage—bravely dashing into the fight or plunging into an abyss of destruction—is only a *species* of courage, whilst the *genus,* far above all *species,* is to *scorn death,* whether by word or deed. Now as justice (i.e., being just) is a quality liked and coveted for its own self, for its intrinsic beauty, the same applies to *truthfulness,* except perhaps in the case of such people as never tasted how sweet it is, or know the truth, but deliberately shun it, like a notorious liar who once was asked if he had ever spoken the truth, and gave the answer, 'If I were not afraid to speak the truth, I should say, no.' A liar will avoid the path of justice; he will, as matter of preference side with oppression and false witness, breach of confidence, fraudulent appropriation of the wealth of others, theft, and all the vices which serve to ruin the world and mankind.

In his other famous work called *Chronology of Ancient Nations,* Al-Beruni also emphasizes that historical research should be free from emotions and prejudices which so often blur human vision and disable men from comprehending the truth with clarity. He points out that rigorous comparative method alone can insure objectivity and impartiality in research. In the preface to the above book he says that his purpose "cannot be obtained by way or ratiocination with philosophical notions, but solely by adopting the information of those who have a written tradition—and by making their opinions a basis on which to build up a system; besides we must compare their traditions and opinions among themselves, when we try to establish our system. But even that we must clear our mind from all those accidental circumstances which deprave most men, from all causes which are liable to make people blind against the truth, e.g., inveterate custom, party spirit, rivalry, being addicted to one's passion, the desire to gain influence."

From the Greeks the Muslim borrowed their tremendous love for logic. Although theologians like Ibn Taimiyya condemned Greek logic vehemently as something against the canons of Islam, the history of Muslim scholarship shows that logic as an instrument of intellectual synthesis and philosophical articulation continued to exercise considerable influence in research and studies in Islam. Josef Van Ess has explained its uses for the Muslims as follows :

> This assertion seems somewhat in question; no Islamic jurist, or any other jurist, could do without logic ; he had to use most subtle hermeneutic methods to interpret the Quran, and he had to apply all kinds of logical processes to adjust the commands found by this interpretation to the individual cases of daily life. The same is true of *kalam,* Islamic theology : theology is by definition nothing more than logical demonstration of believed truth.

Abu Said Al-Sirafi (280-368/893-979), a reputed theologian of his time in Baghdad, made distinction between two types of logic. One which was used by Muslim theologians (*Ulama*) and Fukaha (Jurists) and the other which was strictly of Greek origin. In his opinion scholars in Islam were keen and anxious seekers after truth. They looked into each issue diligently and spread no effort in uncovering right and wrong through intelligent interpretation. Their achievements he believed were impressive and intellectually satisfying.

The strict logicians on the other hand wasted most of their time in wallowing around in barren argumentation. In other words, logical argumentation should not be an end in itself; it must further the cause of knowledge. Logic which does not help either in resolving problems of life, or in strengthening our beliefs is a wastage. Some scholars knowing that Islam does not allow meaningless hairsplitting, have castigated it as a religion based on intolerance and fanaticism. Such a view, however, is patently contrary to the spirit of Islam. There is nothing in the Quran or the Traditions of the Holy Prophet from which it could be construed that independence of judgment or difference of opinion are disallowed. In fact all the available evidence goes to prove that Islam perhaps among the great religions of the world, is the only religion which maintains that difference of opinion, provided it is not based on malice is the surest way to wisdom and rectitude.

The Tolerance : Intellectual and religious tolerance is a sign of social and emotional maturity. In all areas of Islamic scholarship, i.e., philosophical, theological and mystical, there were always deep and unbridgeable divergencies. Ikhtilaf (difference) was considered to be a legitimate right of the individual. The result was that intellectual saber-rattling became a very prominent feature of scholarly circles in Islam. Most of the *Asul-ul-Fiqh* (Principles of Islamic Jurisprudence) were products of continuous debate and discussion, and endless controversies which were generated by serious differences among various schools of thought. The only time when Ikhtilaf would not be tolerated was when it was apprehended that scholars were indulging in dangerously innovative interpretation of the Quranic faith. Jean-Paul Charnay has summed up the role of Ikhtilafat (Divergences) in the intellectual life of Islam as follows :

> Ikhtilafat played a primary role in the development of Muslim thinking : intellectual technique, practical utilization, function in the Muslim community's evolution through diverse historical phases. Ikhtilaf is first an expression and consequence of the creative intellectual flowering of demogeographic conquests, of local and social disparities. It multiplies as it is influenced by political and religious passions and regional deviationism.

Search for Knowledge

An attempt has been made in following few lines to articulate certain philosophical and conceptual aspects of the nature of Prophethood and Prophecy and to use these concepts in outlining an Islamic theory of education.

Nature of Prophethood : The first thing to notice about Prophethood is that the birth of a Prophet had invariably taken place in a noble family with a long tradition of piety and good deeds. If this event is to be explained in the modern political terms, then the relevant concept would be that of 'elitism' and not of 'democracy'. Allah had choosen His Prophets entirely according to His own Wisdom.

The second thing of which we must take note of is that before the mission of Prophecy was bestowed upon an individual, he had already shown, without doubt, that he was a person of exceptional conduct and character and of outstanding merit. In other words, a person on whom the Prophethood was to be bestowed had to meet certain pre-qualifications.

The third thing of which we must make a special note is that a would be Prophet was, without exception, a thinker. He was an individual who was not satisfied with the prevailing environment of morality and human conduct. He was pained to notice the prevailing injustices. All this led him to think about the social order in which there would be no more injustice and usurpation of the rights of the poor. We thus find that the individuals on whom Allah had bestowed the mission of Prophecy had usually faced a fairly long period of intellectual struggle and personal anguish. We see them withdrawing into deserts or into the hills. It is interesting to note that there appeared to be, mutatis mutandis, a certain optimum period for this intellectual and spiritual striving; it was neither too short for the tempering of the Prophetic soul nor too long that it might have led to frustration. Thus, it is not that Allah had thrown away the honour of Prophethood on anyone; the person awarded the Prophetic mission had already been searching for the Truth and was eventually granted a vision of the Truth.

A paper read at the auspicious occasion of Eid Milad-un-Nabi celebrations at the Embassy of Pakistan, Cairo, Arab Republic of Egypt on 12th Rabi-ul-Awwal, 1400 H (30th January, 1980).

Allah had used various means for conveying His word to His Prophets, while Allah had rewarded some of the Prophets with His own Vision or with the reflection of His own Vision, a larger part of His message was received as perceptions and inspirations of truth or in other words as Revelations (Wahy). The Ascension of the Prophet Muhammad (Peace and Blessings be upon him) to 'the Heavens (Miradj) was the ultimate grace of Allah bestowed upon him, wherein he was admitted into the presence of Allah. There is a deep philosophical meaning of the Ascension. This event points to be the place of man in Allah's Design. It tells us that man has been bestowed with an inherent capacity to rise the threshold of Allah, but by following the 'Straight Path'. The 'Miradj' points to the highest point, which the human intellect or ego could possibly attain. Thus, it also fixes the outer limits of knowledge.

In the above context, it would seem desirable, to distinguish between the mystic experience and the Prophetic perception. The mystic feels the bliss of his finite personality melting in the infinite ocean of Reality. The mystic, given a choice, would never wish to return from the repose of 'unitary experience' and his experience remains largely private and incommunicable. On the other hand, the Prophet perceives the reality in its totality. His return is creative and he asserts himself to mould the forces of history with a view to creating a fresh world of ideals.

Theory of Education : The above important facts serve as a background to the articulation below of an Islamic theory of education.

The first duty of a Muslim student is hardwork in the search of knowledge and knowledge should lead him to Certainty (Yaqin), which in turn should strengthen his Faith (Iman). Please note that Islam does not believe in blind faith; in Islam faith is based on intelligence (Aql) and not only on emotions. Quran describes three distinct levels of knowledge: First is ilm-al-yaqin, knowledge through information; second, 'ayn-al-yaqin, knowledge through experience and third and highest, haqq-al-yaqin, knowledge through being.

The second duty of a Muslim student is to do the above search with good intentions, because if his intentions are not right, his hardwork would come only to a naught. Good intensions mean good intentions for all. It is important to note here that the Quranic concept of 'Good is based not only on justice (Adl) but also on the principle of 'Ihsan', which means that not only we should do 'Adl' but also on the principle of 'Ihsan' which means that not only we should do 'Adl' but also make special compensations for the individuals who are suffering from various deficiencies, whether physical, economic or spiritual.

The third point in this theory of education is that of "Blessings" (Faydh), which on one hand, is a product of our own good intentions and on the other, of the grace of our teacher. Unless we are able to establish a special bond between ourselves and our teacher and give him all the due respect (Adab), we will not have these 'blessings' and therefore, our knowledge would remain incomplete

Another factor of great importance to keep in mind is that unless we purify our heart of all ill will and evil, we could not possess good intentions for all. Therefore, in the first place, we have to cleanse our heart, if we want to perceive true knowledge. One Quranic word for heart is 'Fuad', which means both mind and heart.

With the Westernization of our minds, we have forgotten about one very important source of knowledge. One pillar of knowledge, of course, is the objective knowledge, based on the concepts of deduction and induction and the emperical knowledge about causation, but we have forgotten about the other equally important pillar of knowledge - the intuitive knowledge. A Prophet's perception of truth is the most advanced form of this knowledge. Of course, a common individual cannot be privy to Prophetic perception (Wahy), but he can strive towards its lesser aspect i.e. 'Basirah'. We could build a sort of equation for this qualitative knowledge. We can prepare the ground for it by our hard work; we lay its foundations with our good intentions; we cement the foundations with the blessings of our teacher and we correct the direction of this building by the purity of our hearts. We are then ready to receive this knowledge in a great abundance. Indeed, Allah is the Great Grantor of knowledge to those who seek.

However, when we have read all the books and claim to have acquired all the Knowledge, we may still face a great danger, which may nullify all our previous efforts and life's work and this destruction may be brought about by the doubts created in our heart about the Truth (Haqq). In other words, we may lose our faith (Iman) of course if we lose our faith, we lose everything. Therefore we must always pray to Allah that He should not put us in doubt and make us faithless. A faithless person is like a building built on sand. But, if we have faith, then we would have that great quality of mind which would further brighten the building of our knowledge i.e. the 'unity of thought' (Wahdat-ul-Fikr).

Now if we have passed all the above stages, indeed we have done extremely well and deserve the praise of our brothers. However, our work is not finished yet. In fact, our real work starts from now onwards. Its now that we must assume the role of preaching good and in Islam, only preaching of good is not enough; simultaneously, we must also forbid evil and do that with a force and if necessary lay down our lives in doing that. However, many of us may lack enough courage to do that. But, we can have this courage by developing this great quality, this final force which cannot be readily explained by an English word. This force is that of 'Ishq' - Love of Allah and his Prophet.

True Objectives : Of course, we should direct this 'force' toward the true objective, otherwise there is a danger that we may become ineffective. This direction is given by the vision of a better world, as outlined in the Quran-a world in which everyone is equal and free, in which there is complete justice and in which there is no poverty. We must, therefore, strive to establish the Quranic Social Order of the 'Rububiyyah', which would enable full realisation of the latent potentialities of every individual through both sustenance and fostering of his body, as well as the fulfillments of his personality and spirit, which indeed is the ultimate purpose of Islam. We must not forget that the central theme of Islam is 'Welfare' and not 'Salvation'.

7

Ethical Dimensions

Ideal Person

Good character is the sum of personal virtues which guarantees correct and agreeable behaviour in daily social interaction. A person of good character will invariably conform in his behaviour to a strict code of ethics.

What should be the underlying principle of this code of ethics? According to a hadith it is simply this: you should like for others what you like for yourself, that is, you should treat others just as you want to be treated by others.

Everyone likes to be addressed with good manners and pleasing words. So everyone should speak gently to others. Everyone wants his existence to be problem-free, so he should avoid creating problems for others.

Everyone wants others to deal with him in a sympathetic and cooperative manner. So what everyone ought to do while dealing with others is to give them his full sympathy and cooperation.

This standard of ethics is very simple and natural. It is so simple that anyone may easily learn it, be he literate or illiterate, able bodied or disabled, and regardless of his likes and dislikes. This hadith has given such a criterion for human ethics that no one can find difficult to understand. In this way Islam has set forth, in the light of everyone's personal experience, what behaviour may be indulged in and what behaviour has to be refrained from.

According to another hadith, the best of us is one who is best in moral character. Accordingly, becoming a good human being has nothing ambiguous about it. Its simple formula is that of avoidance of double standards. One who lives his life by this formula is indubitably a person of the highest moral character.

The Determination

Islam attaches the utmost importance to intentions (*Niyyat*). No action is acceptable to God purely on the basis of its outer appearance. He accepts only such actions as are performed with proper intention, and rejects those performed with ill intention. Right intention is the moral purposiveness which underlies all actions performed solely for God's pleasure. One who acts on such feelings will be rewarded by God in the Hereafter.

An ill-intention, on the other hand, is a negative spur to worldly attainment. Ostensibly religious acts, if performed for worldly gain or public commendation, are in this sense ill-intentioned. Any fame, honour or popularity which ensues from an ill-intentioned act is a hollow triumph and is looked upon by the Almighty with extreme disfavour.

Intention is rooted in man's inner thinking and feelings. A common man is unable to penetrate the inner recesses of a person's mind but God knows full well what a man's thought processes and feelings are. People can be deluded by appearances, but God has complete knowledge of everything. He will deal with people according to His knowledge and will reward everyone exactly as he or she deserves.

Intention has to do with the inner reality. A thing which loses its reality or its meaningfulness is valueless. Similarly, an act which is performed with ill intention or with no good intention, has no value-neither in the eyes of man, nor of God.

Things are of value only when they are pure, without any adulteration. An act done with right intention is a pure act, and an act performed without right intention is an impure act.

The Reality

A believer in God is also necessarily a truth-loving person. He always speaks the truth. In all matters he says just what is in accordance with reality. A true believer cannot afford to tell lies, or hide facts. What does it mean to speak the truth? It is to have no contradiction between man's knowledge and the words that he utters and for that matter, whatever he says should be what has come to his knowledge. Falsehood, by contrast, is the utterance of statements which do not tally with knowledge.

Truth is the highest virtue of a believer's character. A believer is a man of principle. And for such a person telling the truth is paramount. For him no other behaviour is possible, for he finds it impossible to deny the truth.

The world of God is based wholly on truth. Here everything expresses itself in its real form. The sun, the moon, rivers, mountains, stars and planets are all based on truth. They appear just as they really are. In this unfathomably vast universe of God nothing is based on untruth. There is nothing which shows itself in any form other than its real form.

This is the character of nature, which is spread out on a universal scale. A believer too has exactly the same character. He is totally free from falsehood or double standards. A believer is all truth. His whole existence is moulded to truth. From the very first he appears to be a true person both inside and out.

Speaking the truth is not only a matter of policy for the believer it is his very religion. Compromising in the matter of truth is not possible for him. He speaks the truth as he cannot live without doing so. He speaks the truth because he knows that not speaking the truth is the negation of his own personality and commitment to something which is the negation of the self is not possible for any worthy person.

The Toleration

Patience (Sabr) is the exercise of restraint in trying situations. It is a virtue which enables the individual to proceed towards worthy goals, undeflected by adverse circumstances or repeated provocations. If he allows himself to become upset by opposition, taunts or other kinds of unpleasantness, he will never reach his goals. He will simply become enmeshed in irrelevancies.

The only way to deal with the irksome side of daily living is to exercise patience. Patience will ensure that whenever one has some bitter experience, he will opt for the way of tolerance rather than that of reaction to provocation. It will enable one to absorb shocks and to continue, undeterred, on one's onward journey

Patience, as well as being a practical solution to the problems faced in the outside world, is also a means of positive character building. Failure to exercise patience, gives free rein to negative thoughts and feelings, resulting in the development of a negative personality. While one who remains patient is so morally bolstered by his own positive thoughts and feelings that he develops a positive personality.

Sabr is no retreat. Sabr only amounts to taking the initiative along the path of wisdom and reason as opposed to the path of the emotions. Sabr gives one the strength to restrain one's emotions in delicate situations and rather to use one's brains to find a course of action along result-oriented lines.

The present world is fashioned in such a way that everyone is necessarily confronted with unpleasant matters at one time or another. Things which are unbearable have somehow to be borne; harrowing events have to be witnessed and all kinds of pain have to be suffered. In such situations, succumbing to impatience leads to the kind of unnecessary emotional involvement which is counter-productive, while a demonstration of patience has a healing, beneficial effect, allowing one to tread the path of discreet avoidance. Success in the present world is destined only for those who adopt the path of patience in adverse circumstances.

No Discrimination

During the lifetime of the Prophet of Islam many of his fellow men opposed Islam and engaged in plotting against Islam and Muslims. The Quran has mentioned this at several places. But the counter strategy advocated by the Quran was not to unearth their plots and launch movements to defeat them or even finally to wage war against them, On the contrary, the Prophet and his companions were enjoined to place their trust in God alone.

That is to say, ignoring the plots and antagonism, trusting only in God and rising above circumstances, they were to continue all activities which were of a positive nature.

This was an extremely important injunction. By giving this guidance, God set them on a course of positive thinking, which left no room for negative thinking. In short, this Quranic teaching encouraged the early Muslims to live in a self-sufficient way, free of baneful influence of their opponents.

If you have this obsession that others are plotting against you, and that everyone has turned your enemy, it will result in your starting to suspect everyone, to the extent that even if a member of your own community underscores the importance of tolerance and avoidance, you will take it in a negative light and dub him an agent of the enemy. In this way, you will weaken yourselves by turning your own people away from you.

One harmful aspect of such negative obsession is that one loses all objectivity in thinking. One's entire outlook becomes partisan and prejudiced. One is unable to see reality as it is. One becomes like the man who can see only the thorns in a garden of roses or the colour blind person to whom a garden blossoming with flowers will appear in melancholy shades of grey.

No Patience

Tolerance is a noble humanitarian and Islamic virtue. Its practice means making concessions to others, Intolerance on the other hand, means showing a self- centered unconcern for the needs of others. Tolerance is a worthy, humane virtue, which has been described in different terms in the Shariah: for instance, gentle behaviour, showing concern for others, being soft-hearted, being compassionate.

When true God-worship and religiosity is born within a person, he reaches above all those evils which emanate from selfishness. Instead of living within the confines of the self, he begins to live in the world of reality. The truly pious person begins to look upon people with love and compassion. He does not expect anything from anyone, that is why even when others differ from him or do not behave well towards him, he continues nevertheless to make concessions to them, and continues to be tolerant towards them.

Tolerance implies an unswerving respect for others, whether in agreement or disagreement with them. The tolerant man will always consider the case of others sympathetically, be they relatives or friends, and irrespective of the treatment he is given by them, be it of a positive or a negative nature.

Tolerance means, in essence, to give consideration to others. In social life, friction between people does occur in every society, differences arising from religion, culture, tradition and personal tastes persist. In such a situation the superior cause of action is to adopt the ways of concession and large-heartedness without any compromise of principle.

That is to say that the pious man should be a man of principle as far as he himself is concerned, but should be tolerant towards others. He should judge himself in the light of the ideal but in the matter of his fellow men he should show tolerance and broad-mindedness. This being inseparable from human gentility and nobility. Islam aims to produce this fine human quality of gentlemanliness by preaching tolerance.

The Simplicity : A believer is one who finds God. God's discoverer starts living by nature on the plane of higher realities. He rises above outward, superficial things and finds sources of interest in the world of piety.

Such a person by his very nature becomes a simplicity loving person. His motto is: Simple living and high thinking.

One who has acquired the taste for the meaning of the divine reality can have no taste for outward and material things. Such a person relishes simplicity. In his eyes pretensions lose their attraction. His soul finds peace in natural things. Unnatural and artificial things appear to him as if they are causing his inner world disintegrate and creating obstacles to the progress of his spiritual journey.

Simplicity is a support to the believer. It contributes to his strength. By opting for simplicity he is able to put his time to the best use by not wasting it on irrelevant matters. He does not let his attention be diverted to things which are inessential so far as his goal is concerned. And in this way he is able to devote himself whole-heartedly to the achievement of higher goals.

Simplicity is the food of the believer, and, having its own internal beauty, it serves as an apparel for his modesty. It is in an atmosphere of simplicity that his personality finds the scope for its growth. On the contrary, if the believer builds up an artificial glamour around himself, he will eventually feel as if he is imprisoned in a cell.

A believer considers himself God's servant in the ultimate sense of the word. His thoughts and feelings are all perfectly attuned to this servitude, to this condition of being God's servant. One who consistently thinks in this way inevitably finds his whole disposition veering towards simplicity. Since ostentation, artificiality and social pretensions are at variance with his disposition, he resolutely avoids them throughout his life, in his manner of living and in his daily dealings.

The Piety : Taqwa means piety, that is, leading a life of caution and restraint in this world.

Umar Farooq, the second Caliph once asked a companion of the Prophet what *taqwa* was. He replied, "O leader of the believers, have you ever crossed a path which has thorny shrubs on both sides?" But the companion instead of replying asked another question, "What did you do on such an occasion?" Umar Farooq replied, "I gathered my clothes close to me and moved ahead cautiously." The companion said, "Now I know what is meant by taqwa."

The present world is a testing ground. Here, various kinds of thorns have been scattered for the purpose of testing man, such as negativity, false issues raised by non-serious people, the lure of-worldly things. Besides these, there are many unpleasant occurrences which disturb people's minds and lead them away from the path of virtue.

All these things are like thorny shrubs lining both sides of the path of life. At any moment it is feared that man may embroil himself in these thorns and then instead of going forward, remain entrapped in these snares of life.

In such a state of affairs the wise man is one who travels the paths of life by gathering up his clothes to avoid becoming entangled in these unpleasant snares. In this way, he is able to continue his journey unhampered. Yet at all times he must remain conscious of the fact that he must protect himself . He has to adopt the path of avoidance, not of entanglement.

Man has been created with an upright nature. If no hindrance comes in the way, then every man will, on his own, take the right course. That is why, the utmost precaution must be taken against allowing unnatural obstacles to come in the way.

Then, guided by this upright nature, man will continue to walk along the right path until he meets his Lord.

Thanksgiving : Thanks giving for man is to acknowledge the blessings of God acknowledgment first arises in the heart then, taking the form of words, it comes to the lips of the grateful person.

From birth, man has been superbly, adorned in body and mind by his Creator. All his requirements have been amply catered for, every object in the heavens and on earth having been pressed into his service. All the things necessary for his leading a good life on earth and the building of a civilization have been provided in abundance.

Man experiences these blessings at every moment. It is, therefore, incumbent on man to thank God for His blessings at all times. His heart should be eternally brimming with gratitude for these divine blessings.

Thanksgiving is the most comprehensive term of worship: gratefulness is the essence of the godly life. The best expression of that gratefulness is the expenditure of time and money in the way of God. It is God, after all who has given man the reason to worship Him and the means to do so.

The Trial : Man is free in this world. God has not placed any curbs on him. But this freedom is for the purpose of putting man to the test, and is not meant to encourage him to lead a life of permissiveness like the animals and then just pass away one day. Rather its purpose is that man should lead a morally upright life of his own free will, thus demonstrating that he is of the highest moral character.

One who conducts himself in this matter should be reckoned as God's special servant who, without any apparent compulsion chose to be a man of principle; who, without being subjected to any external force, did of his own free will, what his Lord would have desired. This liberty accorded to man gives him the opportunity to gain credit for being the most superior of all God's creatures.

All the things in this world are God's subjects. The stars and satellites rotate in space entirely at their Lord's bidding. Trees, rivers, mountains, and all other such natural phenomena are functioning according to the unchangeable ways of God laid down by Him in advance. Similarly, the animals follow exactly those instincts instilled in their species as a matter of Divine Will. Man is the only creature who has been given, exceptionally, the gift of power and freedom.

This freedom has opened doors of two kinds for man, one leading to success and the other to failure. If, on receiving freedom an individual becomes arrogant and insolent, it will mean that he has failed to pass the test.

But if on the other hand, he remains modest and humble, bowing to his Lord's will on all occasions, he will have made the right use of his God-given freedom: he will, without any compulsion, have bound himself by divine principles. One who chooses this course will succeed in the test of freedom. He will be handsomely rewarded by God as no other creature. Held to be the chosen servant of God, he will remain in an everlasting state of blissfulness and blessedness.

The Salvation : What is the greatest issue facing man in this world? It is how to secure salvation in the life after death so that he may find his true abode and have a share in God's eternal blessings.

Every man who is born in this present world has to enter another world after death. In this world man was granted life's opportunities as a matter of being tested by them. Whatever man receives in the next world will be purely on the basis of his deeds in this world. This means that in the world before death, man has been given a great number of things and opportunities, whether or not he deserved them. But after death, the criterion of receiving will only be a matter of his just deserts; nothing will be given to him to try him.

This means that those who are held to be deserving will be granted not out of God's blessings but more that they actually merited. But those who have done nothing to deserve God's blessings will have nothing whatsoever in store for them. They will be compelled to live in a state of utter deprivation.

This is man's greatest problem. To what should he give the greatest attention so that he may not be held undeserving in the life to come? Everyone has to exert himself to the utmost in the consciousness that in the next stage of his life he may by default be considered without merit. Then there would be no further scope for him to earn God's blessings, salvation would elude him completely.

The next world is the most perfect and eternal world. There, all kinds of pleasures and happiness which have been stored up for mankind. It is that world which man should cherish most, and it should be the place to which he most earnestly aspires But the time for action to secure a place in that blessing-filled world is not the world after death, but the world before death. The present world is the place for action, while the next world is the place for reaping the reward for one's deeds.

Salvation in the life Hereafter is only for those who prove themselves deserving of it.

8

Moral Codes

Ethical Values

Mankind, according to the Prophet, are a fold, every member of which is a shepherd or keeper unto every other, and accountable for the welfare of the entire fold (Bukhari). Further, mankind are the creatures of God, and most beloved of them before Him is he who is the best to His creatures (Baihaqi). These and other sayings of the Prophet stress the point that one has to identify his interests with the interests of others. The duties to one's self and the duties to others are here placed side by side as the component parts of one's responsibility in life. Only when the individual has a developed sense of such responsibility that he is a moral being and of greater service to society.

Duties are generally expressed in terms of duties to God and duties to society, but the spirit underlying duties to God is the spiritual development of one's self so as to be mindful of duties to others—a harmonious interaction between the sense of God and the sense of fellow-men resulting in righteousness. Such is the concept of morality in Islam and, therefore, Islamic law is the law of duties rather than of rights. Generally, rights have corresponding duties but in Islamic law duties are more than rights. This has its own advantages.

Right is a claim on someone and duty is a responsibility to someone. The emphasis merely on rights gives rise to the sense of one's own power and authority over others which may be injurious to peace, while emphasis on duties creates harmony in social life and is conducive to peace. A generalized sense of duty is a sense of being bound by that which is right because of its rightfulness. Conformity to the letter of the law ' then takes the place of faithfulness to its spirit, *i.e.*, its usefulness in calling attention to the welfare of not only one's self but also of others.

The sense of duty, thus, reminds us of our responsibility towards our fellow-beings. This sensitive is specially needed whenever our desire tends to blind us to everything but itself. There are occasions in life on which, under the influence of strong desire, we are apt to lose control upon ourselves and it is the sense of duty to God and to our fellow-men which keeps us away from evil-doing and directs us to the right path—the path of eternal peace and prosperity. Here we realize the importance of duty and comprehend why Islamic law is the law of duties.

Universal Perfection

The Model World according to Islam, is a world of peace. Islam in itself means a religion of peace. The Quran says: And God calls to the home of peace. This is the message of Islam to mankind. It means that a world of peace on earth so that you may be granted a world of peace in your eternal life in the Hereafter.

Now what are the basic elements of building of a culture of peace, according to Islam to be brief, these are three—compassion, forgiveness and respect for all.

Let's take compassion first. If you go through the Quran and Hadith, you will find many verses in the Quran and Hadith which lay great stress on compassion. For instance, the Prophet of Islam said: O people, be compassionate to others so that you may be granted compassion by God.

Thus, Islam makes compassion a matter of self interest for every man. As one's own future depends on one's compassionate behaviour to other fellowmen. In this way Islam motivates us to be compassionate in our dealings with each other. One who wants to receive God's grace will have to show compassion to others.

Let's take forgiveness. The Quran has to say this in this regard "when they are angered, they forgive." There are a number of verses in the Quran which promote forgiveness.

Then there is a hadith. Once a person came to the Prophet and asked him, "O Prophet, give me a mature advice by which I may be able to manage all the affairs of my life." The Prophet replied: "Don't be angry." It means that 'forgive people even at provocation.' That is, adopt forgiveness as your behaviour at all times.

Respect Others to be Respected : Now let's take the third principle—Respect for all. There is a very interesting story, recorded by al-Bukhari in this regard.

The Prophet of Islam once saw a funeral procession passing by a street in Medina. The Prophet was seated at that time. On seeing the funeral the Prophet stood up in respect. At this one of his companions said: 'O Prophet, it was the funeral of a Jew (not a Muslim), The Prophet replied: 'Was he not a human being?' What it meant was that every human being is worthy of respect. There may be differences among people regarding religion and culture, but everyone has to respect the other. For, according to Islam, all men and women are blood brothers and blood sisters. And all are creatures of one and the same God.

These three principles are the basic pillars to form a peaceful society. Wherever these three values are to be found the result no doubt will be a society of peace and harmony

The above references are enough to show that Islam is a culture of peace. It is true that some Muslims are engaged in violence in the name of Islam. But you will have to differentiate between Islam and Muslims. You have to see Muslims in the light of Islam and not vice 'versa.

Perception of Peace

A believer is necessarily a lover of peace. In his mind faith and a desire for peace are so closely interlinked that, regardless of the circumstances, he will strive to the utmost for the maintenance of peace. He will bear the loss of anything else, but the loss of peace he will not endure.

The life that the true believer desires in this world can be lived only in the propitious atmosphere which flowers in conditions of peace. Conditions of unrest breed a negative atmosphere which to him is abhorrent.

But if peace is to be maintained, it calls for a certain kind of sacrifice. That is, when conditions become disturbed, the believer must overlook both the misdeeds leading up to this situation and the identity of the wrongdoers. He must suffer all the harm and injustice done to him without making any attempt either to retaliate, or to bring the miscreants to book, so that a state of peace should continue to prevail. The believer has to be willing to pay this price, so that his pursuance of constructive ends should proceed unhampered.

The believer is like a flower in the garden of nature. Just as a hot wind will shrivel up a bloom and cause it to die, so will constant friction distract the believer from achieving positive goals. And just as a cool breeze will enable the flower to retain its beauty for its natural life-span, so will a peaceful atmosphere enable the believer to fulfil the obligations of divine worship in a spirit of great serenity. Peace is thus central to the life of the believer.

Islam is a religion of peace. And peace is a universal law of nature. That is because God loves the condition of peace, and disapproves of any state of unrest. God's predilection for peace is quite enough reason for the believer also to love peace. In no circumstances will the true believer ever tolerate the disruption of peace.

Social Justice

A believer has important responsibilities towards both God and man. His duty towards God means believing in Him with all His attributes, worshipping Him, regarding himself accountable to Him; and making himself ready to carry out wholeheartedly any such demands that God may make upon him.

Another responsibility of the believer is one which concerns the rights of human beings. This responsibility devolves upon him in his relations with others. Every man or woman, a relative or neighbour, a fellow townsman or compatriot or one with whom he has dealings in business - everyone has some rights over him. It is incumbent upon a believer to fulfil those rights, failing which he will not be deserving of God's succor.

What is meant by recognising the rights of human beings (Huquq ul-Ibad)? This means that whenever and wherever a believer meets another person, he should give him such treatment as is in accordance with Islamic teachings. He should refrain from such behaviour as does not come up to the standard of Islam.

Examples of proper Islamic behaviour are giving respect to other, never humiliating others while giving them help, acting for the good of others, and if unable to benefit them in any way, at least doing no one any harm, fulfilling trusts, never breaking them; never usurping the wealth and property of others; dealing justly with others regardless of the circumstances; giving the benefit of the doubt to others, not believing in allegations made against others without proper proofs; advising others in earnest.

Everyone has a duty to fulfil these responsibilities towards other human beings according to the Islamic Shariah. This is called Huquq-ul-Ibad, or human rights.

Liberty to Speak

Islam grants human beings total intellectual freedom. Rather it would be truer to say that it was Islam which for the first time in human history brought about a revolution in freedom of thought. In all the ages of history prior to Islam, the system of despotism prevailed, and man was consequently denied freedom of thought. This was a matter of the utmost gravity for it is a fact that the secret of all human progress lies hidden in such freedom.

The first benefit of intellectual freedom is to enable man to achieve that high virtue which in the Quran is called "fearing the unseen." That is, without any apparent compulsion or pressure from God, man, of his own free will, acknowledges God and leads his life in this world, going in fear of Him. In the absence of an atmosphere of total freedom, no one can undergo this spiritual experience-an indescribable spiritual pleasure-which is called in the Quran, going in fear of the Lord. Without such freedom it is not possible to give credit to anyone for this highest of human virtues.

Man is a thinking creature. Of necessity he forms opinions. If curbs are placed on the independent expression of his views, the content of his thought may remain unchanged, but his ideas will never find expression in his speech and writings. Curbs of this nature, imposed by a community or a state, will ultimately produce a society of hypocrites. No sincere person can ever flourish in such a repressive atmosphere. It is only freedom of thought and expression which can save man from hypocrisy.

Moreover, intellectual freedom is directly related to creativity. A society with freedom of thought will produce creative human beings; a society which places curbs on freedom of expression will necessarily witness intellectual stagnation; it will stop producing creative minds, and its development will come to a standstill.

In matters of criticism or expression of differences, the right approach is for people to end unnecessary, sensitivity to it instead of attempting to put an end to criticism and differences. This is the demand of Islam as well as of nature.

According to the hadith it is a virtue on the part of believers: to accept the truth without any reservation when it is presented to them. That is to say, a believer is one who has the ability in the perfect sense of the word to accept the truth. Whenever truth is brought before him, whenever his faults are pointed out to him, no complex comes in the way of his accepting of the truth.

This quality is present to the maximum degree in one who is ready and waiting to accept the truth when it is brought before him. Eager for his own improvement, he accepts the truth with pleasure. This keenness for self-reform through acceptance of the truth is perfectly expressed in the words of 'Umar ibn al-Khattab: "May God bless the man who sends me gifts of my own shortcomings."

It is a fact that acknowledgment of truth is worship, nay, it is the greatest form of worship. It is an act for which man has to make the greatest sacrifice. What makes it such a great sacrifice is that it involves the setting aside of one's prestige.

It amounts to the sacrifice of one's ego. But that is the occasion when man assures his entry into heaven.

When does one find the opportunity for this great form of worship and this great good fortune? This opportunity comes one's way only when there is full freedom of expression. When one can criticise another with impunity. When such an atmosphere prevails in a society which permits the speaker to air his views freely and the listener may freely appreciate what is being said. Just as a mosque is the right place for the performance of prayer in congregation, similarly freedom of expression is the right atmosphere in which to foster the great virtues of expressing the truth and acceptance of the truth.

Social Levelling

According to Islamic tenets, all human beings are equal. In prayer, all members of the congregation stand in the same rows together, and on the Hajj pilgrimage, all the believers belonging to different countries don identical white seamless robes for the performance of the obligatory rites. On the occasion of the Final Pilgrimage, it is noteworthy that the Prophet of Islam declared that no Arab was superior to a non-Arab and that no white was superior to a black. All were equally servants of God. In Islamic society, everyone is accorded the same status, there being, ideally, no higher or lower social strata.

How then can we rationalise what are apparently very great differences in human beings in terms of colour and race, etc., considering that the concept of human equality ranks so high in the value system of Islam? We find the answer in the Quran, which makes it clear that such outward differences are meant to serve as means of identification and were never intended as indicators of superiority (or inferiority). People in different parts of the world may have a diversity of skin colourings and other distinctive racial characteristics, but that is only so that they may be easily distinguished from each other. By Islamic standards, this is designed to facilitate social and national interaction.

The sole basis of superiority in Islam is *taqwa* - the earnestness with which one leads a God-fearing life; as such, it bears no relation to colour or race. Physical attributes certainly have their effect on the social interaction of this world, but in the Hereafter, no value is attached to them. There, the only things which count are inner qualities, for upon them depends the essential excellence of man's distinctive character. That is why, according to a hadith, God sees the heart and not the body. He reserves a place in Paradise only for those found deserving in terms of their inner worth.

According to Islam, all greatness belongs to God. God as the Supreme Being is ineffably superior to all men. While there is this infinitely great difference between God and man, there is no difference whatsoever between man and man.

Equality for All

According to Islam, all human beings have been created by one and the same God, and for this reason belong to one great brotherhood. So far as their earthly origin is concerned, they are all descendants of the first pair of human beings ever created by God -Adam and Eve. In their subsequent spread over different parts of the world, variations in geographical conditions produced a diversity of skin colourings, languages and other racial characteristics.

The teaching of Islam in this regard is that despite differences of colour, language, etc., people should harbour no ill-will towards those who are apparently unlike themselves, for differentiating between one man and another is not approved by God. They should rather promote fellow feeling towards others, even if at first glance they appear like total strangers to them. Bearing in mind that they are all traceable back to Adam and Eve, they should be each other's well-wishers and willingly come to one another's assistance, like members of the same large family.

Ideally, the relation between one man and another ought not to be one of strangeness but one of familiarity; not of distance but of nearness; not of hatred but of love.

When all human beings are descendants of the same progenitors, that means that all are equal: no one is superior or inferior. The distinction between great and small is not between one human being and another, but between God and man. And before

God, certainly, all human beings are equal; all are equally His creatures and His servants. For God does not discriminate between one or the other of His creations.

Peaceful Dealings

Islam is a religion which teaches non-violence. According to the Quran, God does not love *fasad*, (violence). What is meant here by *fasad* is clearly expressed in verse 205 of the second surah. Basically fasad is that action which results in disruption of the social system, causing huge losses in terms of lives and property.

Conversely, we can say with certainty that God loves non-violence. He abhors violent activity being indulged in human society, as a result of which people have to pay the price with their possessions and lives. This is supported by other statements in the Quran. For instance, we are told in the Quran that peace is one of God's names (59:23). Those who seek to please God are assured by verse 5 of the sixteenth surah chat they will be guided by Him to "the paths of peace." Paradise, which is the final destination of the society of God's choice, is referred to in the Quran as "the home of peace'" (89:30), etc.

> The entire spirit of the Quran is in consonance with this concept. For instance, the Quran attaches great importance to patience. In fact, patience is set above all other Islamic virtues with the exceptional promise of reward beyond measure. (39:10)
>
> Patience implies a peaceful response or reaction, whereas impatience implies a violent response. The word *sabr* exactly expresses the notion of non-violence as it is understood in modern times. That patient action is non-violent action has been clearly expressed in the Quran. According to one tradition, the Prophet of Islam observed: God grants to *rifq* (gentleness) what he does not grant to *unf (violence).*
>
> (Sunan, Abu Daud, 4 /255)

The word *rifq* has been used in this hadith as an antithesis to *unf*. These terms convey exactly what is meant by violence and non-violence in present times. This hadith clearly indicates the superiority of the non-violent method.

God grants on non-violence what He does not grant to violence is no simple matter. It has very wide and deep implications. It embodies an eternal law of nature. By the very law of nature all bad things are associated with violence, while all good things are associated with non-violence.

Violent activities breed hatred in society, while non-violent activities elicit love. Violence is the way of destruction while non-violence is the way of construction. In an atmosphere of violence, it is enmity which flourishes, while in an atmosphere of non-violence, it is friendship which flourishes. The method of violence gives way to negative values while the method of non-violence is marked by positive values. The method of violence embroils people in problems, while the method of non-violence leads people to the exploiting of opportunities. In short, violence is death, non-violence is life.

Both the Quran and the hadith have attached great importance to jihad. What is jihad? Jihad means struggle, to struggle one's utmost. It must be appreciated at the outset that this word is used for non-violent struggle as opposed to violent struggle. One clear proof of this is the verse of the Quran (25:52) which says: Perform jihad with this (i.e. the word of the Quran) most strenuously.

The Quran is not a sword or a gun. It is a book of ideology. In such a case performing jihad with the Quran would mean an ideological struggle to conquer peoples' hearts and minds through Islam's superior philosophy.

In the light of this verse of the Quran, jihad in actual fact is another name for peaceful activism or non-violent activism. Where qital is violent activism, jihad is non-violent activism.

Non-violence therefore should never be confused with inaction or passivity. Non-violence is action in the full sense of the word. Rather it is more forceful an action than that of violence. It is a fad that non-violent activism is more powerful and effective than violent activism.

Non-violent activism is not limited in its sphere. It is a course of action which may be followed in all matters.

Whenever individuals, groups or communities are faced with a problem, one way to solve it is by resorting to violence. The better way is to attempt to solve the problem by peaceful means, avoiding violence and confrontation. Peaceful means may take various forms. In fact, it is the nature of the problem which will determine which of these peaceful methods is applicable to the given situation.

Peaceful Beginning : When the Quran began to be revealed, the first verse of the revelation conveyed the injunction: "Read!" (Iqra) (96:1). By perusing this verse we learn about the initiation of Islamic action. It begins from the point where there is hope of continuing the movement along peaceful lines, and not from that point where there are chances of its being marred by violence.

When the command of 'Iqra' was revealed, there were many options available in Mecca as starting points for a movement. For instance, one possible starting point was to launch a movement to purify the Kaaba of the 360 idols installed in it. But, by pursuing such a course, in such a case the Islamic movement would certainly have had to face a violent reaction from the Quraish. An alternative starting point could have been an attempt to secure a seat in the Dar-ul-Nadwa (Mecca's parliament). At that time almost the whole of Arabia was under the direct or indirect influence of the Roman and Sasanid empires. If the freeing of Arabia from this influence had been made the starting point, this would also have been met with an immediate violent reaction on the part of the Quraish.

Leaving aside these options, the path followed was that of reading the Quran, an activity that could be with certainty continued along peaceful lines: no violent reaction would ensue from engaging in such an activity.

> The Prophet of Islam followed this principle throughout his life. His policy was that of adopting non-violent methods in preference to violent methods. It is this policy which was referred to by Aishah, the Prophet's wife, in these words: Whenever the Prophet had to opt for one of two ways, he almost always opted for the easier one. (Fath ul Bari 6/654)

What are the advantages of non-violent activism over violent activism? They are briefly stated as under:

1. According to the Quran there are two faculties in every human being which are mutually antipathetic. One is the ego, and the other is the conscience called respectively *nafs ammara* and *nafs lawwama*. (The Quran, 12:53; 75:26) What the violent method invariably does is to awaken the ego which necessarily results in a breakdown of social equilibrium. On the other hand, non-violent activism awakens the conscience. From this results an awakening in people of introspection and self-appraisal. And according to the Quran, the miraculous outcome of this is that "he who is your enemy will become your dearest friend." (41:34)

2. A great advantage of the non-violent method is that, by following it, no part of one's time is wasted. The opportunities available in any given situation may then be exploited to the fullest extent-as happened after the no-war pact of Hudaibiya. This peace treaty enabled the energies of the believers to be utilised in peaceful constructive activities instead of being dissipated in a futile armed encounter. One great harm done by violent activism is the breaking of social traditions in the launching of militant movements. Conversely, the great benefit that accrues from non-violent activism is that it can be initiated and prolonged with no damage to tradition.

Generally speaking, attempts to improve or replace existing systems by violent activism are counter-productive. One *coup de tat* is often the signal for a series of coups and counter-coups, none of which benefit the common man. The truly desirable revolution is that which permits gradual and beneficial changes. And this can be achieved only on the basis of non-violence.

Way of Living

Since the objective good is known to God alone, the good life is that which is lived in accordance with the law of God and men ought to behave in the manner which pleases God and what pleases God most are the righteous deeds. We are given a beautiful description of righteousness:

> "It is not righteousness that ye turn your faces towards East or West ; but it is righteousness— to believe in God and the last Day, and the Angels and the Book, and the Messengers; to spend of your substance, out of love for Him, for your kin, for orphans, for the needy, for the wayfarer, for those who ask, and for the ransom of slaves; to be steadfast in prayer, and practise regular charity; to fulfil contracts which ye have made; and to be firm and patient, in pain (or suffering) and adversity, and throughout all periods of panic, such are the people of truth, the righteous'. (2 : 177).

The emphasis laid upon this verse is so great that most of the Quran seems to be nothing else than the exposition of its implications. Among the duties; enumerated in this verse, the first and foremost is to believe in the Unity of God. This is the basic concept into which the Quran desires to initiate human mind. The late Rev. C. F. Andrews has said :

> "One of the greatest blessings which Islam has brought to East and West alike has been the emphasis which at a critical period in human history it placed upon the Divine Unity. For during those Dark Ages both in East and West, from 600 to 1000 A.D. this doctrine was in danger of being overlaid and obscured in Hinduism and Christianity itself, owing to the immense accretions of subsidiary worships of countless demi-gods and heroes. Islam has been, both to Europe and India, in their dark hour of aberration from the sovereign truth of God's Unity, an invaluable corrective and deterrent. Indeed, without the final emphasis on this truth, which Islam gave from its central position,—facing India and facing Europe—it is doubtful whether this idea of God as one could have obtained that established place in human thought which is uncontested in the intellectual world today"
> (*The Genuine Islam*, Singapore, Vol. 1, No. 8, 1936).

Unity of God is to express itself in the Unity of man. The enforcement of the sense of Unity and brotherhood has been the chief aim of Islam. Every one who embraces Islam, enters into its fold and is treated as a brother, since believers are but one brotherhood (49 : 10). Suffice it to quote from the Prophet who says:

> "A Muslim is a brother of another Muslim, he neither wrongs him, nor leaves him helpless, nor humiliates him" (Muslim).

> "It is forbidden for a Muslim to take the life, honour and property of another Muslim" (Muslim and Bukhari).

> "In mutual compassion, love" and kindness, you will find the faithful like a body, if one of its parts feels pain, the whole body responds with wakefulness and fever" (Muslim and Bukhari).

Believe and work righteously are the injunctions to be strictly observed. These are the words that reverberate and echo in the Quran. The Quran expects man who believes in God to express that belief in an earnest endeavour to promote the unity of man, it is by action that he has to prove his belief in God, even as the Prophet said:

> "God doth not accept faith if it is not expressed in action, and doth not accept action if it does not conform to faith" (Bukhari).

Next to belief in God is the importance attached to the deeds of charity. So mindful is the Quran of the economically depressed classes of society that it calls upon every earning member to assign, in his earnings a share to the needy and the poor: "And in their wealth is a share of the needy and deprived" (51: 19). The supreme note in regard to social security is struck in the verse (3 : 92). It runs:

> "Ye shall never attain righteouness unless ye give (the needy and poor) of that which ye love (particularly your wealth); and whatever ye give of a truth God knoweth it well."

Charity is not to give something worthless but it is to give what we love and value greatly. Faith is not merely a matter of words, we must be prepared to show it in deeds of charity to our fellow-men. Practical deeds of charity are of value when they proceed from love, and from no other motive. In this respect our duties take various forms in the gradation as arranged in the above cited verse (2 : 177). The importance attached to these duties is manifest from the fact that their mention precedes that of the duties to God such as Salat (Prayers) which is one of the five pillars of Islam. These are the pillars devised to purify the soul of man and build his character in such a manner that he takes pleasure in self-sacrifice—the essence of righteousness.

The above verse is remarkable in that it renders the individual conscious of his duties on which depends the welfare of society and also teaches him to be firm and patient in pain (or sufferings) and adversity and throughout all periods of panic. The virtues of firmness and patience help man preserve his dignity and enable him to bear with fortitude all that falls to his lot of the vicissitudes of life.

The Arabic word 'Sabar', which occurs in this verse, is translated as patience but it implies many shades of meaning which is impossible to comprehend in one English word. In addition to its meaning of not being hasty, the word 'Sabar' connotes perseverance, constancy, steadfastness, firmness of purpose, self-restraint, endurance of sorrow, pain, and other evils. But it is never used in the sense of despair and disappointment for Islam is not passivity but active striving with the hope for the better. 'Sabar', thus, means patient perseverance and firmness of purpose which bear good fruits. In proof of the importance of this word it is enough to say that it has appeared in the Quran on more than ninety occasions and the Caliph Umar is reported to have stated that he had found the best way of life in patience, for patience is the key to success.

Here, it may be said that there is no peculiarity about Islam, for all the revealed religions profess the same truth. But their teachings are not in the original form. Further, they cannot claim to be the religions of universal character. Islam is the only religion, universal and for all time, for the Prophet Muhammad was sent as a Universal Messenger to mankind (34 : 28), and the Quran is the Book preserved in the original purity. Being universal in character Islam is neither Judaism which has the concept of a particular covenant or a specially chosen people, nor is it Christianity whose mission, as Jesus made it clear, was confined to recovering the 'lost sheep of Israel'. Further, the Christian view of the 'Kingdom of God in heaven and Kingdom of Caesar on earth' has no place in Islam.

Says Kerr : 'In professing to provide man with a political and legal system as well as a spiritual faith, Islam denies, at the outset, the conception familiar to Christendom of a separation between temporal and spiritual matters' (*Islamic Reform*, p. 3).

Observes Hitti : 'Moses was a prophet, so were Ibrahim, Nuh, Christ and others, each with a dispensation appropriate for a certain time or place. But Muhammad's dispensation, sums up as well as supersedes all earlier ones. It is final. After it there is none' (*The Near East in History*, p. 197).

Being the last of the Prophets, the message delivered by Muhammad is final and for all time and the law contained in the Quran is perfect and comprehensive. Good life is, therefore, to live in conformity with such a law.

Rules and Regulations

Islamic law is the Command of God revealed to the Prophet Muhammad. It precedes the state and is not preceded by it; it controls the society and is not controlled by it; state and society both have ideally to conform to its dictates. Observes Jackson:

> "Islamic law finds its chief source in the will of Allah revealed to the Prophet Muhammad. It contemplates one community of the faithful, though they may be of various tribes and in widely separated locations. Religion, not nationalism or geography, is the proper cohesive force. The state itself is subordinate to the Quran, which leaves little room for additional legislation, none for criticism or dissent. This world is viewed as but the vestibule to another and a better one for the

> faithful, and the Quran lays down rules of behaviour toward others and towards society to assure a safe transition. It is not possible to separate political or juristic theories from the teachings of the Prophet, which establish rules of conduct concerning religious, domestic, social and political life.
>
> This results in a law of duties rather than of rights, of moral obligations bindings on the individual, from which no earthly authority can relieve him, and which, he disobeys at peril of his future life"
>
> (Jackson, Foreword to *Law in the Middle East*, pp. vi, vii).

The doctrine of the Umma or one Community of the Faithful lies at the root of Islamic political concept. The Umma consists of the totality (jamaa) of individuals bound to one another by ties, not of kinship or race, but of religion, in that all its members profess their belief in the One God, and in all their relations to Him, all are equal, without distinction of rank, class or race. Differences of function are recognised, but 'the noblest among you is the most god-fearing' (49:13). See Gibb, 'Constitutional Organisation' in *Law in the Middle East*, p. 3.

According to Plato, law belongs to the class of convention; it rises through use and wont, while Islamic law is based upon Divine Revelations. Being Divine in origin, Islamic law is distinct from human law which is the product of reason and outcome of customary rules which can never, with perfectness, produce uniformity of conduct within the field of action to which they apply as do the Divine laws with their specified norms of good and bad, virtue and vice.

Divine laws are the standards of right conduct and provide guidance not only in establishing a well ordered society, but also in distinguishing between 'good' and 'evil'. As a well-knit system of obligations, they safeguard the rights of all and as a product of Divine Wisdom which alone knows what the objective good is, they ensure the welfare of the entire humanity.

The peculiarity of divine law is that it is eternal and immutable. The basis of life, as conceived by Islam, is spiritual. A society based on such a conception must have eternal and immutable laws, but since it does not lose sight of the material world which is subject to change, the laws contain broad principles that admit of interpretation so as to accommodate the change in life and to provide for the growing needs of society. Over and above is the Rule of Necessity and Need to provide facilities to those who are confronted with hardships.

> Divine laws, thus, take in their sweep not only this world, but the world to come : 'Ye prefer the life of this world although the Hereafter is better and more lasting' (87 : 17). Islamic life, as such, is the harmonious blend of the material with the spiritual. Bare spirituality is never preached in Islam as it says 'yes' to life and to the worldly things. God has made all things in nature available for man so that he may harness them to suit his purpose: 'Whatever is in the heavens and whatever is in the earth are made of service unto him' (45 : 13).

Divine law is unique in that it has its own permanent standards of justice. Hence justice according to Divine law is much higher than all other systems of justice, be they Greek, Roman or any other human law, for it searches the innermost motives. Justice, as conceived by Islam, is not only to give each his due, but also to return good for ill. What Islam suggests is the objective approach to the problem of justice, to put ourselves in the place of another, to see things from the standpoint of an impartial observer. Here are some of the Quranic verses to give an idea of impartiality :

> 'And when ye judge between people, judge with fairness' (4:58). 'O ye who believe! stand fast to justice, and for the sake of God always be truthful in giving evidence, though it be against your own selves or (your) parents or kinsfolk, whether the party be rich or poor: God safeguards the interests of both (parties). Therefore follow not your own inclinations lest you should swerve from justice. If you prevaricate or decline (to speak the truth), then verily God is aware of what you do' (4:135). 'O ye who believe! For the sake of

> God, stand up to uphold justice and let not ill-will towards any people impel you to deviate from justice. Act justly. This indeed is akin to piety. Be mindful of God ; for assuredly, He knoweth all that ye do'
>
> (5 :9).

Justice in Islam is conceived as a sacred trust, a duty imposed upon man to be discharged in all sincerity. 'To render justice', says Sarakhsi, 'constitutes one of the most noble acts of devotion' (*Mabsut*, vol. 16, p. 67). According to Kasani, 'it is one of the best acts of devotion and one of the most important duties after belief in God' (*Badai al-Sanai*, vol. 7, p. 4). Says the Caliph Abu Baker:

> 'By God, to me the powerful among you will be weak, and the weak among you powerful until I have taken for them their right'
>
> (Abu Ubayd, *Kitab al-Amwal*, p. 8).

The Caliph Umar is reported to have said :

> 'No one will be allowed by me to treat others unjustly or to encroach upon their rights. Should anyone do so I will punish him severely so that he returns to others their rights' (Abu Yusuf, *Kitab-al-Kharaj* p. 167).

The above sayings are in obedience to the Command of God which lays a preponderant stress on moral values :

> 'Verily, God enjoineth fairness of dealings and kindly behaviour (with others), and the giving to kindred (out of what you have) ; and forbiddeth lewdness and wrong-doing and oppression' (16 : 90). 'And do not touch the property of the orphan except to replace it with something better until he comes of age; give measured weight with, (full) justice;—no burden do We place on any soul but that which it can bear;—whenever ye speak, speak justly, even if a nearer relative is concerned; and fulfil the covenant of God: Thus doth He command you, that ye may remember' (6 : 152). Such is the morality and law of Islam. For details we refer the reader to our work Philosophy of Islamic Law I and the *Orientalists*, Islamic Publications, Lahore (Pakistan).

The Goals

This has been the most disputed problem in the past and continues to be so in the present. For, if everything is determined or predestined by God, why should man be held responsible for his acts? This issue has given birth to two parties of opposite-views—Jabriyya or Fatalists and Qadriyya who are opposed to Fatalists.

To Fatalists, God must be tyrant and unjust if He punishes man for acts which, are not under his^ power and control. As opposed to this view, the Qadriyya hold that God is Just and is bound to be so. He would not punish man for such acts as are not in his power. Man, they say, has complete power over his actions: he has free-will and also choice and, as such, responsible for his acts.

Before we enter into further details, let us try to know, in the light of Quranic verses, the scheme of God and how it is carried out. It cannot be denied that God has power over all things (67 : 1), He created all things and ordered them in due proportions (2 : 52). He also created Death and Life, that He may try which of His creatures (men) is best in deed (67 : 2). Creation, therefore, is not without a purpose. God has created things with a measure (54 : 49) and also created their opposites, for things are known through their opposites. Night has been created to "know the importance of Day and vice versa. Thus, world has been made a glittering show with all sorts of things to test the quality of man: 'That which is on earth, We have made but a glittering show for the earth, in order that We test them—as to which of them is of best conduct' (18 : 7). Evil and Good are both created by God as a trial, and test for us: 'And We test you by evil and by good by way of trial, to Us must ye return' (21 : 35).

As to the Will of God, 'He doeth what He will' (2 : 253). This is further supported by the Quranic verses: 'Thy Lord is doer of what He will' (11 : 107). 'His verily is all Creation and Commandment (7 : 54).

It may be noted that there are two aspects of His Commandment—Commandment relating to Creation (*amr takwini*) and Commandment relating to Right Conduct (*amr tashrii*). Creation includes both what He likes and what He dislikes, for example, He created the Devil and wickedness, while Righteousness is His love and approval. Man has to choose for himself, what is liked by God, with the help of the Rules of Right Conduct. Wickedness and sin do not fall under His liking and approval: 'He loveth not mischief (2 : 205). Ha liketh not ingratitude from His servants' (39 : 7). And when ingratitude and wickedness transgress their limits punishment becomes inevitable. Even then God's Mercy gives every chance to the wicked to mend themselves and to repent.

They are given a definite warning and if they still persist in their wickedness, the charge is proved against them and it is at this stage-that God's Commandment takes effect: 'When We decide to destroy a township, We send Commandment to its folk who live at ease, and afterwards they commit abomination therein, and so the Word (or doom) hath, effect for it, and We destroy it utterly' (17: 16); and it was never God's (part) that He should send a folk astray after He had guided them until He had made clear unto them what they should avoid' (9 : 115).

God's will is expressive of His unlimited power which renders everything possible for Him. 'He cannot be questioned for His acts but men will be questioned for theirs (21: 23). He may forgive whom He pleaseth and punish whom He pleaseth but, at the same time, He is Oft-Forgiving, Most Merciful (3 :129). This shows the tremendous Power which He commands and can use it at His Will and Pleasure but His Mercy gives chances to men so that they may correct themselves. If they fail to do so, it becomes just and fair for God to set seal on their hearts and on their hearing (2 : 7), and give rope to such as do not receive guidance and try them in their contumacy and then mete out a severe punishment for them. All this shows that God is not tyrant.

The Quranic verses which deal with God's severe penalty indicate His Power and Possibility to do any thing but the use of such power is not without justice-Although God can deal with His creatures in whatever manner He Hikes and is not bound by any law) to be just, yet 'not one will He treat with injustice' (18 : 46); 'nor shall He suffer to perish the reward of any who do a (single) righteous deed' (18 : 30). 'He never harms those who serve Him' (3 : 182); 'nor is He unjust' (41: 46).

From the foregoing it is proved that God is just and deals justly and as such, His determining of good and evil cannot be without justice. Further what is predetermined is not known to us, so why dispute it and call its fairness in question and why not believe in His Justice and Mercifulness.

The best course is, therefore, to have implicit trust in the justness of God and ascribe every good to Him and evil to ourselves: 'Whatever good (O man!) happens to thee, is from God; but whatever evil happens to thee is from thyself (4 : 97). We have no reason to doubt God's fairness Who takes into consideration even an atom's weight of good and evil and passes His judgement in accordance therewith: 'And who so doeth good an atom's weight will see it then, and who so doeth the atom's weight of evil will see it then' (99: 7,8).

We cannot evaluate our acts. May be, we pride ourselves on our works and take them to be the righteous ones but in the judgement of God they are quite reverse. We may be under the impression that our efforts will be rewarded, while we are among 'those whose efforts have been wasted in this life, but they thought they were acquiring good by their works' (18 : 104). We cannot judge our acts, God alone is the best judge.

Coming to the question of the Fatalists we feel that they are unnecessarily obsessed with the idea of determination. They must always expect good from God, for He does not intend anything evil for His creatures. Even' in the severe punishment which He has meted out there is our welfare. To meet the strict claims of justice equality is prescribed in cases of murder (2: 179). Life is taken for a life and in this law of equality, says the Quran, is the saving of life. And, indeed, it saves lives, being a lesson for all. Though the life of the murderer is lost but it brings peace to the society. Likewise hands of the thief are cut off (5 : 41) and in this lies the safety of property and protection of innocent people from crime. All the acts of God are, therefore, a Mercy to mankind and in their own interest.

We do not know what is really good for us and what is evil, 'Perchance ye dislike a thing which is good for you and that ye like a thing which is bad for you but God knoweth and ye know not' (2 : 216). So instead of questioning the predestination, of which we know nothing it is profitable to beseech God for His guidance and entreat Him to give what is good for us.

The Prophet has rightly prescribed *istikhara* (asking good of God) in place of discussion on this topic. God in all His bountiful Mercy may grant us, what we ask for. 'Call Me', says He, 'I will answer your prayer.' (40: 60). Further, He has the power to efface the evil: God doth efface what He will and establishes what He will and with Him is the source of ordinance' (13 : 39).

Here the question may arise that God's knowledge of things would be defective if such changes take place. To this we answer that He is All-Powerful and can withhold Decree of Command which brings destiny into existence.

And it is for this reason that the Prophet laid stress on prayers. Pray often and in real earnest,' said he, 'for prayers can avert that which is inevitable (destiny).' We have to act upon it, for it is possible that God might have intended for us a better destiny on account of our entreaty and earnest prayer. Thus, His knowledge of things cannot be defective.

The followers of the Prophet asked him once as to what actually predestination meant and whether they should cease to work, for what is predestined is bound to happen. The Prophet in answer, exhorted them to work and to do righteous deeds and cited the Quranic verse:

> 'As for him who giveth (in charity) and is dutiful (toward God) and believeth in goodness: surely We will make smooth for him the Path of Bliss. But he who is greedy miser and deemeth himself self-sufficient and disbelieveth in goodness; surely We will make smooth for him the Path of Misery. (92 : 5-10).

This is the best solution offered by the Prophet. Obsessed with the idea of determinism we should not cease to work, nor be indifferent to the world. The Path of Bliss will be made smooth for us if we have faith in God and do righteous deeds. For details, we refer the reader to our work Islam, its Theology and the Greek Philosophy, Islamic Publications, Ltd. Lahore (Pakistan).

The Evaluation

On analysis we find that ethics is not a finished and complete subject. Socrates has rightly remarked: 'No system of ethics could be constructed until full attention had been devoted to the special features of moral experience and to the vagueness and contradictions of ordinary moral opinions. This required the philosophical intellect of the first rank concentrated on the problems of conduct' (*Ency. Britannica,* vol. 10, p. 762).

He went about showing that those who claimed to teach men how to live, poets, orators, and sophists were unable to define their views by argument or even to give adequate definitions of what they were claiming to explain. They were both inconsistent and ignorant. The problem is, therefore, to find what is absolute or objective good.

Nietzsche adopts an attitude of moral relativism. To him, that only is good which leads to enhancement of the will to power, and because in different times and climes it is possible to achieve this result with the help of different moral devices, he did not see any point in prescribing a universal code of morals. He insisted on the inversion of values because he saw in the prevailing Christian values nothing but nihilism and decadence.. Morality, he says, has been only a weapon in the hands of those who had the will to gain power, hence various systems to suit the various ends. He who is strong and powerful is on the right side, and who is weak is destined to be reckoned as false.

The classical ethical theories are characterised by their efforts to answer two questions: 'What is the good life ?' and 'How ought men to behave ?' Moral theories like Hedonism, Cynicism, Stoicism, Utilitarianism and so on seem to be of highest complex nature. We find ourselves constrained to support G. E. Moore who claimed, in his *Principia Ethica*, that the classical theories were attempts to deduce moral precepts from theological, metaphysical or scientific premises and that such arguments are fallacious, since one cannot argue from premises of one logical type {i.e., descriptions) to conclusions of a different logical type (i.e., prescriptions).

Moral theories which appear plausible at a first glance, such as Hedonism, are found upon careful examination to suffer from serious defects. How can the good life be identical with a life of pleasure, since there are pleasures which are bad ? For example, pleasures such as drinking alcohol, give us momentary pleasure but may result in a life of subsequent pain and travail.

The various answers which classical theories give are in the form of advice rather than an effort to define moral words like 'good', 'bad' and so on. Hedonism, for instance, may be regarded as advising men that good life consists of pleasure, and further that they ought to act so as to acquire pleasure. But the word 'good' is not defined and, indeed, 'good' like all moral words, is indefinable and that 'goodness' is an unanalysable property. Any attempted definitions of moral words will be in terms only of their descriptive meaning and no more.

> Good and evil are thus, described in terms of pleasure and pain. So far as 'Utilitarian Ethics' is concerned it assumes that man is motivated by the desire to secure pleasurable and avoid painful experiences. The Utilitarians have their own suspicions of reason and look to human observation and experience in order to find what men actually value. Instead of judging the conduct by the feelings and motives, they would judge it by its consequences. Each individual, they held, is really seeking his happiness above everything else. If then we are to find a moral standard in what men actually value, we must find it not in the heavens alone but in human happiness.
>
> (Dewey, *Ethic*, p. 167).

> The essence of Bentham's philosophy is that nature has placed man under the empire of pleasure and pain. We owe to them all our ideas; we refer to them all our judgements, and all the determinations of our life. He who pretends to withdraw himself from this subjection knows not what he says. His only object is to seek pleasure and shun pain... .These eternal and irresistible sentiments ought to be the great study of the moralist and the legislator. The principle of utility subjects everything to these two motives'
>
> (Bentham, *The Theory of Legislation*, p. 2).

Bentham's theory is criticized as contradictory in itself. According to its conception of desire and motive, the whole object of all actions is the obtaining of personal pleasure, while the proper standard for judging the morality of act is its contribution to the welfare of others. In Bentham's theory 'desire for private pleasure as the sole motive of action and universal benevolence as the principle of approval are at war with each other'.

'It would be only a poor sort of happiness' remarked George Eliot in her *Romola*, 'that could ever come by caring very much for our narrow pleasures'. Personal pleasure is indeed a low sort of pleasure and it is better to be a human being dissatisfied than a pig satisfied.

Further, pleasure has no sound basis, for it depends mostly upon the existing state of a person:

> 'What is agreeable at one time, disagrees at another; what pleases in health is distasteful in illness; what annoys or disgusts in a state of repletion is gratifying when one is hungry and eager. And on a higher scale, that which is pleasant to men of generous disposition arouses aversion in a mean and stingy person; what is pleasant to a child may bore an adult; the objects that gratify a scholar are repulsive to a boor'
>
> (Dewey, Ethics, p. 213).

In fact, there can be no standard of judgement as to know what exactly constitutes pleasure and, morally speaking, pleasure as an end cannot be considered 'good', for a villain takes pleasure in his wickedness. The Utilitarian theory, that pleasure is the good and the end, is baseless and immoral.

It may have been clear by now that Morality cannot be adequately defined and Ethics fails to be a science. But the subjectivists, for instance, Hedonists contend that their moral judgements are not false but true. Moral theories, in this respect, are classified into subjectivistic and objectivistic. This raises the question of defining subjectivism and objectivism.

Subjectivism : Subjectivism is the doctrine that all knowledge is subjective only and incapable of objective proof. It is commonly held that there is no reality other than the reality of things which we see, touch, hear, smell or taste. This leads to deny the existence of an order of reality which is not open to the investigation and subject to the laws of science and equally denies, with regard to human conduct, that there is anything real in the psychological ·realm other than the series of emotions, desires, impulses, hopes and thoughts which make up the stream of our consciousness. Hence a thing is good not because it is characterized by goodness or is really good but because we desire it and it gives us happiness.

Suppose if someone denies this sort of conclusion as ascetics are said to have done, maintaining that we should mortify the flesh here for the happiness to be attained in the Hereafter, what will be the reply? Further, if we ask a subjectivist, 'How do you know that pleasure is a good ?' He has no reasoned answer, he just sees to be so. Finally, as we have already-explained pleasure has no definite meaning.

The argument which is advanced in support of subjectivism may be called the argument from Sentience. The subjectivists argue that no question of good or bad can arise in a world which has no sentient being —beings that are capable of feeling, for it would not make sense to say that anything good or bad could happen to inanimate objects such as a rock or stone. It is only if some sentient being is affected by these events, or could be affected by them, that it makes sense to say that they are good or bad. Goodness and badness thus seem to depend upon the feelings, attitudes and desires of sentient beings. From considerations such as these it is argued that some form of subjectivism must be true.

But if we probe deep into such argument it becomes evident that what it proves is not the good or bad as it actually is but as it is thought or felt. Moral judgements of this type cannot be called sound ethical judgements since they depend not only upon emotions,, desires, and feelings of persons making such judgements but also on their ethical, traditional, social, economic and other sentiments. It is on this account that these judgements not only differ from one another but are also conflicting so much so that even vices and crimes-are considered virtues. Says Canon Rashdall, a well-known authority on ethical philosophy:

> 'There is hardly a vice or crime (according to our own moral standard) which has not at some time or other in some circumstances been looked- upon as a moral and religious duty. Stealing was accounted virtuous for the young Spartan and among the Indian caste of Thugs. In the ancient world Piracy, i.e. robbery and murder, was a respectable profession. To the Mediaeval Christian religious persecution was the highest of duties, and so on'
>
> (C. E. M. Jood, *Philosophy*, P- 31).

Under the circumstances it may be said that just as science is content with a world of matter in motion, the subjectivist ethics is content with a world of human consciousness which consists of nothing except the stream of emotions, desires, impulses, hopes and thoughts. The peculiarity of the subjectivist theories of ethics is that they do not accept the view that there is an 'object' which possesses ethical qualities of its own, with the corollary that there can be correct ethical judgement.

For a better understanding of subjectivist theories let us call a person making an ethical judgement 'the subject' and the character to which the judgement refers 'the object'. The ethical judgements are called subjectivistic as they do not refer to the object which they support but to the subject, being judgements to the effect that the subject is experiencing certain feelings. The good according to such theories is not the good in its own right but according as is experienced by the subject, i.e., the maker of ethical judgement. It, therefore, follows that if such theories are considered to be correct then 'good' has no ethical quality of its own, for, the good, in such a case, is only what is thought 'good'. Let us turn to objectivism and see whether its ethical judgements are correct.

Objectivism : Objective means actually existing, not Subjective only. Hence objectivism is the tendency to lay stress upon what is objective or external to the mind.

> The main argument in favour of objectivism is that; it provides a theory which corresponds more closely to the views of men of common sense about moral matters

> than subjectivism. To mark the difference between subjectivism and objectivism we cite an example of 'two persons who have just entered a room and asked to guess its temperature; the one is supposed to have recently emerged from a refrigerator, the other from a hot-house; the former guesses 75°F., the latter 70°F. It is clear that two subjective conditions prevailing in the bodies of the two judges have determined the guesses that they make as to the temperature of the room; what they do not determine is the temperature of the room. What both judges are purporting to assess is a certain condition which prevails in the world independently of their judgements, and most of us would agree that, since the temperature of the room can be measured by a thermometer, there is a perfectly definite sense in holding that judgement according to thermometer is Objective and correct, while another judgement to the effect that it is something else is wrong and incorrect'
>
> (C. E. M. Jood, *Philosophy*, pp. 133,134).

The difference between the case in which we judge about the temperature and the case in which we judge about ethical qualities is that in the former we can refer to an instrument, the thermometer, by reference to which we can determine what the objective temperature is and pronounce our judgement to be nearer to the truth than the other, whereas there is no equivalent instrument wherewith to measure ethical judgements. Here is the difficulty and it is perhaps for this reason that the subjectivists contend that all knowledge is subjective and incapable of objective proof. Let us turn to Kant and see if his moral theory can solve this problem.

In his analysis of human impulses and desires Kant goes all the way with subjectivists that man is merely a creature of likes and dislikes, of wants and needs, of impulses and tastes, of preferences and prejudices, but, he says, there is one characteristic unique in nature, and man being possessed of it, cannot be adequately regarded as wholly a child of nature. In addition to the impulses and desires which tell him -what he would like to do, he is, on occasion, conscious of something else, namely, what he ought to do which may be very opposite to what he would like to do. Thus, for man there is a distinction between 'want' and 'ought', between 'desire' and 'duty'; moral sense is innate in him and not derived from experience. Moral sense, says Kant, is our unescapable feeling in the face of our temptation that this or that is wrong. An act is good not because it has good results or because it is a right, but because it is done in obedience to the inner sense of duty. Morality is not properly the doctrine how we make ourselves happy but how we make ourselves worthy of happiness.

To comprehend the unique significance of 'ought' Kant insists that man must be a member of some other order of reality. Thus, he can win free from the influences of heredity, circumstances and environment which otherwise determine his psychology. To see Kant's moral philosophy in its proper setting we have to study it in its association with his metaphysical theory.

Kant says that when we will to do our duty in pursuance of ought' and in the face of disinclination, we are making direct contact not with the familiar world which appears to our senses, but with the world as it is independently of ourselves—a moral world and an order of reality which contains the value of morality such as right and good. It is not with our minds and our intellects that we recognize what is right and realize what ought to be done, but by the 'practical' as opposed to the 'theoretical' reason—a faculty similar, in modern concept, to intuition. The central feet of morals appeared to him to be the voice of duty from within the soul itself.

Thus the familiar world of common sense is not the only world, there is another world and order of reality which is spiritual and which contains values of morality. This implies the existence of a mind, other than our own, which not only knows but also creates values—a Law-giver who lays down the moral law or order of the universe. The argument, in this way, passes over from ethics to religion.

With God as the Law-giver the problem is solved. He alone knows the objective good and we cannot know it as we often dislike a thing which is good for us and like a thing which is bad for us:

'Perchance you dislike a thing which may be good for you ; and perchance you like a thing which may be bad for you'. To know the objective good is beyond our power and it is in His law alone that we find the required instrument and standard for correct ethical judgements. 'Good', here is not what is thought 'good' but the 'objective and absolute good'. The question, is now, 'What is the good life, in its real sense, and' how ought men to behave?'

Values and Traditions

Plato: Evil is Due to Lack of Knowledge : In most of the classical theories it is assumed that if we know what the good life is we will naturally behave in such a way as to try to achieve it.

Platonism, for instance, holds that evil is due to lack of knowledge; if a man discovers what is right he will never act wickedly. But the problem is how to discover 'the right' or 'the good' and how can this be done when men hold different and conflicting opinions about the good life?

In answer to this Plato says that the discovery of the nature of things is an intellectual task, hence to discover what the good life is one must be trained in various disciplines such as mathematics, philosophy and so on. It is only through such intellectual training that men would have the capacity to know the nature of the good life. Even without this sort of training it is possible for some men to lead good life but they will do so haphazardly or blindly. There may be some men who do not have intellectual power to apprehend what the 'good life' is, but they will act virtuously if they follow those who have knowledge of the good. This finds expression in Plato's famous work 'The Republic', which speaks of Philosopher King as the most efficient ruler, for he is possessed of knowledge of 'the good' and can lead men to the good life.

According to Plato, there is fundamentally one and only one good life for all men to lead because goodness is something which is not dependent upon man's inclinations desires or wishes but is absolute as it exists independently of men and remains to be discovered if men can be properly trained. Such is the absolutism in Plato's philosophy.

From the above it is evident that Plato regards morality as

being a matter of knowledge but only a few are intellectually gifted to have such ability. It is not sufficient to say that those of us who have not the ability- can live good lives by being led by those who have, since to behave morally presupposes that one has responsibility for one's actions and an action is not truly moral or immoral unless it is the result of free choice of the individual performing it. Aristotle seems aware of these defects in Plato's theory, since he adopts his own doctrine of morality.

Aristotle: Doctrine of the Golden Mean : Aristotle, though a great metaphysician, but, curiously enough, in his ethical writings he adopts a scientific or empirical approach to ethical problems. Instead of trying to discover the nature of the good life for all men by reflection alone, he examined the behaviour of various people in every day life. He noticed that the various lives that men of common sense consider to be good all contain, one common characteristic, i.e. happiness. Hence he frankly admits that the aim of life is not goodness for its own sake, but happiness.

His doctrine of Golden Mean is explained as follows:

> Being happy, according to Aristotle, is like being well-fed. How much food should a man eat in order to be well-fed? To Aristotle, there is no general answer to this question in the sense of specific amount. It depends on the size of the man, what sort of work he does, whether he is ill or well, and so on. The proper amount for anyone to eat can be ascertained by trial and error: if we eat a certain amount of food and still feel hungry, we should eat more ; if we eat the same amount and feel uncomfortable, then we should eat less. The correct amount is a 'mean between eating too much and too little.

But the 'mean' cannot be interpreted as being synonymous with 'average'. Suppose that one pound of food per day is too little, and that two pounds is too much. Does this suggest that the average amount (i.e., one pound and a half) is the correct amount? Aristotle's answer is that it may or may not be—but in general, one cannot say that the correct amount is exactly one pound and a half ; all one can say is that it is an amount somewhere between one pound and two pounds; and this is what Aristotle intends by the word 'mean'. Further, it will be seen from the above that Aristotle's mean varies from man to man.

The golden mean, however, is not, like the mathematical mean, an exact average of two precisely calculable extremes; it fluctuates with the collateral , circumstances of each situation and is subject to flexible reason.

The theory of Aristotle is subject to some criticism as in certain situations it is difficult to follow the mean. For example, there is no 'mean' between keeping a promise and not keeping one. The same applies to telling the truth: either one does or does not tell the truth. But we have to bear in mind that the question of mean arises only when there is the possibility of going to extremes.

Hedonism : To Plato, the good life is in no way connected with pleasure, but Aristotle moderated this doctrine in holding that 'pleasure must be in some way an ingredient of happiness'. Epicurus disagreed with both of them and held a view which is called 'Hedonism', the doctrine that pleasure is the sole good. To him, morality is identical with expedience.

The ethical philosophy of Epicurus consists mainly of advice for living moderately but pleasantly. While discovering pleasure to be good he also realized that if a person pursues pleasure too arduously, pain will follow. For example, if a man drinks too much, it will result in headache. Since some pleasures are obviously followed by pain, Epicurus distinguished between those pleasures which are followed by pain and those which are not and regarded only the latter as good. He called the former 'dynamic' pleasures and the latter as 'passive' pleasures. Sexual love, for example, is bad because it is accompanied by fatigue, remorse and depression. He advocated avoidance of such pleasures as are bad, for he believed that it is better to avoid pain than to seek pleasure if it will produce pain.

Hedonism, though theoretically attractive, may be seen to violate our ordinary feelings about what constitutes behaviour. The objection is not that it seeks superficial and narrow pleasures but, more fundamentally, that pleasure is not the sole object which men should strive for.

Cynicism : It is the philosophy of the Cynics, founded by Antisthenes, a pupil of Socrates, who condemned ease, -wealth, and enjoyment of life. The most famous was Diogenes who carried principles to an extreme. This is the philosophy which holds that if salvation is to be found it is to be found in a rejection of society and in a return to simple life—to a life of asceticism.

The word 'Cynic' comes from the Greek word 'Kunos', which means 'dog-like'. Diogenes, for example, is supposed to have lived in a large tub, and rejected all refinements—of dress, food, personal cleanliness. The Cynics believed that the world was fundamentally evil; in order to live properly a man must withdraw from participation in it. Cynicism is not only anti-social, but also contributed largely to undermine the social standards, contending that only individual virtue was of essential importance. As a philosophy Cynicism has had a great influence upon plain man and is considered to have been a major factor in the development of early Christian philosophy. The monk is no better than a Cynic for he casts aside the world and lives the life of a cave or monastery, while monasticism is not permissible in Islam.

Stoicism : Stoicism has been the most influential ethical doctrine of the ancient Western World before Christianity. Zeno was the founder of Stoicism and is supposed to have lectured in the third century B.C. from a porch, and stoicism gets its name from this fact, since 'stoa' is the Greek word for 'porch'. The basic tenet of stoicism for achieving personal salvation is just like that of the Cynics and can be summed up in one-sentence. Learn to be indifferent to external influences! It is a philosophy of indifference. By practising indifference one becomes independent of the world.

The Stoics believed in predestination, i.e. that all happenings in the world are fixed by God according to some preconceived plan, and that virtue consists in a will which is in agreement with the happenings of nature. Further, they considered it important to free oneself from desires and passions.

Stoicism differs from Cynicism in that the Cynics felt that they were powerless to prevent the collapse of the world in which they lived and hence they renounced it, while the Stoics argued that this sort of renunciation was unnecessary, for man need not renounce the material things of the world provided that he does not become involved in them. If he remains indifferent to them and uneffected by them there is no reason why he should not continue to enjoy them.

The Stoics hold that man is not free but instead is chained to his destinies in accordance with the divine-plan. But this view is inconsistent with their view that, a man can alter his character and can change his frame of mind in such a manner that he will become-indifferent to things that he formerly prized. If man is free and has power to alter his character and to-change his frame of mind, then the thesis that all events are predetermined by some master plan must be false.

The problem of Freedom of the Will is the most baffling one. It has not only appeared in Stoic-philosophy but also occurs in religious philosophy as-well as in modern psychology. Islam is the religion, which has found a clue to its solution as will be explained later.

Spinoza: The Ethics : Spinoza is reckoned as one of the towering figures in the history of Ethics. He was a rigid determinist as he says, 'All things come to pass, come to pass according to the eternal order and fixed laws of Nature'. Thus he was in the metaphysical tradition of the Stoics-In holding that nothing is good or bad in itself, but is only so in relation to someone, Spinoza is a relativist. From this point of view of Spinoza riches, fame and sensual pleasure are all not inherently worthwhile. They are not worth acquiring for their own sake but only as means to making human life more happy. When these things affect men in desirable ways, they are good, but when they affect them in undesirable ways, they are bad.

According to him good life consists in the recognition of the truth that all events are determined and a man will be happy when he comes to understand that there are limits to human power and that everything which happens must happen necessarily. This sort of attitude, says he, if developed, will liberate men from fear, anxiety and unhappiness. These arise only when a man becomes slave to his emotions.

Spinoza's masterpiece is The Ethics which is considered to be his great work by many philosophers but he did not effectively resolve the conflict that exists between determinism and freedom. He believed that all events in nature are determined which means that man is essentially powerless. The question is: 'how can he change his attitude and frame of mind towards life and be free from anxieties when he is powerless ?'

Bentham and Stuart Mill: Utilitarianism : One of the earliest exponents of this moral theory was Francis Hutcheson but the most famous exponents of it are Jermy Bentham and John Stuart Mill who attempted to lay down a principle for determining the rightness or wrongness of an act and called this maxim the Principle of Utility. According to this principle an action is right in so far it tends to produce the greatest happiness for the greatest number and happiness is taken to mean pleasure. The fundamental point is that it is consequences of a given action which determine its rightness or wrongness, not the motive from which it is done. The object is to separate the rightness or wrongness of an action from the goodness or badness of the person who performs the action.

There are certain objections raised against Utilitarianism and Nietzsche describes Mill as a 'block head' for his assumption that in computing the amount of happiness or unhappiness, which an action creates, each man will count equally for one unit of happiness. Nietzsche believed that some people were inherently more important than others and their happiness or unhappiness counted for more than the happiness or unhappiness of the average man. Carlyle, on the other hand, condemned Utilitarianism as 'a universal syllabus of sentimental twaddle'.

Further, there are some philosophers who rejected Utilitarianism on the ground that consideration in assessing the moral worth of our action must be given to the motive from which it is done.

Kantian Moral Philosophy ; According to Kant ethics is the most important subject in philosophy. He believes in the moral basis of religion. He even used ethical arguments to establish the existence of God. Since men who are not virtuous are happier in this world there must be another world for virtuous men to be rewarded and this leads him to the conclusion that there is God and an eternal life.

'What is the nature of morality' is the main question which Kant's moral theory was formulated to answer. Kant believed that the key to answer this question lay in distinguishing between acts done from 'inclination' and acts done from a 'sense duty-or obligation'. An obligations that which a map ought to do despite his inclination to do otherwise.

Some philosophers have held that in matters of morality one should act upon his inclinations but Kant rejects such an account of morality. For him, a man is acting morally only when he suppresses his inclinations and obeys the command of duty. Further, he makes a distinction between actions which are 'in accord with duty' and those done 'from duty'.

The former are not moral acts but the latter are. Most parents, for instance, are inclined to take care of their children because they are fond of them but this does not amount to moral act as it is in accordance with duty and not from duty. A man who understands the nature of his duty and acts upon it is moral and not otherwise. According to him the concept of goad and evil must not be determined before the law. But only after it and by means of it'. Thus he subordinates good to moral law. Briefly, a moral action is that which is done from 'a respect for duty and a moral person is he who acts 'from duty', not from inclination or even in accord with duty.

Kant differs sharply from the Utilitarians in that he stresses the point that the essence of morality is to be found in the motive from which an act is done. A man who keeps promises by accident is not a moral man. Every action, says he, must be judged in the light of how it would appear if it were to be a universal code of behaviour. All that is required is to know our duty in a particular case and ask ourselves if the motive of that act can be made universal without falling into self-contradiction. For example, says he, 'May I when in distress, make a promise with intention not to keep it?'

Evidently, this principle, if made universal, simply contradicts itself, for with such a promise there would be no such thing as a promise. No one would like to be content with a false or deceitful promise. The principle of right action, in this light, may be summed up as: 'Act in a way that you would like to be paid back in your own coin' or 'Act as if the maxim of thy action were to become by thy will a universal law of nature'. This is according to Kant, the unconditional command of our conscience—a categorical imperative. Another categorical imperative formulated by Kant is: 'So act as to treat humanity, whether in thine own person or in that of -another, in every case as an end, never as a means only.' Another way of putting such maxim is 'Do unto others as you would have them do unto you.' We should treat others as ends in themselves because that is how we regard ourselves. To treat another man only as a means to achieve our end is to disregard his humanity, hence immoral.

It is said that Kant's theory is inconsistent in that he has not held to his original claim that he is concerned solely with motive and not consequences. The objection is on the basis that Kant introduces consequences of the act in tacitly showing that the effect of not behaving in accordance with the categorical imperative would be to make human life impossible.

9

Believers' Unity

The Islamic community is governed by a sense of both individual and collective responsibility to Allah, who has defined the limits of human behaviour. In discussing the collective aspects of human interaction in any community, it is only logical to start at the beginning, that is, with the family. The Islamic teachings are designed to strengthen and protect this important nurturing ground of future generations with the utmost care and concern. Marriage, which is the cornerstone of the family is strongly encouraged in Islam. The purpose of marriage, according to Islam, is that a man and woman build a home, live together in love, kindness, support and companionship, meet each other's sexual needs and bring up children together. By their marriage, they form a family unit which also supports and strengthens the existing families of the pair.

Since men and women have different natures, Islam assigns different but complementary roles to each, dividing the work between them in a way that best suits their capacities and natures. It assigns the leadership role, the financial responsibility and the support and maintenance of the women and children, to men. Women are responsible for looking after their family and husband's comfort and well being, guarding their honour and properties, providing for the physical and emotional well being of their children and bringing them up as true Muslims. That a woman must do the household work is not required by Islam, as she is free to hire domestic help if she can afford it. She can pursue her own work and interests, provided the family is not neglected. They are not required to provide for the family's maintenance because Islam has made this the responsibility of men.

Islam lays great stress on raising children properly. Young people, on their part, are required to develop a sense of responsibility for their own conduct from an early age. A young Muslim is considered by Islam as accountable for his actions from the age of puberty by which time he is considered to be capable of possessing a sufficient understanding of the Islamic teachings and of what is allowed and what is prohibited. Thus, there is a continuity of values from one generation to the other and rebellion against them is not only a rebellion against parental guidance but against Allah.

Islam also requires that Muslims take responsibility for their elderly parents or relatives who may need their care and support.

Islam considers the honour of women sacred and insists that they be treated with dignity and respect. Women are required to guard their modesty and purity. The Islamic community should be free from the exploitation and degradation of women and of any influences which weaken marriage, the family life or people's morals. Islam lays down certain limits to govern the relations between men and women so that their interaction may be characterized by integrity, purity and honesty.

The material development of the community is considered a religious obligation in Islam. However, the aim of all such efforts must be the welfare of the people and the community, keeping in mind the needs of future generations as well.

Charity and feeling of brotherhood which is unique amongst Muslims is intended to distribute wealth equally so that wealth is not concentrated among a few people while the rest live in poverty. Every Muslim is expected to help and to accept responsibility for those living in his community as far as his means allow.

The social life of a Muslim is based upon principles that are designed to secure happiness and prosperity for the individual as well as for the community. There can be no superiority due to class or origin or wealth according to the Quran and the sayings of the Holy Prophet (PBUH). On the contrary, there are many Quranic verses and sayings of the Holy Prophet (PBUH) which remind mankind of the fact that all humanity represents one family springing from the same parents.

The relation between the individual and the community is based on this unity of origin. The role of the individual is complementary to that of the community. Between the two, there is solidarity and cooperation. The individual is responsible for the welfare and prosperity of his community. The community life of Islam is marked by cooperation in goodness and piety. The individual is enjoined to play an active part in the establishment of sound social morals by inviting the members of the community to good and forbidding evil. In doing so, not only does he himself avoid evil and does good, but he also helps others to do the same. The individual who feels indifferent to his community is a selfish and irresponsible person.

Thus, the structure of community life in Islam is very lofty, sound and comprehensive. Among the main elements of this structure are sincere love for one's fellow human beings, mercy for the young, respect for elders, comfort and consolation for the distressed, visiting the sick, genuine feelings of brotherhood and solidarity, respect for the rights of other people with regard to life, property and honour, and mutual responsibility between the individual and the community.

Way of Life

> The believers are brothers. Quran: Sura 49: 10 *The Apartments*

None of you can be a believer unless he loves for his brother what he loves for himself.

Tradition of the Prophet Muhammad

Muhammad was both a prophet and a ruler. The first few years of his mission were spent in his native Mecca. It was a flourishing centre of trade, and persecution grew as one person after another joined him in a way of life that threatened the prevailing materialism.

To escape assassination, he and his followers moved to Medina. There for ten years he ruled a community which has always been regarded as the embryo of the Islamic state. He was succeeded by four of his close companions, the "just" caliphs: Abu Bakr, 'Umar, 'Uthman and 'Ali.

The role of the Prophet as a social reformer, and of the first Muslim community in Medina as a social order, are still a stimulus to political thought in the Muslim world.

This section gives one man's answer to the question, "What does the life of the Prophet of Islam mean to us today?": and another man's insight into the relation between an individual and the community to which he belongs.

What Does the Life of the Prophet Mean to Us? Each year the Birthday of the Prophet gives an opportunity for general rejoicing and family parties, and also for fresh assessment of the role of Muhammad and of the relevance of his life and message to contemporary needs.

One such assessment was made in the mosque at Zurich, on the occasion of the Prophet's Birthday, 1972, by Dr. Ismail Izzet Hassan, Doctor of Music and formerly of Cairo.

Fourteen centuries ago, in a land which was at that time backward and out-of-the-way, a successful and happily married young businessman retired to Mount Hira near Mecca to pursue quiet meditation. At the age of forty he was shaken to his depths by a vision of the Archangel Jibbrail, and after that he understood that God had chosen him as a prophet.

When he died at the age of sixty-three, his life's work had completely transformed his native land. Not only did a new, pure faith prevail. The whole of existence had become different. The status of the poor and of the slaves, the rights of women, the protection of minors, had been put on a totally new basis; politics and economy were reorganised, democracy brought into public life, all in a manner incredibly audacious for those days.

A hundred years after the quiet meditation of Mount Hira, Islam had spread a new civilisation from Central Asia to the Atlantic. It challenged other civilisations to rid themselves of decadence and barbarism. One single man had initiated a revolution and a renaissance that had spread across the known world. How was this possible?

The Prophet of Islam always maintained that he was only a man like all others, but that he had been called by God to be His messenger and God had revealed His Word, the Holy Quran, to him. The secret of Muhammad's effectiveness lies in his complete obedience to his Lord, in his total self-dedication to the execution of the instructions he received from Him. He did not fulfil his task out of his own strength, but as an instrument of a Higher Power. A *Hadith* (tradition of the Prophet) says: "My Lord has formed my character and formed it well."

No personal ambition drove him on. Again and again it cost him great inner struggles and conquest of self to hold to his mission. Temptations, crushing difficulties, bitter enemies opposed him. Dedicated friends helped him. He experienced successes, some of which could hardly have been expected by human foresight. First he arose to proclaim a faith. Later he acted as law-giver, as head of state, as military commander. He was a husband and a father, as well as a friend and counsellor to many people. He was active in the world - a human, like us - yet always completely for God.

In this manner the Prophet Muhammad fulfilled the true task of Man, the purpose of humanity, and so he is also called "the perfect human" *(al-insan-ul- kamil)*. According to Islamic teaching, God has appointed Man as His agent on earth, has made him responsible for executing His Will and commanded him to stand up for Good against Evil. The Prophet taught the Muslims in the new community which grew around him how to live and be effective in this manner.

The Founder of Islam has not only shown a way to salvation in a future life, but has also brought practical answers to the problems of this life. He leaves us not only a theory that is preached, but concrete experience and historical facts.

And we do need concrete facts. In today's situation of crisis the call for renewal, change and progress is heard everywhere. The Prophet Muhammad is a prime example of a personality who understood how to bring about revolutionary progress and build a community of true brotherhood.

The deep trouble and distress in today's world may have a

simple root cause: that we humans - and, unfortunately, we must also add, we Muslims too - have not properly obeyed God's essential instructions and thereby have missed our main goal. Whoever studies the life of the Holy Prophet of Islam in earnest finds himself confronted with the question: "Are you also ready to follow the highest that God shows you?"

Individual versus Society : There are two sources of social legislation in Islam. One is the Quran, which contains the laws on which life in Muhammad's Medina was built. The second is the *Sunna,* the "custom" of the Prophet: what he said and what he did. His personal life was recorded in detail by his family and friends. Each of his sayings is known as a "tradition", *hadith.*

Dr. Hassan Hathout, writer, poet and surgeon, illustrates his theme, "Individual versus Society", by examples drawn from the experience of the Prophet and his immediate successors. These stories are part of the furniture of the mind of every Muslim — told to children as well as studied by lawyers. They are, he says, "formative elements in the Muslim mentality."

In our present-day world, both the capitalist and the communist camps suffer from a conflict between the right of the individual and the right of the community. Whereas capitalist societies protect the individual and his rights, often pushing this so far as to trespass on communal welfare, communist countries almost disregard the individuality of the individual for the sake of society as a whole. The results of both are far from satisfactory.

The so-called "free world" boasts of political freedom, and freedom of thought and expression. Yet under the banner of private enterprise such perversions as greed and selfishness have become acceptable. Freedom to become rich has often added to the miseries of the poor. Freedom of thought has often been converted into freedom to pollute thought. As people become more and more material-minded, they become less and less God-guided. The result is an unhappy society.

When we turn to communist societies, the scene is even worse. Individuals are but the bricks used for a building. Society looks like a beehive or an ant colony - very active, very disciplined. In this atmosphere, a sign of individuality is looked upon as political opposition. Since the conception of God is non-existent, it is difficult to imagine any source from which values such as conscience, love, self-restraint and charity can derive. The inevitable result is also an unhappy society.

It seems that both sides have been willing to reconsider their systems. The communist camp has had to permit some kinds of private ownership. In capitalist countries it has been found inevitable to impose certain limitations on the absolute rights of the individual: rising taxation, state ownership, the welfare state, for example.

The ideal ratio of individual to communal interest has not yet been found. Against this background, it may be asked how Islam views this question. It is interesting to note that the views here given are not derived from the theories of communism and capitalism. The religion of Islam as conveyed by the Prophet Muhammad is nearly fourteen hundred years old.

The communal and individual viewpoints have been so blended in Islam that it is difficult to separate them. Fraternity and love are the cement which binds various individuals to form a society. In the Prophet's words: "The faithful are to one another like (parts of) a building - each part strengthening the others." And: "The faithful in their mutual compassion, sympathy and love are exemplified by the whole body. If one of its organs falls ill, the remainder will suffer."

These ideas are not merely of moral value. They are legally implemented, for Islam brought with it a legal system. A legal principle introduced by the second caliph 'Umar decrees that if a person dies of starvation, the penalty for wrongful death should be imposed on all the citizens of the town, as though they had killed him.

Duties and Rights : Many of the teachings of Islam bear a dual nature. An individual's right may also be his duty, and as such cannot be surrendered. Islam thus protects vital communal rights by asking the individual to be clear about his own rights.

The right to be educated - recognised by law - is also the duty to learn. The Prophet said: "Seeking knowledge is a duty for every Muslim, man or woman."

The right to express an opinion involves the duty to speak out.

If you believe that something is right, you have not the right to remain silent about it. The Prophet teaches: "He who remains silent about truth is a dumb devil." Related to this is the duty to give testimony in court, and this may also be applied to the duty to vote. The Quran says: "Do not withhold testimony, and whoever does so must have a wrongful heart."

The right of political opposition and of honest criticism of authorities is also a duty. The first caliph, Abu Bakr, in his inaugural speech, said: "If I do right, support me. If I do wrong, correct me." The second caliph, 'Umar, asked: "What will you do if I go wrong?" One of those present stood up and shouted: "By God, we will put you right with the edge of our swords." 'Umar replied: "If you do not do so, you will lose God's blessing. And if I do not accept your correction, I shall lose God's blessing."

This attitude is not confined to political issues, but concerns every aspect of life, in accordance with the saying of the Prophet: "Whoever sees wrong being done must change it - with his hand, if he can, or else with his tongue or his heart." Even obedience to government, commendable as it is in Islam, may become a crime if the government disobeys God. The Prophet said: "There is no obedience if it entails disobedience to God." The first caliph declared: "Obey me as long as I obey God. If I disobey Him, then you owe me no obedience."

The right to work is coupled with the prohibition of unemployment, for it is also a duty to work. Beggary is forbidden in Islam. If a person is completely unable to earn a living the community has to provide for him. The Prophet said: "It is better to collect wood and sell it, than to seek charity." 'Umar said: "No one should be lazy, for the sky does not rain gold and silver."

Liberty, Fraternity and Equality : It puzzles the Muslim to find that historians in the West date "Liberty, Fraternity and Equality" from the French Revolution. And never a word about Islam!

Freedom is sacred in Islam. The basic freedom is to free oneself from passions and desires. For instance, the main aim of fasting all through the month of Ramadan (no food or drink from sunrise to sunset) is to train the individual to be able to say "No" to himself whenever it should be said. This type of freedom is so important that the Prophet likened it to winning a major battle. Returning from a battle, he commented, "We are back from the minor *Jihad* (holy war) to the major *Jihad,"* referring to conquering one's moods and passions. And again. "Might is not to be assessed in terms of physical strength. The strong man is he who can control himself when angered."

Freedom from greed is stressed, and freedom from the fear of other mortal men. The Quran is very rich in verses emphasising full regard for God alone. "Fear them not, and fear Me." "Worship God, and let nothing share (worship) with Him." "They fight in the cause of God and they never fear blame from any blamer."

Freedom from the fear of men is much encouraged by the fact that in Islam man's relation with God is a direct one, without intermediary. There are no clergy in Islam and all are equal in the eyes of God. The Quran stresses this direct relationship: "When those who worship Me ask you concerning Me, I am indeed close to them. I listen to the prayer of every suppliant when he calls on Me. Let them also with a will listen to My call, and believe in Me, that they may walk in the right way." Other aspects of freedom were stressed by Islam fourteen centuries ago. Freedom of religious belief is expressed in the Quran. "Let there be no compulsion in religion. Truth stands out clear from error." Personal security and freedom from unlawful arrest are established Islamic rules. The second caliph 'Umar, for example, was unable to prosecute people caught drinking (illegally) in their own houses because he had no right of entry. As to equality before the law, and equality of opportunity, there is only one respect in which one person can be considered better than another, and that is in good deeds and the fear of God. "Dearest to God are those that fear Him most," says the Quran.

Status of Non-believers

An Islamic society is not formed of Muslims only, but of Muslims, Christians and Jews living together under the legal system of Islam.

The legal principle applying to Christians and Jews is: "They have the same rights, and owe the same duties (as we do)."

As a religion, Islam does not put itself in an attitude of conflict towards other God-sent religions. The word *Islam* literally means surrender (to God). God's guidance has been sent through a succession of messengers and prophets who are all revered by a Muslim. Islam is thus the last link of a chain. The Quran reads, "Say (O believers) we believe in God and in that which has been transmitted to us, and in that which has been transmitted to Ibrahim, Ismail, Ishaq, Jacob and the Tribes; and that which was given to Moses and Jesus; and that which was given to the Prophets from their Lord. We do not discriminate between them and to Him do we surrender."

Muslims and the People of the Book (Christians and Jews, who have their own sacred writings) can eat each others' food, unless it is specifically prohibited, like pig and alcohol.

A Muslim can take a Christian or a Jewess for a wife, and she has the right to stick to her faith. The People of the Book have freedom to worship in churches and synagogues, which are to be protected by the Muslim ruler. They are equal under Islamic law. Yet on legal points specified in their own religions concerning their private affairs (marriage, divorce, inheritance, etcetera) the Islamic law does not apply and they are left to settle these matters according to their own religion. This is an example of preserving the rights of minorities.

Equality is not only in the court room. Minorities also share the benefits of the principles of social security and "welfare state" laid down since the earliest days of Islam. One day the caliph 'Umar saw a blind old man - a Jew - begging. The man told him, "I beg so as to be able to pay the tribute." (The tribute was a tax imposed on non-Muslims, who were exempted from military service.) 'Umar took him by the hand to his own house and gave him what he needed. He sent orders to his treasurer: "Look after people like him. It would not be fair to take from him when he is young and neglect him when he is old." He decreed that old age should be a reason for exemption from the tribute, as well as illness and disablement. On his way to Damascus, 'Umar once encountered a group of Christian lepers, and ordered food and money to be given them.

The Right of Ownership — Private Property : Private

ownership in Islam is a concept radically different from that of either communism or capitalism.

In Islam total ownership is God's.

The right of ownership that has been bestowed on us is secondary to this.

"To God belongeth whatever is in the heavens and the earth." "Give them something yourselves out of the means which God has given you."

The owner of property should realise that he is God's agent. In his capacity as owner, he must behave in accordance with the ways of God.

Indeed, God's ownership extends to the owner himself. Islam pervades all aspects of life, all the time. In the eyes of a Muslim, whatever he does or thinks, while at work or at leisure, be it private or public, personal or social, concealed or revealed, popular or unpopular, is a matter of the relationship between God and himself.

Private ownership in Islam entails a God-owned owner, given the right to own a God-owned property and to exploit it fully in the ways of God. This right of ownership, once assumed, is very strongly protected in Islam. But in its respect for private ownership. Islam does not foster greed or materialism. These are tempered by conscience, and by legal safeguards. For instance, it was conscience, and that ever-vivid mutual relation with God, that induced the third caliph 'Uthman to give away a caravan full of foodstuffs free, rejecting an offer to sell it at tenfold price, when Medina was struck by famine.

The right of ownership is the rule. Limitations on it are the exception (contrary to communist theory). Ownership in Islam is a social function, and is interpreted in Islamic law as aiming at the welfare of the community. Where the actions of the owner conflict with this welfare he can be restrained: for instance, in cases of mental incapacity, hoarding, abuse of others' rights, injury to the community (such as monopoly), or neglect of the needs of the poor.

A prerequisite of enjoying the right of ownership is recognition of the rights of the needy. The Prophet was heard to say: "He cannot be a believer. He cannot be a believer. He cannot be a believer." When asked "Who?", the Prophet answered: "He who sleeps the night with a full stomach, while his neighbour is hungry." Private ownership is so sacred that in ordinary circumstances a thief might have his hand amputated: but if he proves needy the punishment is suspended. It is the duty of the governor to fulfil this need for food. If the alms tax *(zakat)* together with money given for charity do not suffice, the governor must impose heavier taxes on those better off, in favour of the needy.

In times of war or famine resources are to be shared. In a year of famine, 'Umar suggested that each household should double the number of people they were feeding, "for people will not perish of half-empty stomachs."

No individual right or freedom can be regarded in isolation. The Prophet told this story. A group of men shared a ship - some on the upper deck, some on the lower. Whenever they wanted water, those below had to come up.

So they thought it might be a good idea to cut a hole in their part of the vessel so as not to bother the ones above. If those on deck allowed them to do this, the ship would sink and all would be drowned. If they prevented them, all would survive. Whole nations today are faced with similar dilemmas.

The State: Authority and Responsibility : Islam couples authority with responsibility, as in our day the welfare state sets out to do.

The fourth caliph 'Ali wrote instructions to his viceroy in Egypt: "Fear God in regard to the lowest class in society, who are helpless, poor and miserable. You are responsible to God, for He entrusted them to you. The distant should receive as much as those who are near. Give each his due, and if you think this is beneath your dignity, do not make excuses. You will not be forgiven if you ignore minor matters to concentrate on those which seem important. Look into the affairs of those who are so weak that they cannot reach you. Appoint Godfearing and humble persons to bring their affairs before you. Give attention to the helpless orphans and the young who would never beg. The burden of responsibility on a viceroy is indeed a heavy one."

The caliph Umar ibn Abd el-Aziz said: "If a mule stumbles in Iraq (far away in the empire) I shall find myself responsible to God for it on the day of judgment: why had I not paved the road properly?" There are innumerable examples of this coupling of authority with responsibility. As the Prophet said: "Every one of you is a shepherd and is responsible for his flock. The governor is a shepherd - so is the man with a family, the woman in her household, the servant with his master's money. All these are shepherds, responsible for the flock entrusted to them."

This is a passing glimpse of Islam, And it has much to offer to our restless world. But it seems to be an abandoned treasure, abandoned by those who bear its name. No wonder they are so different from the glory I describe, And unless they go back to it again, they will remain Lost in bewilderment, at the rear of Humanity's procession. For it is the remedy, the light and the guidance from God For them - and for the world.

No Show-off

Modesty plays a vital role in character building. It restrains a man from behaving in an undesirable manner. It also acts as a shield against immoralities. It holds the key to piety. It is related by Zaid bin Talha that the Holy Prophet (PBUH) said:

> "Every religion has a distinctive quality and the distinctive quality of Islam is modesty."

This Hadith shows that in every faith, some particular aspect of moral behaviour receives importance and an extraordinary emphasis is laid on it; in Islam modesty is of fundamental significance as the Holy Prophet (PBUH) said:

> "Modesty is a part of faith."

The word, modesty, in common use, signifies that a man should abstain from indecent acts. However, in the terminology of the Quran and the *Hadith,* it is used in a wider sense. In Islam, it stands for a feeling which is intolerant of everything that is not desirable or produces disgust in a person.

Faith and modesty are so closely related to each other that either both will be present in an individual or community or none of the two would be present. It is related by Abdullah bin Umar that the Prophet of Allah said:

> "Modesty and faith exist together and when one of them goes out, the other too goes out,"

The rule of modesty is prescribed for both men and women that is, to lower their gaze and not stare at each other as the Quran says:

> "Say to the believing men that they should lower their gaze and guard their modesty." (24: 30)
>
> "And say to the believing women that they should lower their gaze and guard their modesty. " (24: 31)

Modesty is not to be observed only in relation to human beings. The Almighty Creator comes first. No one can be more unfortunate than the person who, knowing that Allah sees and hears all that he does and speaks, feels no shame in saying dirty and deplorable things in His presence. If the sense of modesty is alive and active in a person, his life will not only be clean in the sight of his fellow beings but also in the eyes of Allah. The primary requirement of modesty is that a person should feel disgusted at everything that is displeasing to Allah. Therefore, he should abstain from it.

It is related in *Tirmidhi* that once the Holy Prophet (PBUH) observed while speaking to his Companions:

> "Practice modesty towards Allah as it ought to be practiced towards Him. "

The proper way of observing modesty towards Allah is that you take care of the head and all the ideas and notions that are contained in it, and you take care of the belly and all that is contained in it (i.e., protect the mind against evil thoughts and the stomach against unlawful food).

Lessons in Economy

Islam provides guidance to its followers in all phases and activities of life. Its teachings with regard to economics are mentioned in several passages of the Holy Quran. Islam encourages sharing and a just distribution of wealth.

"To those weak of understanding make not over your property, which Allah hath made a means of support for you, but feed and clothe them therewith, and speak to them word of kindness and justice." (4:5)

In another place Quran says:

"Seek with the (wealth) which Allah has bestowed on thee, the home of the hereafter, nor forget thy portion in this world: but do thou good." (28:77)

The Quran reminds us in Surah Baqara:

" There are men who say: "Our Lord give us (thy bounties) in this world!" But they will have no portion in the Hereafter. And there are men who say "Our Lord give us good in this world and good in the Hereafter and defend us from the torment of fire" To these will be allotted what they have earned;" (2:200-202)

In an Islamic society adequate fulfilment of basic material needs is as necessary for human welfare as spiritual uplift. Therefore, while arranging for the spiritual guidance of men through prophets, Allah has also provided all necessary resources for his material well-being. The individual is required to fulfil his material needs through his own efforts. Islam condemns begging and laziness and places great stress on hard work. The Prophet (PBUH) is reported to have said:

"Beg not anything from people,"

and also:

"A man has not earned a better income than that which is from his own labour."

Hadrat Umar once said: "Seek of the bounty of Allah and be not a burden on others."

The economic life in Islam therefore is based upon Divine instructions. Earning one's livelihood through labour is not only a duty but a great virtue as well. Dependence of any able person on somesone else for a livelihood is a sin and disgraceful humility.

All kinds of work and hard labour is respected in an Islamic society. The Holy Prophet (PBUH) is reported to have said that it was far better for a person to take his rope, cut wood, pile it up and sell it in order to eat and give charity than to beg for sustenance from others. According to Islam, the status of honest hard working men cannot be lowered because of the kind of work they do for a living.

The economic system of Islam is based upon a comprehensive system of morals and principles. A person employed by another or by a company has the moral responsibility to do his work efficiently and honesty. The Holy Prophet (PBUH) said that if any of you undertakes to do any work, Allah loves to see him do it well and with efficiency. Upon the completion of work, the worker is entitled to a fair wage. Failure by the employer to pay just wages or to cut it down is a punishable act, according to the Law of Allah.

Honest trade is permitted and blessed by Allah. This may be carried out through individuals, companies or agencies. But all business deals should be conducted with honesty. Cheating, hiding defects of goods and exploiting the needs of customers are all sinful acts and punishable by the Islamic law. All methods of earning a living have to be honest, anybody brought up on unlawful provisions, according to the Holy Prophet (PBUH) will be a fuel for the fire of Hell. Islam forbids usury or charging interest in return for lending money to the needy. This is to show man that he rightfully owns only what he works for and that any exploitation of other people's needs is immoral and inhuman and against the teachings of Islam. There are several traditions of the Holy Prophet (PBUH) excluding the cheaters, exploiters and dishonest businessmen from the band of true Muslims.

It is essentially the responsibility of the individual to support his family by earning an honest income. However it may not always be possible. In all societies there are some people who cannot achieve that goal and so become dependent upon the state or on others. It then becomes the responsibility of the Islamic State to play a positive role in guiding and regulating the economy to ensure a respectable standard of living for all the people who are unable to take care of their own needs and require assistance. The Holy Prophet (PBUH) clearly declared:

"He whom Allah has made an administrator over the affairs of Muslims but remains indifferent to their needs and poverty, Allah will also be indifferent to his needs and poverty."

In order to fulfil this obligation, the Islamic state needs financial resources. The means of income for the Islamic state are:

Zakat: Islam has instituted a social security system with religious sanctity. It is a part of the religious obligations of a Muslim to pay Zakat at a prescribed rate. The significance of the institution of Zakat in Islam is so great that whenever the Quran speaks of the obligation, to establish prayers, it also simultaneously stresses the obligation of Muslims to pay Zakat. The Holy Prophet (PBUH) went so far as to say that whoever offers prayers but does not pay Zakat, his prayer are in vain.

The purpose of the establishment of the institution of Zakat is to setup up a society which is like a single family, where wealth is justly distributed where the essential needs of all deserving individuals are met through mutual help with planning and organization by the state.

There is a general consensus among jurists that collection and distribution of Zakat is essentially the duty of the Islamic state. This was the practice during the day of the Holy Prophet (PBUH) and the first two khalifas. However Hadrat Uthman, the third khalifa, allowed the payment of Zakat directly to the needy.

Income from Natural Resources: Natural resources have been provided by Allah for the welfare of all people, therefore, the monetary benefit derived from these resources should be distributed to all people, and not to any particular group or individual.

Taxation: The right of the Islamic State to raise funds through taxes is defended on the basis of the Holy Prophet's (PBUH) saying:

"In your wealth there are also obligations beyond Zakat."

Most jurists have upheld the right of the state to levy taxes, because if these funds benefit the people themselves, it is their obligation to bear the cost. However, only a just tax system has to be applied in harmony with the spirit of Islam. The khalifas are reported to have stressed that taxes should be collected with justice and kindness, that they should not be beyond the ability of the people to bear, and should not deprive the people of the basic necessities of life.

Borrowing: If total revenue from all the above mentioned sources is not sufficient, the Islamic state would stand in need of borrowing. In this case because of the Islamic injunction against interest, the borrowing would need to be free from interest.

Although man is encouraged to work, is free to engage in business and trade, is entitled to earn and possess wealth and has the authority to invest and spend, he is guided by principles which save him from going astray. There are certain rules of expenditure to be followed. God enjoins upon man to fulfil his financial obligations towards his fellowmen and to be moderate in his spending.

The Quran says:

> "And render to the kindred their due rights, as (also) to those in want, and to the wayfarer: But squander not your wealth in the manner of a spendthrift. Make not thy hand tied (like a niggard's) to thy neck, nor stretch it forth to its utmost reach, so that thou become blameworthy and destitute."17:26, 29)

The main purpose of the Islamic laws that deal with economic and commercial matters is to secure the rights of the individual, to maintain the solidarity of the society, to encourage morality in the world of trade and to enforce the law of Allah in business as well. It is logical that Islam should be concerned with such aspects as these, because it is not merely a spiritual formula but a complete system of life.

10

Institution of Family

The Relationship

Show kindness to parents ...

Lower to them the wing of humility

out of tenderness.Quran Sura 17: 23-14 *The Israelites*

Parents and Children in the Quran : Profound issues of love and obedience often arise between parents and children. An Indian mother and daughter discussed their mutual duties, and a subsequent study of what the Quran has to say on the subject revealed an emphasis somewhat different from what they expected. To parents, the utmost kindness is due: and to God, obedience.

Four well-known passages from the Quran are quoted here, followed by some notes from the commentary of Yusuf Ali:

> Thy Lord commanded, "Worship none but Him, and show kindness to parents. If one or both of them attain old age with thee, never say unto them any word expressive of disgust nor reproach them, but address them with excellent speech. And lower to them the wing of humility out of tenderness. And say, 'My Lord have mercy on them even as they nourished me in my childhood.'"
>
> Quran: Sura 17: 23—24 *The Israelites*

> We enjoined on man kindness to his parents. But if they strive to make thee associate with Me that of which thou hast no knowledge, then obey them not. Unto Me is your return, and I shall inform you of what you did. Quran: Sura 29: 8 *The Spider*

> We have enjoined on man concerning his parents - his mother bears him in weakness and his weaning takes two years — "Give thanks to Me and to thy parents. Unto Me is the final return." ... And if they contend with thee to make thee set up equals with Me concerning which thou hast no knowledge, obey them not. Be a kind companion to them in all worldly affairs: and in spiritual matters follow the way of him who turns to Me. Then unto Me will be your return and I will inform you of what you used to do.
> Quran: Sura 31: 14-15 *Luqman*

> We have enjoined on man to be good to his parents. His mother bears him in pain and brings him forth in pain ... When he comes to maturity he says, "My Lord, make me grateful for Thy favour which Thou hast bestowed upon me and my parents, that I may do such good works as please Thee. And make my seed righteous for me. I do turn to Thee, and truly I am of those who submit to Thee." ... But the one who says to his parents, "Fie on you both! God's promise ... is nothing but tales of the ancients," ... will be utterly lost.
> Quran: Sura 46: 15-18 *The Sandhills*

In his notes on the passages in the Quran dealing with parents and children, Abdullah Yusuf Ali makes the following comments:

> In matters of faith and worship even parents have no right to force their children ... Children and parents must all remember that they have to go before God's tribunal, and answer each for his own deeds. In cases where one set of people have lawful authority over another set of people (as in the case of parents and children), and the two differ on important matters like mat of Faith, the latter are justified in rejecting authority:

> the apparent conflict will be solved when the whole truth is revealed to all eyes in the final judgment.

Where the duty to man conflicts with the duty to God, it means that there is something wrong with the human will, and we should obey God rather than man. But even here, it does not mean that we should be arrogant or insolent. To parents and those in authority, we must be kind, considerate and courteous, even when they command things which we should not do and therefore disobedience becomes our highest duty...

In any apparent conflict of duties our standards should be God's Will, as declared to us by His command. That is the way of those who love God: and their motives in disobedience to parents or human authority, where disobedience is necessary by God's law, is not self-willed rebellion or defiance, but love of God, which means the true love of man in the highest sense of the word. And the reason we should give is: "Bom you and I have to return to God; therefore not only must I follow God's Will, but you must command nothing against God's Will."

These conflicts may appear to us strange and puzzling in this life. But in God's presence we shall see their real meaning and significance. It may be that was one way in which our true mettle could be tested: for it is not easy to disobey and love man at the same time.

Told to the Children : Teaching children religion is reckoned as one of the most important aspects of family life. This is primarily the responsibility of the parents. Children are taught to pray by the time they are seven, often by older brothers and sisters.

Much of the teaching comes in story form: tales of brave and generous men and women who did great things for their fellow men, or about rich and poor people who are unequal in possessions and yet are equal before God.

"Muslim women have a great responsibility for passing on tradition and culture. So it is important to give the children the right examples. Prophet Muhammad's life is rich in this way," said one mother. It may be one of the older members of the household - grandmother or even great-grandmother - whose story-telling is unforgettable.

The Prophet's life - his boyhood as an orphan, his honesty in business, his calling, his escapes, his struggles as well as his victories is told and retold, as are the lives of other prophets. "After the Prophet," said another mother, "my favourite characters are Virgin Mary and Caliph 'Umar. Girls can learn much from Virgin Mary. They can be pure and virgin till they are married - dedicated in a way as she was."

'Umar, the second successor to Muhammad, is especially popular. He was not only a warrior, but a father to his people. He used to move about Medina at night, to find out how his poorer subjects were living. One of many tales is of his hearing the cry of a hungry child, and himself fetching and cooking food for the family. His conversion—from violent opposition to Muhammad — was a dramatic turning point in the early growth of Islam. The story is told here from the Children's Page of *The Islamic Review and Arab Affairs* (Working, September 1967). It is part of a series on the life of Muhammad, written by Mrs. Olive Toto.

Conversion of Umar : Please remember, all you little girls who will grow up to be women, that Muhammad's first believer was a woman, Khadijah his wife ...

His next believers were 'Ali and a little slave boy Zayd, who were about twelve or fourteen years old. Maybe they were young, but they were very serious boys and knew what they believed to be right! Abu Bakr, an old and trusted friend, joined Muhammad. Other friends also came forward. A small band of fifty people joined Muhammad in his belief.

Now a change came about. The citizens of Mecca turned against Muhammad and his followers were persecuted. After three years an open opposition was organised and acts of violence started. A youth leading prayer was attacked and he fought back. Islam does not say turn the other cheek. It is common sense that one has to defend oneself.

In the fourth year of his mission, Muhammad was given a friend's house to hold meetings for people who wanted to know about God. The name of this friend was Arqam ...

There was a man called 'Umar. He thought about things and decided to have his peace of mind by killing Muhammad, and then his followers would forget him. So he took his sword in his hand and went to Muhammad's house to kill him. 'Umar was a man of great influence in Mecca. He did not know that his sister Fatima and her husband had become Muslims. On his way to the Prophet's house with his sword in his hand he met a man who had recently embraced Islam. Seeing the sword the man said, "Where are you going?" 'Umar said, "To kill Muhammad." "Oh," said the man, "don't you know that even your sister and your brother-in-law have embraced Muhammad's religion?"

'Umar was furious: he decided his relations must die first and then Muhammad. On reaching the house he heard his relatives reading verses that had been revealed to Muhammad from God. 'Umar was so furious that he beat his brother-in-law very badly. 'Umar's sister was hurt whilst trying to stop the fight. 'Umar snatched away these verses and started to read them. One could have heard a pin drop, so engrossed was 'Umar. His rage had calmed down, and his breathing was once more like a human being's. Gradually, as he was reading the words, peace came into his heart. He was reading something that calmed his soul with its truth and beauty. It had set him thinking.

On seeing this altered man, the followers talked to him, and soon the harsh and proud 'Umar joined Islam.

'Umar then went to the house of Arqam, where Muhammad met him at the door. 'Umar said, "O Prophet of God! I declare my faith in God and believe in His Prophet." Things became much easier with 'Umar on Muhammad's side.

Mary and Jesus : Of all the women honoured in the Quran, Mary mother of Jesus stands highest. Her own family upbringing is recounted in the third sura of the Quran, which is named after her father 'Imran. The visit of the angel, and the birth of Jesus, are told more than once. Here is the story as it is given in the chapter named after Mary:

> In the name of God, the Merciful, the Compassionate.
>
> And make mention of Mary in the Scripture, when she had withdrawn from her people to a chamber looking East,

> And had chosen seclusion from them. Then We sent unto her Our spirit and it assumed for her the likeness of a perfect man.
>
> She said: Lo! I seek refuge in the Beneficent One from thee, if thou art God-fearing.
>
> He said: I am only a messenger of thy Lord, that I may bestow on thee a faultless son.
>
> She said: How can I have a son when no mortal hath touched me, neither have I been unchaste?
>
> He said: So (it will be). Thy Lord saith: It is easy for Me and (it will be) that We may make of him a revelation for mankind and a mercy from Us, and it is a thing ordained.
>
> And she conceived him, and she withdrew with him to a far place.
>
> And the pangs of childbirth drove her unto the trunk of the palm tree.
>
> She said: Oh, would that I had died, and had become a thing of naught, forgotten!
>
> Then (one) cried unto her from below her, saying: Grieve not!
>
> Thy Lord hath placed a rivulet beneath thee,
>
> And shake the trunk of the palm tree toward thee, thou wilt cause ripe dates to fall upon thee.

So eat and drink and be consoled. And if thou meetest any mortal, say:

> Lo! I have vowed a fast unto the Beneficent, and may not speak this day to any mortal.
>
> Then she brought him to her own folk, carrying him.
>
> They said: O Mary! Thou hast come with an amazing thing.
>
> Oh sister of Aaron! Thy father was not a wicked man nor was thy mother a harlot.

> Then she pointed to him. They said: How can we talk to one who is in the cradle, a young boy?
>
> He spake: Lo! I am the slave of Allah. He hath given me the Scripture and hath appointed me a Prophet, And hath made me blessed wheresoever I may be, and hath enjoined upon me prayer and almsgiving so long as I remain alive,
>
> And (hath made me) dutiful toward her who bore me, and hath not made me arrogant, unblest.
>
> Peace be upon me the day I was born, and the day I die, and the day I shall be raised alive!
>
> Such was Jesus, son of Mary.Quran: Sura 19: 16-34 *Mary*

Domestic Life

> The family is a divinely-inspired institution that came into existence with the creation of man. The human race is a product of this institution and not the other way round.
>
> Khurshid Ahmad

Woman must be regarded as equal to man and must shed the remaining shackles that impede her from taking a constructive part in life.

> The family is the primary cell in society, and as such it must be afforded every protection in the national interest.
>
> Abdul Moghny Said

Of all the questions that exercise the minds of Muslims, those connected with family life are the most sensitive. Muslims are proud of their traditions, and wish to maintain them. Western culture with its permissive standards has an impact on their sons and daughters which they see as a threat to their whole way of life. Advance in technology is regarded as essential: but there is widespread fear of the retrogression in character that often seems to accompany it.

Certain practices are an essential part of religion.. Others are a matter of custom, and can be set aside. Every Muslim community is in process of some degree of adjustment in regard to the position of women, to marriage customs and to relations between the generations.

These dilemmas are reflected in what Muslims say about their family life. But in comparison with the ever-increasing rate of marital breakdown in the Western world they understandably feel that they have something of value not only to preserve, but to offer. Mr. Khurshid Ahmad, Chairman of the Islamic Foundation, Leicester, writing on "Family Life in Islam", says, "It is the family that provides the most congenial climate for the development and fulfilment of human personality." Marriage and the family in Islam should be studied in the context of the scheme of life Islam wants to establish. "We refuse to accept the value-neutral approach that willy-nilly fashions the life and perspectives of man in the secular culture of the West today. We think the disintegration of the family in the West is, in part, a result of confusion about the place and the role of the family in society and about the purpose of life itself."

About a third of the legal injunctions in the Quran deal with family matters, and with the network of rights and obligations that provide the basis for family life. These aim to produce the attitudes and behaviour patterns that Islam wants to foster in society. The Muslim family is an extended family, normally with three or four generations within its circle. Marriage in Islam is not a temporary union and is meant to last for life. Dissolution of marriage is, however, permitted if it has irretrievably broken down: but before divorce the law demands an attempt at reconciliation by the families concerned. "The natural prevalence of monogamy as the normal type of sexual relationship" is more and more the practice in Muslim countries. Nevertheless, a limited polygamy is seen as a realistic need in certain circumstances: and indeed as preferable to the "concealed polygamy" without responsibility, in some ways tolerated in Western society. "Islam is a practical religion and is meant for the guidance of human beings made of flesh and bones." The ideal is a loving, stable family in which the best of human nature can flower.

An Arab Family : A Muslim lawyer, Mr. Jamil Nasir, head of an Arab family in Jerusalem, made the following observations on the social traditions of Arab family life. In 1966, his daughter invited me to spend an evening in her home. She was then Vice-Principal of a Teacher Training College, and had just returned from a course in "counselling" in the United States. She is one of ten children, who include two medical doctors and a Ph.D. Three of her sisters were living at home: two of them principals of schools, and the youngest a teacher. Present also was an Irish sister-in-law, whose doctor husband had refused better paid posts so as to continue to work in Jerusalem.

Awkward questions arise as one sits in such homes. "What is happening to your life in America, in Britain?" "What about these attacks on old people for their money?" "Why do you let young people treat your lovely parks as bedrooms?" On this particular evening, the conversation turned on a tragic event. In London, the sons of a mutual friend had been attacked in the street. One had lost an eye and was in a serious condition.

My friend's father, the lawyer, said: "How can these things happen in a civilised country? Here, the police find and punish thieves within a few days. In your cities, I hear, they cannot find them. Our young men feel responsible to their families. They are more afraid of what the family would do or say than they would be of the police."

I asked him to tell me more about the ties which bind Arab families, and which, he said, still implant a sense of privilege and responsibility in each member, young and old. He said:

> Arab social life is based on ancient traditions, and on the teaching of the Quran. The individual is responsible to the family, and the family to the tribe or community. If an individual commits wrong, the family and community will be held responsible: and if wrong is done to an individual his family and community automatically support him.

Thus an individual is very cautious in his dealings and behaviour, because he will be subject to reprimand by his relatives and his community, all of whom he will have involved by his wrongdoing. The reputation of the individual man or woman reflects on his family and community, and they have to pay any fine he incurs.

From an early age, children are taught not to cause any inconvenience to parents and relatives by bad behaviour. They grow up in this spirit, and there is therefore hardly any juvenile crime, theft or injury committed. They learn to respect older people, to help their neighbours and to be generous to guests. Thus we find a high level of security in Arab countries.

When a man marries, he remains closely connected with his father and mother, sisters and grandparents. Together they share happiness and sorrow, and meet the events and accidents of life, and take the lawful and customary procedures if their rights are infringed. If necessary, all the relatives will act together. Marriage and funeral expenses are corporate responsibilities.

Girls are treated equally with boys, and every man is obliged to protect his women relatives as far back as the connections of the "fourth grandfather". A woman after marriage retains her father's family name, rather than taking that of her husband, as an indication that her father is responsible for her all her life. Her parents must visit her during every big holiday season, and take her a present. Thus she feels the strength and protection of her male relatives. This encourages her, and if she gets into difficulties it helps to deter her from wrongdoing.

There are customary procedures to be followed, as well as legal ones, if something goes wrong between families. For example, news came that my son had been involved in a car accident in Amman. While he was driving, a boy was knocked down. The police completely exonerated the driver, but this was not the point as far as the family was concerned. We went straight to Amman, found three respected men of standing, and sent them to the boy's family to arrange a week's truce between the families. (Among the Bedouin, if someone is killed and such a truce is not quickly settled, a life will be taken to restore the family honour.) The boy was lying in hospital with concussion. After a week, the truce was renewed for two months. The boy was unconscious for fifteen days. If he had died, we would have had to pay the sum enjoined by the Prophet Muhammad to be paid for an accidental death, now reckoned as £350. Every one of our family — "until the fourth grandfather" and the cousins connected in this degree - would have been liable to contribute. But, thank God, the boy recovered.

When the two months were over, there was a ceremony. A sheep was killed and many members of both families were present at the feast. "Thank God, the boy is well," we said. "We forgive you and realise it was an accident," they said. Peace was restored, and documents signed to say so.

The father is responsible for his sons and his daughters. If a girl does something wrong with a man, the family honour is at stake. There are cases when the brother kills her, or kills the man who wronged her. The law takes into consideration "defence of life, property and honour," and a lenient sentence may be given: three years' or seven years' imprisonment, rather than hanging.

Hospitality is another side of Arab tradition. There still exists the custom among Arab chiefs of generously welcoming a guest for three days before asking him his name and the purpose of his visit. Then he is offered any help he needs.

> Mutual assistance and cooperation; help for the poor and needy; respect for others' faith and rights as well as safeguarding one's own; obedience to law and custom; the inclination to treat others as one wishes others to treat oneself: all these are part of the Arab attitude and way of life. Jamil Nasir, Jerusalem'

Position of Women : The traditional place of women in Islam is a high one. Modern writers all stress the improvements the Prophet Muhammad brought about in their position and rights. Undue restrictions prevalent at certain periods of history have been, it is said, a matter of social custom, not of religion itself.

Equal and Different : According to the Quran, women are equal to men as human beings - different in their role. In the presence of their Creator, their basic duties are the same. Daily prayer, fasting and pilgrimage are incumbent on them. They are alike in their hopes of paradise and certainty of judgment.

> Men who surrender unto Allah,
>
> And women who surrender,
>
> and men who believe,
>
> And women who believe,

> And men who speak the truth,
> And women who speak the truth,
> And men who persevere in righteousness,
> And women who persevere,
> And men who are humble,
> And women who are humble,
> And men who give alms,
> And women who give alms,
> And men who fast,
> And women who fast,
> And men who guard their modesty,
> And women who guard their modesty,
> And men who make mention of Allah much,
> And women who make mention of Him,
> Allah hath prepared for them forgiveness and a vast reward. Quran: Sura 33:35 The Clans

> If any do deeds of righteousness - be they male or female - and have faith, they will enter paradise.
> Quran: Sura 4:124 Women

Women have the right to own property, and to inherit it, and to run their own businesses. It is often pointed out that these measures of equality were only won in western society in the Nineteenth Century, whereas they have existed in Muslim law since the time of the Prophet. At the same time, men have duties towards the women of the family. A wife must be maintained by her husband, even if she has means of her own. This is used to explain the inequality of inheritance — a man receives a larger share of a family legacy than does a woman.

Women in History : Women played an important part in the early days of the Prophet's mission and the coming of Islam. His wife Khadijah - a business woman in her own right - was the first to support him in his calling. In their home in Mecca their daughter Fatima and her sisters grew up. After Khadija's death, and his move to Medina, much of our knowledge of what he said and what he did is owed to the loving insight and acute perception of his young wife Aishah. These three names are very often given to Muslim girls.

In seeking their role in society, today's Fatimas, Khadijahs and Aishah's have the example of these early pioneers of Islam, and also of many others who played their part later in the flowerings of Islamic life and civilisation. In every age some outstanding women make their mark.

Many saintly women are recorded, among them Rabia al-Adawiyya, whose life of poverty in Basra challenged the rich and powerful in the early days of the Abbasid empire. The great philosopher and mystic Al-Ghazzali quoted what he learned from her about the love of God, and her prayers still sift the motives of those who use them.

Oh my Lord ! the stars are shining and the eyes of men are closed and every lover is alone with his beloved, and here I am alone with Thee.

Oh God ! if I worship Thee for fear of hell, burn me in hell, If I worship Thee in hope of Paradise, exclude me from paradise, But if I worship Thee for Thine own sake grudge me not Thine everlasting beauty.

In contrast with Arabia's life of dedication in poverty, many women have been honoured for the use they made of their wealth. One of the most famous of these a generation after Rabia was Zubaida, wife and cousin of the caliph Harun al-Rashid. She is still remembered with gratitude by pilgrims to Mecca for the beneficence of her provision of water in the city and along the road from Iraq.

Most women who have wielded influence in Muslim society have done so through their sons. The position of the mother in the family is central, and an often-quoted saying of the Prophet is, "Heaven lies at the feet of a mother."

Education for Women : The present resurgence of Islam was already gathering momentum at the beginning of this century. Leading thinkers - the Egyptian Muhammad Abdo and the Indian Amir Ali among them - called for the restoration to women of rights given to them in the Quran but often ignored in practice. During the Ottoman period women's education had been almost totally neglected, and in the early 1900's experiments in the education of girls began simultaneously in different parts of the Muslim world. Today, such education is given high priority by the governments of Muslim countries, including Saudi Arabia. Women are graduating from scores of universities, and there is a growing body of skilled professional women: doctors, nurses, teachers, lawyers, also architects and engineers. There are also widespread literacy programmes, reaching the country women.

Freedom for Service : Many tensions arise in the effort to give maximum service to the community without disrupting the pattern of family life and without losing prized traditions and identity. To understand these tensions it is necessary to take into account the revulsion against elements of decadence in western society. The idea that "progress" lies in imitation of the West is rightly rejected. The excesses of some upholders of "liberation" for women have made it more difficult for women in Muslim countries to pursue their own path towards fuller responsibility. To find the way to this, without eroding the importance of motherhood, or of loyalty to Islam, is the challenge this generation is facing.

Two quotations show these concerns from very different points of view. The first comes from a woman who has held cabinet office in Jordan, the second from a Shite scholar in Iran.

Mrs. Inam Mufti was appointed Minister for Social Affairs in Jordan in January 1980. She was formerly Principal of the UNRWA Women's Vocational College, Ramallah, in the West Bank. She has been a pioneer of education in many forms, and in the 1940's was herself one of the first girls to go to college from her home town in Safad, in Northern Palestine. She is concerned with what women will bring with them into public life, with questions of values as well as of skills. Women, she thinks, can bring into every branch of a nation's work a sense of service and a care for individuals. As they do so, they will become pace-setters for standards of excellence and integrity.

We want to find a balanced formula for partnership which takes into consideration all the responsibilities of women. The role of the mother in the community must never be underestimated. But apart from women with young children, there are many who do not find full employment and expression in their homes. Here is a potential that the nation cannot afford to neglect.

Certain old attitudes and prejudices must change, and they are changing. In the past, these have limited the activities of women, and their freedom of expression. But there is nothing in the true tradition of Islam to hold women back. The Quran says that every man and woman must search for knowledge, and also tells them to engage in honest work.

We need to move with caution so as not to lose the family life we prize. We do not want to find ourselves neglecting either our children or our old people. There is a give and take between the generations, a mutual interplay of service and responsibility, which we must maintain. The preparation of women citizens must be personal, as well as vocational. They bring up the men, and character building for the future is their most vital role.

Sayid Mujtaba Musawi Lari is the son and grandson of respected Shite scholars in Iran. His grandfather was one of those instrumental in bringing into being the Iranian constitution of 1906. He himself studied theology for ten years in the city of Qum, an ancient centre of religious training not far from Tehran. He then spent some time in Germany for health reasons. His shrewd observations and wide reading during this period of ill health formed the basis of a book *Western Civilisation through Muslim Eyes.*

He portrays the inconsistencies, the absurdities, alongside the arrogance, which he finds in western society. The workless, the hungry, the lonely old and the delinquent young, the pampered dogs and battered wives, for him mirror the callousness of a society which appears to have lost its heart and soul. If the picture is overdrawn, it is nevertheless a genuine expression of views widely held. It makes it understandable that western strictures on other societies are not better received.

To his picture of the West he adds his own reflections on Islam's contribution to the solution of social problems. In a chapter on the family he speaks of marriage, and the importance of "steering the life-force into its God-given legitimate channels where peace of mind and calm of conscience accompany the happiness of a shared life."

Modern disrespect for the bond of marriage is due to the neglect of this high conception of wedlock. It has been degraded by a mass of petty dreams and twisted imaginations. Men's thinking about marriage was in ruins before their families began to fall apart.

On the position of women Sayid Musawi Lari writes:

> The West's vociferous partisans of Women's Lib have no idea of the revolutionary leap forward in women's position which Islam brought about. Islam regards both man and woman as created by God to rise to the full stature of the perfect human. Each is a precious soul. They are complementary to each other. Many women possess such personal excellence and intelligence that they attain great heights of true humanity and happiness. Many men, alas, fall to the lowest depths because they flout reason and abandon themselves to their passions.

A woman, he says, tackled the formidable caliph 'Umar on a legal point in public. 'Umar could not deny the accusation and said, "It was a man who erred and a woman who uttered the truth." He contrasts the property rights of the Muslim woman with the legal position of women in Europe until recent years, quoting the Sura of Women (4: 33) "Whatsoever a man earns is his own. Whatsoever a woman earns is her own." He continues:

> It is true that today far too many women are condemned in the East to an unsatisfactory way of life. But this is not due to Islam's regulations. It is due to the neglect of religious precept in political, social and financial institutions.

Poverty is one important reason for the bad conditions under which Eastern women have to live. A few are too rich; but the majority far too poor, victims of hunger and wretchedness. The resultant weakness has deprived people of the strength to rise up and insist on a change in their environment, for the sake of their families and their children. Nor have the women the power in such a situation to make use of their legal rights and to take men to court for the violence and tyranny of their behaviour. Women fear the difficulties of having to live without a male companion in a man's world.

Economic needs cause a diminution in morals and in human affections. Violence and injustice replace moral values.

Although Islamic lands are amongst the worst sufferers from these modern disasters, it is not Islam itself, but the deliberate neglect and abandonment of Islamic principles by Muslims and their leaders which has brought these tragedies upon us. For Islam is the very acme of the counterforces to poverty and injustice, and insists that wealth must be fairly divided amongst people of all classes, declaring that it is wrong for people to have to live under the torture of indigence and its pressure on hearts and souls, not least those of women and children.

Have we not men wise and just enough to eradicate these wrongs? To cure the bitterness which they produce? To reenact sound Islamic measures? To restore respect for the dictates of piety and reverence for God and men? Should not the same Islam which once rescued woman from degrading depression, now raise her again by instituting a new society?

The Veil : "The true veil is in the eyes of the men," runs a saying of the Prophet. Women on pilgrimage are not allowed to veil their faces. What is clearly commanded in the Quran is a modesty of dress and behaviour - for both men and women.

The relevant passages are as follows:

> Tell the believing men to lower their gaze and be modest. That is purer for them. Lo! Allah is Aware of what they do. And tell the believing women to lower their gaze and be modest, and to display of their adornment only that which is apparent, and to draw their veils over their bosoms, and not to reveal their adornment save to their own husbands or fathers or husband's fathers, or their sons or their husband's sons or their brothers or their brother's sons ... and turn unto Allah together, Oh believers, in order that ye may succeed. Quran 14:30-31 Light

> Oh Prophet! Tell thy wives and thy daughters and the women of the believers to draw their cloaks close round them when they go abroad. That will be better, that so they may be recognised and not annoyed.
>
> Quran 33: 59 The Clans

The commentator Abdullah Yusuf Ali says in notes on these two passages, "The rule of modesty applies to men as well as to women." "The times were those of insecurity, and the women were asked to cover themselves when walking abroad. It was never contemplated that they should be confined to their houses like prisoners." "The object was not to restrict the liberty of women, but to protect them from harm and molestation under the conditions then existing in Medina."

The covering of the face by a veil has never been universal in the Muslim world. Country women go to the fields without a veil, women in some parts of the Muslim world have not adopted it, others during the last decades have discarded it. But the Quranic injunction to modesty, however it is applied, cannot be set aside. Its interpretation has varied, and does vary, but its importance is basic. One interpretation of what constitutes modesty is the long skirt and head scarf worn by many young women — a stricter interpretation than that of some of their mothers.

Some Muslim women note an obsession among western observers with the question of the veil, an emphasis that tends to trivialise an important debate. The point at issue in the many discussions on the subject of women's role and women's dress is not the veil itself, but the values which Muslim society treasures and seeks to maintain. High among these are honour and good faith, premarital chastity and fidelity in marriage. "If the veil still exists, it is because those who are wearing it feel it is part of their tradition and part of their lives," says one woman lawyer.

Asked about the question of the veil, a western-educated Iranian woman student said:

> I think the profound reason for the veil in Islam is that a woman should not draw the attention of others. But if deeply inside her aim *is* to draw attention to herself she will do so even by being covered. Therefore it is

> a question of motive. If our motive is to gain the respect of others we will do this through the way we are: our behaviour, our acts, our thoughts, what we say and what we wear.

A woman can be a centre of attention or she can decide to give attention to others. She can be a cause of crime or a cause of creation. It depends on her deep motives.

Today we talk a lot about "la femme objet", the woman as a material object and not a real human being. And we often blame men for this attitude. They may deserve part of the blame, I do not know. But we are the real cause. We must be able to attract through our naturalness, our freedom from jealousy, hate and selfishness, and through what we think. Dressing in an extravagant fashion must not be the test of being charming and attractive. We can change such values by rethinking our role and our place in society and the world.

The Prophet's Marriages : On the Prophet's own family life, the following comment comes from Professor Seyyed Hussain Nasr, author of *Ideals and Realities of Islam, Man and Nature,* and other works:

> During the period of youth when the passions are most strong the Prophet lived with only one wife, who was much older than he, and he also underwent long periods of abstinence. And as a prophet many of his marriages were political ones, which, in the prevalent social structure of Arabia, guaranteed the consolidation of the newly founded community ... The multiple marriages of the Prophet, far from pointing to his weakness towards "the flesh", symbolise his patriarchal nature and his function, not as a saint who withdraws from the world, but as one who sanctifies the very life of the world by living in it and accepting it with the aim of integrating it into a higher order of reality.
>
> Seyyid Hussain Nasr

Origins of Muslim Marriage : The fourth chapter of the Quran is called *Women,* because it deals largely with women's rights. It begins:

> O Mankind! Be careful of your duty to your Lord Who created you from a single soul and from it created its mate and from them twain hath spread abroad a multitude of men and women.

It goes on to urge respect for mothers and for the rights of orphans, then continues:

> Marry of the women who seem good to you two or three or four; and if ye fear that ye cannot do justice (to them) then one (only) ... Thus it is more likely that ye will not do injustice.

The trend today is to interpret this as a clear discouragement of polygamy. One man commented, "The Quran tells us, 'Marry more than one if you can be fair to them — but you never will be fair.' The Prophet for certain special reasons married more than one wife and treated them justly. But how can we disregard the word of God in the Quran telling us that we shall not act justly?"

The origins of Muslim marriage, and the special circumstances in which arose its permission of a limited polygamy are explained in *A Muslim Commentary on the Declaration of Human Rights.* The author is Sultan Hussain Tabandeh, leader of the Nematullahi Sultanalishahi Sufi Order, Iran.

A glance at the situation in the Arab communities of the Pre-Islamic Times of Ignorance reveals how much Islam in fact advanced women's status and improved the conditions of their life.

The enemies of the Muslims attacked them with military force and in the ensuing battles so many men perished that great numbers of women were left without a protector, an almost impossible situation in the desert society of the Arabia of those days. It was to ensure the safety of women bereaved ... that the Prophet was told to grant permission to the Companions each to take one of the bereaved women with her children under his aegis as part of his own family ... and so to extend to the solitary women the assurance of protection and family life.

The new religion at once set to work to purge society of abuses. The imposition of a strict limit of four on the numbers of marriages allowable was one of the first beneficent new regulations.

The legalising of the number of four wives was not a command to take four wives. It was not an order but a limit. This permission is hedged about with many conditions. For instance, the man's finances must be sufficient, his circumstances favour a multiple establishment. His intention must be to be absolutely fair to each wife, his companionship and provision for each be equally shared.

> If polygamy is not allowed, circumstances may arise which cause difficulty, sin, confusion or unnecessary strain ... Many reasons make polygamy sensible, reasonable and right. But if a man's motive is merely to satisfy his carnal lusts, polygamy is frowned on, since men are commanded to allow their reason to control their passions. The acceptance of this inner discipline increases the intellectual powers and diminishes the force of fleshly desire.
>
> Sultan hussein Tabandeh

Marriage : An eminent Indian lawyer, A. A. A. Fyzee, discusses the legal aspect of marriage in his authoritative text book, *Outlines of Muhammadan Law.*

Marriage, in its legal aspect, is a contract and not a sacrament. There can be no marriage without consent. In its social aspect, three important factors must be remembered.

(i) Islamic law gives to the woman a definitely high status after marriage.

(ii) Restrictions are placed upon the unlimited polygamy of pre-Islamic times.

(iii) The Prophet, both by example and precept, encouraged the status of marriage. He positively enjoined marriage for all those who could afford it. And the well-known saying attributed to the Prophet, "There is no monkery in Islam", expresses his attitude to celibacy briefly and adequately.

In its religious aspect... marriage is recognised in Islam as the basis of society. It is a contract, but it is also a sacred covenant. Marriage as an institution leads to the uplift of man and is a means for the continuance of the human race. Spouses are strictly enjoined to love and honour each other.

> Muslim law permits polygamy but does not encourage it, and the Quranic injunction (Sura 4: 3) shows that in practice perfect equality of treatment on the part of the husband is, for all practical purposes, impossible of achievement. Hence Muslim law as enforced in India has considered polygamy as an institution to be tolerated but not encouraged. Asaf A. A. Fyzee

Divorce : There are strict rules and safeguards in the Quran in regard to divorce. Abdul Moghny Said discusses these in his book, *Islam - A Progressive Faith for a Dynamic World:*

> Marriage is a noble communion between man and woman, a communion which is blessed by Allah and based on freedom of choice. It is to be made or dissolved by the free consent of both parties.
>
> Islam leaves room for divorce as an undesirability, but not as a right to be excessively used. If it is deemed impossible for a couple to live together, after exhausting all means of conciliation and arbitration, they have but to separate. "If you fear a breach between the two of them, appoint an arbiter from his folk and an arbiter from her folk. If they desire amendment Allah will make them of one mind." (Quran Sura 4: 35 *Women)* It is clear that divorce is permitted only as a last resort. As Prophet Muhammad said, "Divorce is the most hateful to Allah among that which is permitted." When divorce is deemed inevitable it must be carried out in a decent and kind way. "Divorce must be pronounced twice and then (a woman) must be retained in honour or released in kindness." (Quran: Sura 2: 229 *The Cow)*
>
> We would like to emphasise that humanity has learned through its long experience that divorce is an unavoidable necessity in certain cases. This is why divorce is permitted even in countries whose religion does not allow it. As regards this issue, Islam has proved to be realistic. Abdul Moghny Said

Family Planning : Statements by Muslim religious authorities have been sought on the question of the use of contraceptive methods, in view of Family Planning programmes. These statements agree that contraception - but not sterilisation - is permissible under Muslim law:

> The use of medicine to prevent pregnancy temporarily is not forbidden by religion, especially if repeated pregnancies weaken the woman due to insufficient intervals for her to rest and regain her health. The Quran says: "... Allah desireth for you ease; He desireth not ... hardship for you ..." (Sura 2: 185) "... And hath not laid upon you in religion any hardship ..." (Sura 22: 78) But the use of medicine to prevent pregnancy absolutely and permanently is forbidden by religion.
>
> The Fatwa Committee, Al Azhar University, March 10 1953"
>
> There are genuine traditions which allow methods for restricting procreation, such as coitus interruptus ... A corollary of this is the dispensation for the use of medicine for contraception.
>
> The Grand Mufti of Jordan, December 1964

In his book, *The Lawful and the Prohibited in Islam,* Dr. Yusuf Al-Qaradawi, Dean of the Department of Shariah, University of Qatar, says:

> The preservation of the human species is unquestionably the primary objective of marriage, and such preservation of the species requires continued reproduction. Accordingly, Islam encourages having many children and has blessed both male and female progeny. However, it allows the Muslim to plan his family due to valid reasons and recognised necessities.

Valid reasons given for the use of contraceptives are: fear that the pregnancy or delivery might endanger the life or health of the mother; fear that the burden of children may straiten the family's circumstances so much that one might do something *haram* (forbidden) to satisfy their needs; fear that the children's health or upbringing might suffer, especially that a new pregnancy might harm a previous suckling child. Dr. Qaradawi adds:

> Imam Ahmad bin Hanbal [founder of one of the four traditional schools of Islamic Law], is of the opinion that contraception requires the consent of the wife, because she has the right both to sexual enjoyment and to decide whether or not she wants a child. It is reported that 'Umar forbade the practice of coitus interruptus without the consent of the wife. This was, on the part of Islam, a noteworthy step toward establishing the rights of women in an age in which they had no rights.

Abortion : While Islam permits preventing pregnancy for valid reasons, it does not allow doing violence to the pregnancy once it occurs, says Dr. Yusuf Al-Qaradawi. However, there is one exceptional situation, he says. If it is reliably established that the continuation of the pregnancy would necessarily result in the death of the mother, then, in accordance with the general principle of the Muslim legal code, that of choosing the lesser of two evils, abortion may be performed.

The Islamic position on abortion is examined by Dr. Hassan Hath out, FRCSE, Chief Medical Officer, Maternity Hospital, Kuwait.

In February 1971, a seminar was held in Beirut by the International Planned Parenthood Association, on "Induced Abortion - a Hazard to Public Health". Among divergent views, says Dr. Hathout, there was a strong current in favour of abortion, but a new impetus was given to the discussion when Islam's attitude was broached. The need was expressed for a study of Islam's stand on planned parenthood from all angles, and especially in relation to abortion, so as to clarify what Muslim law sanctions and proscribes in regard to it.

Dr. Hathout's paper, "Induced Abortion", was presented at a further gathering of the association in Rabat, December 1971. A summary of his argument follows:

> I am no stranger to the subject (of abortion) as I encounter it almost daily as obstetrician and gynaecologist. Quite a sizeable part of my life has been spent in study of the human foetus. And I am a believer in Islam who holds that Islam is and should

remain the foundation upon which the life of the Muslim should rest.

History shows that man's civilisation has rested on one unique concept, namely man's control over his passions. Without this, he would not have scaled the heights of moral glory nor would his intelligence have proceeded along the path of scientific research. If man were to give his passions free rein, mankind would become a community bent on self-destruction - a disintegrating civilisation.

Lust today is portrayed as an irresponsible beast. Chastity is held to be unreasonable and unacceptable. In Muslim societies, however (and among Christians living among them), virginity before marriage is practically one hundred per cent. This means it is not beyond the reach of possibility. It might be argued that fear and social pressures contribute largely to this figure. But fear is not - and should not be -the sole reason for chastity. Indeed I have known men who practise self-restraint not out of fear but out of self-respect and respect to those they love. If you love somebody you should not subject them to possible harm.

When doctor and patient discuss this question, there is always a third party present: the foetus, the newcomer waiting at the door. Perhaps the foetus has the added privilege of having his whole life ahead of him. I have come to know the foetus in its various phases, arriving at the conclusion that the foetus is an individual. I have been unable to draw a line between the foetus as a human and a non-human. I have moreover been unable to draw a line telling me where I would have to feel concern for the foetus and where I would have to disregard it. It is confusing and contradictory to hear those voices loudest in the defence of the illegitimate baby, which were most willing to have sacrificed him a few months before, when he was a foetus *in utero.*

Muslim legal views on abortion were unanimous on some points, varied on others. Some were based on the early medical belief that "quickening of life" took place when movement of the foetus could be felt, about four months after conception. This is not now scientific.

Abortion differs from contraception, being an assault on life and therefore a criminal act. All agree that abortion is a crime after" quickening" has taken place, and blood money is due. Opinions differ as to before "quickening". Ghazzali and others hold it a crime against existing life. But if the mother's life is endangered, the lesser evil is to be allowed and the mother saved. The foetus has the right to inherit — and the right to live. To deprive it of this right is prohibited by religion, unless there are strong grounds. These may be the certainty of danger in the present or immediate future to the mother's life, or the strong probability of the baby being born deformed.

To say that a foetus is "unwanted" is a delusion. We have conducted a survey on a group of women - married - who had demanded abortion. When they were delivered of their babies, we asked each one if she still felt the baby was unwanted. The reply of one and all was in the negative.

11

Social Life

Essential Elements

Islam has given laws based on the Book of Allah, preached and practiced by the last Messenger of Allah which guarantee the rights of human beings, their life and property, their honour and prestige, security and peace. They guarantee social, religious and political rights to all its citizens, irrespective of race, caste, creed or colour. All enjoy equal rights and equal freedom in an Islamic society.

In the way ward society of Arabia, women were treated as animals, life and honour of none were safe. Men buried their daughters alive. No law existed and men bowed before idols. In that society robbery was not considered a crime, trust had no sanctity and a man could lose all his possessions including his wives and children through games of chance. It was Hadrat Muhammad (PBUH) who brought about a marvellous change in the life of such people.

He cast kindness into their hearts and converted robbers into custodians. People constantly fighting among themselves became brothers. They learnt to stand side by side, shoulder to shoulder in a row while praying. It was Hadrat Muhammad (PBUH) who taught that all human beings belong to one brotherhood and that they are all equal. He made life easier by his teachings of tolerance of other people's views and opinions, especially in matters of faith. The Quran says:

> "Let there be no compulsion in religion." (2:256)

Everyone in the Islamic society is free to practice his religion. This philosophy of religious freedom is further explained in the Holy Quran:

> "If it had been the Lord's will
> They would all have believed
> All who are on earth!
> Will you then compel mankind,
> against their will to believe!" (10:99)

The protection of life and property is fully guaranteed to every citizen in an Islamic society.

> "take not life, which Allah hath made sacred, except by way of justice and law:"
> (6:151)

And with regard to property:

> "And do not eat up your property among yourselves for vanities, nor use it as bait for the judges, with intent that ye may eat up wrongfully and knowingly a little of (other) people's property. " (2:188)

In an Islamic society, wealth should remain in circulation. For this purpose, Islam has established the institution of *Zakat* which is collected from the rich and distributed amongst the poor of the society. *Zakat* is compulsory and, therefore, if one does not pay it, he goes against the commandment of Allah and for him, is prescribed a painful punishment.

As regards the acquisition of wealth, Islam encourages all lawful means and condemns the unlawful ones. Muslims are required to earn livelihood by honest means; it regards begging and unemployment as undesirable. Its emphasis is on lawful and legal trade and it considers hoarding, games of chance and gambling as illegal.

Yet another feature of an Islamic society is justice which is to give every deserving person his right. It is the duty of every individual member of the society to cooperate with the society towards this end, to the best of his ability.

In order to eradicate evil, the Holy Prophet (PBUH) first attacked the basis of corruption. He prohibited all alcoholic drinks and gambling in the Islamic society. He encouraged people to adopt piety, goodness and justice in their individual as well as social dealings. He also discouraged slavery and used all possible methods to get rid of this evil from society.

The social system based on these principles has been working successfully till the present times. In these comprehensive principles, the most balanced Divine Guidance is given to mankind to purify their life and to lay the foundation of a healthy, pious and chaste society in which people can live in peace and happiness. These are the distinctive features of the society set up by Prophet Hadrat Muhammad (PBUH) which provides honour, peace and security to every human being.

Social Features

There seem to be four main types of sexual relations, of which we either have a society of pure homosexuals, an entirely promiscuous society, a society in which no sexual relation exists except between husband and wife, or a *laissez-faire* society in which all these forms are tolerated. Are there any rational and objective bases on which we can choose among these types of society ?

Let us start with the easiest one to rule out. If men continue to be moral then a society of pure homosexuals is a self-defeating one, since it severs the enjoyment of sex from its reproductive function. An entirely promiscuous society seems to many to be the best, and in the long run the inevitable form of sexual relations. In such a society, sex, it is thought, ceases to be a problem, since here we shall for the first time combine complete freedom with the deepest enjoyment as well as the procreation of children. This, however, is a mere dream in which one does not see the facts as they are but as one wants them to be. Here are some of the difficulties that beset such a society.

Far from being the natural or ultimately the inevitable, and even if man is viewed as a mere animal, this is a dream which shall never be realised. This is because the human being is basically and biologically a pair-forming species. As the emotional relationship develops between a pair of potential mates it is aided and abetted by the sexual intimacies they share. The pair-formation function of sexual behaviour is so important for our species that nowhere outside the paining phase do sexual activities reach such a high intensity.

The facts are therefore against those who argue that man is basically promiscuous. "It is true that in many cultures economic considerations have led to gross distortion of the pair-forming pattern, but even where this pattern's interference with officially planned 'pseudobonds' has been most vigorously suppressed, with savage penalties and punishments, it has always shown signs of reasserting itself. From ancient times, young lovers who have known that the law may demand no less than their lives if they are caught, have nevertheless found themselves driven to take the risk. Such is the power of this fundamental biological mechanism."

As a dream, a promiscuous society is one where everybody chooses whoever he likes at whatever time he prefers. As a reality it is a society in which sexual deprivation becomes the main problem.

The young and the beautiful are universally more attractive than the plain or the ugly, and the old. And then there are personal tastes as to voice, form, culture, gesture, dress, etc. And if a person fails to find the mate of his or her liking, then even if he or she is physically satisfied, he or she is most likely emotionally deprived.

In such a society people are sure to be obsessed with sex, the search for the younger, the more attractive, the what not, becomes a full-time job. If time is a valuable asset, then much of it is unnecessarily wasted in such a society.

And this leads inevitably and naturally to the commercialization of this human need, a commercialization which through advertisement, pictures, specialised magazines, the employment of sexually attractive girls and, only very occasionally boys and men, and a hundred other cunning devices, yet increase the obsession with sex.

And the natural outcome of this is a distortion of human values. We do not mean by this anything metaphysically or mysterious. We only mean that in such a society a person's worth will depend on the accident of her or his being of a certain age or having good looks and/or a beautiful body. Girls are rewarded socially, and materially, and even 'crowned', not for anything they achieved but for a thing they had at their hour of birth. By implication the less beautiful girls are punished for no fault of theirs. How manifestly unjust an arrangement, one might say, even cruel !

And the fact of the matter is that a promiscuous society is definitely a cruel one. Even in a normal society, the feeling that one is getting older —and hence less attractive and less wanted therefore—is somewhat annoying, but how much worse it must be in a society where the worth of a person is determined, above all, by the degree of physical attraction, almost to the exclusion of other considerations.

If many criminal tendencies among both the young and the old are discovered to have their origins in broken homes and unstable families, what is going to be the fate of the army of parentless children which a promiscuous society produces? We cannot go here into details of the problems of the mass bringing up of children, but we have pointed to some of the consequences. Contemplating them, some might say : "Well, no-one ever seriously advocated this kind of society. All we stand for is a society where every individual or group of individuals shall have the freedom to lead the kind of sexual life which they prefer. In such a society, married people will live side by side with promiscuous individuals and homosexuals, each appreciating and respecting the ideas and choices of the others and tolerating their behaviour." But, on even a little reflection one will realise that this will not do either.

First, because the bad consequence of homosexuality (with the details of which we are not presently concerned) and promiscuity, will not be eradicated by having those who practise them living among married people. All the complications will be there, though on a narrow scale.

Secondly, if the consequences are admitted to be harmful, then why encourage, and not lessen, the factors responsible for them ? And, the unfortunate fact is that tolerating homosexuality and promiscuity means encouraging them and pushing more and more people to practising them inasmuch as tolerance leads to others to experiment, and in due course, to come to practise them—as is invariably the case with any other aberrance that is 'tolerated.' The inevitable result will be that the society will become more and more homosexual and promiscuous and it is the married people who will come to be looked upon as 'eccentric', as happened in the case of the people of Prophet Lut (peace be upon him):

> "And Lut : (Remember) when he said unto his folk : Will you commit abomination such as no other people ever did before ? Lo ! you come with lust unto men instead of women. Nay, but you are a wanton folk ! And the answer of hie people was only that they said (one to another) : Turn them out of your township. They are folk, forsooth, who keep pure !" (7 : 80-82)

Although wicked people have always been committing this most heinous sin that has given the people of sodom an everlasting notoriety yet it has always been considered a filthy and detestable act. But the only people who have tried to raise it to a moral excellence, were the Greek Philosophers in the ancient world, and the Europeans in the modern world. The latter are doing their utmost to make up the deficiency by making an open propaganda for it, and have succeeded in giving this filthy act a legal sanction. So much so that the legislatures of some countries have legalized it. It does not require elaborate argument to show that homosexuality is a horrible social crime and a heinous sin. For the Creator has made the male and the female of each and every living species different from and complementary to each other for their reproduction. Then this difference in the human species has been created to serve another purpose. This is to urge the two to live together in order to form a family along with their offspring. For this is the foundation of a civilized life for which man has been created. That is why their bodies have been made complementary to attract each other for the satisfaction of sex urges and for the service of the natural function of reproduction of the species. Therefore the one who satisfies this sex urge in an unnatural way becomes guilty of many crimes at one and the same time :

1. Such a one, so to speak, wages a war against the natural and physical functionings of his own organs and those of the victims of his lust. This inevitably produces very harmful effects on their physiques, their minds and their morality.
2. He becomes guilty of treachery and dishonesty against Nature for he enjoys sexual pleasure, without performing the necessary service of his species and civilization and without fulfilling the rights and obligations attached to it.
3. He commits a breach of trust against the society in general for he enjoys all the benefits of the civilized society, but in his turn does not take on himself the responsibilities of the married life and wastes all his powers in the unnatural satisfaction of his sexual desires. This selfish and unworthy attitude is not only useless but also positively harmful to the collective morality. Thus he makes himself unfit for the service of the family and of the human race and produces unnatural feminine characteristics in, at least, one other male, and opens the way to adultery and moral degradation for at least two women.

By elimination then, and also by implication, the society with the least evil and most good is a society of married people who do not tolerate, but do their best to eradicate, all the causes of homosexuality and promiscuity.

Muslim Society

> Islam teaches that God is concerned not only with moral and ethical reform, but also with social emancipation and economic conditions.
>
> Abdul Moghny Said

> Islam strikes a balance between the two extremes of capitalism and socialism.
>
> Muhammad Qutb

> The simultaneous stress on both the material and the spiritual aspects of life is a unique characteristic of the Islamic economic system. This synthesis of the material

> and the spiritual is what is missing in the other two systems, capitalism and socialism. Both the capitalist and the socialist systems have neglected the spiritual needs of the human personality.
>
> Muhammad Umar Chapra

Contemporary attempts to base the life of nations on Islamic principles cover a wide range. All are profoundly influenced by the example of the Prophet and of the early Muslim community in Medina. They are also strongly influenced by reactions to events and trends in the Western world, both capitalist and communist.

The great adjustments that are taking place in Muslim society are happening at a time when it feels itself under threat from a dominant civilisation which, while no longer politically imperialist, is imposing its norms of behaviour and its materialism on others. Reactions towards the "West" face Muslims with difficult dilemmas.

The search goes on for answers to social and world problems that are consonant with Islamic tradition, neither merely reactions to nor adaptations of alien thought.

"The dominant, permanent factor in Muslim countries," says Dr. Fathi Uthman, former editor of the *Islamic World Review,* "is Islam as a comprehensive way of life." It is important to realise, he adds, that those who hold this view can be progressive - recognising that not everything "modern" is tied to secularism. The Islamic revival is many-sided, forward-looking as well as traditional.

The tide of renewal in the Muslim world began to flow more than a century ago, with movements such as that of the Wahhabis in Arabia, the Arab awakening in the Near East, and the expansion of Islam south of the Sahara.

The Twentieth Century has seen a war of ideologies — of powerful ideas regarding man and society. Every tide of ideology that has swept through the world during the course of the past decades has had its observers, its critics and sometimes its supporters in the Muslim world. Liberalism and socialism in turn were interpreted in Muslim terms. The atheistic creed of communism has never been acceptable to Muslims, but the Marxist diagnosis of society and history has had its influence in various quarters. Nationalism, though contrary to the Islamic concept of the universal community, the *Ummah,* helped to raise many local and regional loyalties, as well as to inspire the larger vision of Pan-Arabism. Young men — and women also of each succeeding generation pinned their hopes of radical change to one banner or another: often to suffer disillusionment when the promises of their leaders were not fulfilled.

More and more, hopes of profound change on a national and global scale came to focus on a return to the teachings of Islam. Islam itself could be viewed as an ideology, in the sense of a comprehensive system of ideas that embraces the whole of life.

Some of many trains of thought and action are indicated here: a view on Arab Socialism; the principles of Islamic banking by one of its pioneers; an insight into the universal nature of science; and how the West is seen. Is it irretrievably decadent, or are its people possible partners in fashioning a new age? The key to all progress is in the renewal of faith.

Origins of Arab Socialism : The Islamic principles on which Arab socialism was based differ fundamentally from dialectical materialism.

One of those who contributed to the development of independent Arab socialist thinking is Abdul Moghny Said, until 1975 Under-Secretary in the Ministry of Manpower, Cairo. He is known for his pioneering work in the field of workers' education. In his book, *Arab Socialism,* he traces its origins in the thought and practice of the Quran and the Prophet.

The concept of Arab socialism actually existed for many centuries before modern Arab nationalism came upon the scene. Its roots were planted long before Marx. They lie deep in the soil of Islam and in the cultural heritage of the Arabs.

All the great monotheistic religions were cradled in these Eastern Mediterranean lands which have always been the home of the Arab people. The impulse towards social emancipation is found in all these religions, but it is perhaps most developed in the precepts of Islam. The Quran makes it clear that, as well as setting up moral standards as a basis of decent behaviour and better human relations, religions must bring help to the poor and improve the living standards of the masses. In previous revelations the message was simple: "Do not exploit; be charitable; practise unselfishness." In Islam, for the first time, an economic theory of equal opportunities and fair distribution was outlined.

Without being too theological, it is possible to explore the social and economic implications of Islam and the principles which have influenced contemporary Arab socialist thought... Islam teaches that God is concerned not only with moral and ethical reform, but also with social emancipation and economic conditions.

The Quran provides a basis for a moral interpretation of history; an interpretation which is deeper and broader than that of Karl Marx because it covers both the moral and material aspects, while that of Marx concentrates entirely on the material aspects, being greatly influenced by the materialistic evolutionary philosophies of his time. Religion is not the opium of the people. The great religions aimed at a classless society, where equality, justice and prosperity would prevail. In their principles, and particularly in Islam, which Marx completely ignored, we can trace much that pointed towards socialism.

A New Economic Order : Muslims responsible for the policy of nations - Asian and African as well as Arab — see the teachings of the Quran as having relevance to major questions of economics, and also to the stewardship of money and the distribution of world resources.

Banking is one field where practices based on these teachings have been increasingly explored and expanded. In the 1970's and 1980's numbers of Islamic banks were set up, based on the principles of partnership and the sharing of profit and loss. It is essential that the system should be interest-free, since the Quran specifically forbids usury, and this is generally taken to include any form of interest. But the emphasis is on working out a positive system, not merely on excluding an incentive regarded as wrong. By 1987 there were more than 100 Islamic banks and financial institutions throughout the world, including multinational banking companies. The Islamic Development Bank (IDB) was established in 1975 by the Organisation of the Islamic Conference (OIC) to undertake long-term financing of development projects.

One of the pioneers of these developments is Prince

Muhammad Al-Faisal Al-Saoud, Chairman of the International Association of Islamic Banks. In 1981 he founded the Geneva-based Dar-ul-Mal al-Islami (DMI). The aim is that Islamic banks and interest-based banks should view each other not as competitors but as partners. One of many steps towards this goal was a symposium of bankers held in Baden-Baden, West Germany, in May 1981, organised by the Syma Institute and chaired by Prince Muhammad.

In his inaugural address he outlines some value premises of Islam. (1) The unity *(tawhid)* of thought under God: His power and direction are relevant to every aspect of life. (2) The vice-gerency of man who is God's deputy and who has to act as a trustee: with no extravagance, no waste, but positive utilisation of the available resources. (3) The search for justice, political and social as well as individual. From such a value-framework, he says, the economist will derive a new set of policy conclusions. The thrust of economic analysis will move from what people demand, to what the world needs, and this will be a revolutionary change in economic thinking.

The basic principles of Islamic banking and finance are not new. What is new is only in the application. Our philosophy is based on the Quran in which there are certain things that are given, things which do not bear discussion, because we cannot in any way adjust them. However, there is a wide area in which innovation, new approaches and methods can be applied. We feel we can contribute to the solution of some of the problems in the economies of the world today. We are trying to help in relieving the pressures on the Third World by mobilizing the resources of the Islamic countries through Islamic banking.

Man has been created as God's surrogate in this world. Therefore he is not a totally free agent in his social and economic interactions. There is a certain code. The question of interest is one thing, but more important is the total integration of morality in the dealings of any human being in any endeavour he undertakes.

Economics, as we understand it in its classical form, is the satisfaction of the need for goods and services. With Islam, the definition is slightly different. It is the material satisfaction of the need of society according to the role man plays in this world. This entails certain limitations, which make it different from the western concept of total freedom of action.

Trusteeship brings the idea of accountability in this world before humans, and before God in the life hereafter ... We shall have to develop social accounting over against the type of accounting with which we are familiar at the moment... These concepts are not just ethical norms, but have important economic consequences.

In this new approach, we do not claim that we have all the answers or that we have been able to develop all the solutions. We would like to learn from other traditions, and we would like to see others also adopt a more open attitude to the study of the Muslim approach to economics.

Science and Faith : The search for knowledge is a duty in Islam. European scholarship owes a debt to the Muslim world for its earlier leadership in the scientific field. Now, however, "The Muslim World can and should learn from and profit by the West, particularly in the spheres of modern sciences and technology." Muhammad Asad, author of *The Road to Mecca,* is one among many who develop this theme.

Never have the worlds of Islam and the West come so close to one another as today. Cultural imitation, opposed to creativeness, is bound to make a people small... Not that the Muslims could not learn much from the West, especially in the fields of science and technology. But the acquisition of scientific notions and methods is not really "imitation"; and certainly not in the case of a people whose faith commands them to search for knowledge wherever it is to be found. Science is neither Western nor Eastern, for all scientific discoveries are only links in an unending chain of intellectual endeavour which embraces mankind as a whole.

Every scientist builds on the foundations supplied by his predecessors, be they of his own nation or of another; and this process of building, correcting and improving goes on and on, from man to man, from age to age, from civilisation to civilisation, so that the scientific achievements of a particular age or civilisation can never be said to "belong to that age or civilisation." At various times one nation, more vigorous than others, is able to contribute more to the general fund of knowledge; but in the long run the process is shared, and legitimately so, by all.

There was a time when the civilisation of the Muslims was more vigorous than the civilisation of Europe. It transmitted to Europe many technological inventions of a revolutionary nature, and more than that: the very principles of that 'scientific method' on which modern science and civilisation are built. Nevertheless, Jabir ibn Huyyan's fundamental discoveries in chemistry did not make chemistry an "Arabian" science; nor can algebra and trigonometry be described as "Muslim" sciences, although the one was evolved by Al-Khwarizmi and the other by Al-Battani, both of whom were Muslims: just as one cannot speak of an "English" theory of Gravity, although the man who formulated it was an Englishman. All such achievements are the common property of the human race. If, therefore, the Muslims adopt, as adopt they must, modern methods in science and technology they will do no more than follow the evolutionary instinct which causes men to avail themselves of other men's experiences.

Change through Renewal : The Islamic concept of change in society is renewal *(tajdid),* as the key to reform *(islah).*

The Prophet did not start with a system, or with large numbers. He began with change in the hearts of men and women - his wife, his closest friends. The idea of reform is not the modern one, which begins with the outward, trying to reform the world but never man himself.

Africa south of the Sahara has seen a vigorous expansion of Islam during the nineteenth and twentieth centuries. This renewal of Islam in West Africa may be regarded as "a model of *tajdid",* suggests Dr. A. R. Doi, Director of the Center for Legal Studies, Ahmadu Bello University, Zaria. The revered Shehu (Sheikh) Uthumanu Dan Fodio (d. 1817), scholar and preacher in what is now Northern Nigeria, was regarded by his thousands of followers as the Renewer *(mujaddid)* of his age. In one of his many books he speaks of the character of such a reformer.

It is related [in a saying of the Prophet] that at the beginning of every century God will send a learned man to the people to renew their faith. The characteristics of this man must be that he commands what is right and forbids what is disapproved of, that he reforms the affairs of the people, and judges between them, and that he assists the truth against vanity and the oppressed against the oppressors, in contrast to the characteristics of the other learned men of his age.

The struggle the Shehu declared against rulers he regarded as corrupt began with preaching (the *jihad* of the word). At the risk of his life he took a stand against an injustice, and, his struggle turned into an open revolt (the *jihad* of the sword). With his brother Abdullah and his son Muhammadu Bello he established a state in the new city of Sokoto. This became the centre of a renaissance of poetry, literature and religious study, as well as of prosperous trade. All three were learned and scholarly men: more than a hundred books by them survive. These were concerned with the application of the precepts of Islam to the practical affairs of home, trade and state, and also with the poems, in Arabic and in the vernacular languages, which helped to make the teachings of Islam live for a population largely illiterate. The memory of Uthumanu Dan Fodio is still a powerful influence among the more than 150 million Muslims in West African countries, and also in the Sudan.

Renewal in this spirit is the aim of the Emir of Kano, HH Al haji Ado Bayero. He sees his responsibilities as extending to the contribution a united Nigeria can make to the world. At the end of Ramadan 1988 he invited chiefs from the south of Nigeria, as well as his northern neighbours, to celebrate the Feast, the Eid-ul-fitr. Together with the Anglican Bishop of Kano, he spoke of uniting peoples of all creeds on the firm ground of moral rectitude, selflessness, and dedication for the betterment of mankind. In a situation tense with recent religious conflict, he and the Bishop gave joint witness to "religion as an agent of unity rather than of division and destruction." Amid the blare of trumpets and the thunder of hooves as thousands of horsemen thronged the ancient city, a note was sounded of quiet faith for the future.

Islam and the West : Over the past hundred years, a renewal of faith and confidence has come to the Muslim world. The forms of this renewal have been manifold: its expressions range from the personal to the running of states, from individual integrity to steps towards a new economic order, from scientific research to art and poetry.

The springs of renewal, or resurgence, in the Muslim world may be discerned in the Quran, in the potency of its teachings and of the basic tenets of Islam. What actually occasioned it, at this time in history, was reaction to the domination of western civilisation, in its political form of imperialism and, more insidiously, in the onslaught of its materialism and secularism.

A reaction had to come. Revulsion against the West was inevitable, and might take controversial forms — not always viewed by Muslims as true to the best in Islam. It was not a reaction against Christianity, but against moral corruption as well as economic and political domination.

In face of the threat of a dominant culture, three possible courses present themselves: rejection, surrender or a selective choice, says Sayyid Abul Hasan Ali Nadwi, Rector of the Nadwat-ul-*Ulama* Islamic University in Lucknow. One of the most widely read authors of his time, he has written more than 40 books - in Arabic, Urdu and English. His insights into the world situation and the demands it makes on Muslims have done much to challenge the fears and raise the hopes, especially of the younger generation.

In his book, *Western Civilisation - Islam and Muslims,* he analyses the choices that face them.

An unrelenting battle of ideas and ideals is taking place throughout the Muslim world- a clash between the Islamic and the Western concepts of life, values and traditions. The past history of the Islamic countries, the indestructible attachment of the Muslim masses everywhere to Islam, the ideals which inspired them in their struggle for freedom - all these things demand that Islamic values alone should have a claim on their leadership. On the other hand, the intellectual make-up, education and political interests of the ruling classes in Muslim countries require that Western forms of life should be pushed forward.

The attitude of rejection and withdrawal is emphatically futile. It is bound to fail. No nation can aspire to maintain its individuality which lacks faith in itself and is plagued with an inferiority complex. All its efforts to hold its ground against a mighty civilisation, which has also become the dominant trend of the time, must ultimately fail.

In contrast there is the philosophy of defeatism, capitulation, servility. Its advocates are ardent, though immature, disciples of the West. Modernism to them means westernisation.

A man who does not make the West his preceptor and relegate himself to the rank of a pupil, but treats it as an associate, [can] make his own contribution. He ought to know that if he has to learn a great deal from the West, the West too has to learn no less from him. His endeavour should be to bring about a synthesis between the material and spiritual forces of the West and East and then to evolve from it a way of life the West may also be compelled to adopt, and which may serve as an inspiration to the most highly advanced nations of the present day world.

"Arousing the Conscience of the West": Criticism of western ways does not necessarily regard the fight for values as confined to the Muslim world, nor as irretrievably lost in western society. Dr. Fathi Uthman, former editor of the *Islamic World Review,* in a seminar held at the Oxford Centre for Islamic Studies (February 1987), gave points of common hope and advance, providing grounds for cooperation. As the shadow of colonialism recedes, he said, new friendships are arising. Business relationships enable economic problems to be tackled together. And above all within the structure of western society there are many positive initiatives, "arousing the conscience of the West and countering the impression of an imminent collapse of standards and values."

Response to such initiatives of change, recognised in the conduct of Christians encountered in the West, was confirmed by a Muslim Brother from the Sudan. "I have moved from condemnation to the realisation that there are people we can and should work with," he said. "Absolute moral standards provide the area of cooperation to achieve the Will of God."

Right Path

When you want to understand Islam, where do you go? A learned professor has said that we must go to the dictionary and scholarship, and then to the mosque. Certainly it is necessary to go to these places, but going there alone will be incomplete. Islam is not confined to the mosque - it is a code of conduct and a guidance for everyday life. We have to watch the career of a Muslim who has himself understood the religion of Islam and who practises its principles. Without that watching, the mosque or the textbook will give us only an incomplete understanding.

The Honourable Justice M. M. Ismail, Madras

Islam's conception of life is often put in terms of a road. A road has a beginning and a destination. The individual is somewhere on the road between birth and death. The human race is on the road too -the road from Creation to Judgement.

The millions now turning their faces to Mecca pray many times a day: "Show us the straight way." "Guide us on the straight path." *Al-Fatiha,* the opening chapter *(sura)* of the Quran with its seven verses, is repeated at each of the five times of prayer.

Whole books have been written on these verses. They are the first to be memorised by children, and they are pondered by statesmen. An ex-Prime Minister, asked what was the inspiration behind his success in recent negotiations, went through the Fatiha step by step.

The first volume of one modern "explanatory translation" of the Quran is entirely devoted to this opening chapter. "Let us look at the *Surat Al-Fatiha* as a whole," it says, "and see what type of mind it reflects or tries to build."

"Al-Fatiha": The Opening : In the Name of God, Most Gracious, Most Merciful.

Praise be to God,

The Cherisher and Sustainer of the Worlds;

Most Gracious, Most Merciful; Master of the Day of Judgement.

Thee do we worship, And Thine aid we seek.

Show us the straight way,
The way of those on whom
Thou hast bestowed Thy Grace,
Those whose (portion)
Is not wrath,
And who go not astray.

The Holy Quran, Sura I

Signposts on the Road: The Pillars of Islam : For the traveller who sets out on the road of faith, there are certain signposts or pillars by which to chart his way. The Muslim is taught to mark five such pillars.

The first is his witness to the God he serves: the One God, to whom man must submit or surrender totally. The word *Islam* means such surrender, and *Muslim (Muslima)* is the man or woman who thus submits to God. This "witness" *(shahada)* or creed is:

"There is no god but God (Allaḥ)
And Muhammad is the Prophet of God."

The second of the pillars is prayer.

The third is *Zakat*: the giving of a certain proportion of income for the relief of poverty.

The fourth is the discipline of fasting - from dawn to sunset during the month of Ramadan.

The fifth is the pilgrimage to Mecca - to be performed once in a lifetime by every Muslim able to make the journey.

Of these, the duty which most affects the daily life of the Muslim family is the observance of the five daily times of prayer, starting before sunrise and ending late in the evening. In many of the Muslim homes in which I have stayed, the family are up for the Dawn Prayer that begins the day. It should be performed between dawn and sunrise. My hostess in a Cairo club slipped away to a quiet corner after lunch, so that the midday prayer might not be missed. A cheerful schoolgirl, hurrying in to her home with her books under her arm, went first to pray and then to tea. In the cool of the evening in Bombay's beautiful Hanging Gardens, many of the faithful were praying as the sun set.

The midday prayer on Fridays is the weekly congregational gathering. Shops close, business stops. A sermon precedes the prayers, which are performed together without regard to rank. A gallery or aisle in the Mosque is often set apart for women.

There are many who do not pray, and many for whom it is a mere repetition of a formula. The following quotations come from some of those to whom prayer is a realitv - individuals in widely differing circumstances.

Daily Prayers : In his prayers, a Muslim faces the direction of the city of Mecca. When the time comes, in whatever place he happens to be, he turns towards Mecca and says his prayers. Facing one direction is a symbol of unity of purpose for the millions of Muslims offering their prayers at the same time in the four corners of the earth.

The Muslim says the *Fatiha,* and recites any other portion of the Quran he feels like reciting, because of its particular meaning, or because he happens to remember it. Bowing, and touching the earth with his forehead, he terminates with a formal prayer in which he asks God to bless him and his people "as Thou hast blessed Ibrahim and his people."

The daily prayers are made by practising Muslims individually. A family can join in prayer, or any group which happens to be together. On Fridays, however, the noon prayer should be made collectively.

Voice Within : Prayer reminds man of God and helps him to be receptive to His guidance.

The five daily prayers are the best rest intervals for man in our busy and materialistic world.

The moral foundations of Islam are standards in which human behaviour can be channelled for the good of the individual as well as for the good of the community as a whole. They are not mere preaching stuff which may not keep step with ever-changing conditions. They form together that which we call "conscience" or the good side of us.

The "voice within" reminds us always that God is with us. To believe in God is simply the way to develop this "voice within" by seeking God's remembrance, presence and guidance.

Man Can Choose : The trouble we now see in the world - and in the Muslim world -is the result of listening to self-will when we should listen to God.

If we ask, what does God say in such a crisis as we face today, we can turn to the Holy Quran and find a key in the verse, "God does not change the condition of a people until the people change themselves." Another key is in the *Fatiha,* the prayer we repeat so many times a day. It says, "Guide us in the straight path." This shows us that God wants us to take guidance from Him. If this is so, we have to listen for that guidance. He will not catch us by the ear and drag us along that straight path. We must open our ears to His guidance, which the *Fatiha* makes us ask for.

Man is *ashraf-ul-makhluqat,* the top of creation, the highest of living beings. We have freedom to think for ourselves, about what is right and what is wrong. If we say everything is under God's control, we imply that He wills evil. You may say a leaf falls to the ground — and God wills it. But with man's actions it is different. He can choose between right and wrong, which lead to heaven and hell. Therefore we need to ask God's guidance along the straight path.

A time of quiet listening and asking for Gods guidance in this way is very important for every Muslim.

Haroun S. Kably,

Plaited Kufic ornamentation

"God gathers mankind for the Day of Judgement"

Advocate, Supreme Court, Delhi, and President, All India Cutchi Memon Community

Thy Lord Hath Not Forsaken Thee : Verses may be chosen from the Quran as optional acts of prayer to suit the circumstances of the believer, his joy and sorrow, gratitude and need.

A television programme in Cairo on the Prophet's Birthday (April 1973) included a talk on courage in adversity by the newly-appointed Sheikh al-Azhar, Dr. Abdul Halim Mahmud. The chapter of the Quran named *The Glorious Morning Light* (Sura 93) was read. Afterwards a Palestinian lady, a refugee living in Egypt, said:

> As I knit, I pray - just as Gandhi used to say the name of God as he spun. It is the same with the beads you see in my husband's hand. Men say short prayers as they handle them. One of these is, "Your covering and mercy, oh Lord." It means that the inner life is protected. Whatever the circumstances and defeats outside, the life inside our hearts need not be invaded by evil.

One part of the Quran which is often used in our prayers when we are disappointed or disheartened is the sura called *Al-Doha, The Glorious Morning Light.* It is said that these verses were revealed to the Prophet in Mecca, after he had received no revelations for some time and his opponents were mocking him.

By the morning hours

And by the night when it is stillest,

Thy Lord hath not forsaken thee nor doth He hate thee,

And verily the Hereafter will be better for thee than the present,

And verily thy Lord will give unto thee so that thou wilt be content.

Did He not find thee an orphan and protect (thee)?

Did He not find thee wandering and direct (thee)?

Did He not find thee destitute and enrich (thee)?

Therefore the orphan oppress not,

Therefore the beggar drive not away,

Therefore of the bounty of thy Lord be thy discourse.

Mrs. Fareeza Taji, Palestine and Cairo

Prayers for Forgiveness and Obedience : The following come from a prayer-book in use in the Sudan.

O God! I ask forgiveness for myself and for my father; for all Muslims, both men and women; for all believers, both men and women; for those of them who are alive and those of them who are dead.

Deal with me and with them, whether soon or late, in the faith, in this world and the next, according to what You deserve. Do not deal with us, O Lord ! according to what we deserve. For You are forgiving, patient, generous, bountiful, tender and merciful.

O God ! in Whose hand are all our affairs, put an end to our neglect of You.

We have turned away from You, and from Your Commands, and from listening to the good things You say.

The crime that has caused this is that we have turned towards people who are no concern of ours. These have drawn us away from the benefit of Your speaking with us, and from our fear of You, in spite of our great need of you.

In this there is nothing but loss.

We pray you to turn our desires towards You. For You alone can rescue us from danger in this world and the next.

From *Al-Ratib,* a book of prayers used by the Imam Muhammad al Mahdi

The Call to Prayer : God is great! God is great!

I testify that there is no god but God!

I testify that Muhammad is God's Prophet!

Come to pray! Come to prosperity!

God is great! There is no god but God!

In the Mosque : Here the believer is a fish in water: the hypocrite is a caged bird.

Inscription on the gate of the Masjid Jami' mosque, Isfahan

The Fast of Ramadan : The Muslim calendar consists of twelve lunar months. Because of this the annual festivals occur at different seasons - thirteen days earlier in each successive year.

The ninth month is the month of fasting, Ramadan. All through it, from the first glimpse of the crescent moon to its reappearance a month later to mark the feast, no food or water may be taken from dawn till sunset. Before light, the sound of a drum is often heard in the street, with its summons to awake and eat in the twilight, before a white thread can be distinguished from a black, and the day's fast begins. Ramadan is a time of discipline— and also of surprising gaiety, of family visits and neighbourly calls for the *iftar* (break-fast) parties in the evenings when the fast is over.

There are various aspects of Ramadan. One is the recollection of the revelation of the Quran, especially on the "Night of Power" or "Night of Destiny", the 26th-27th of the month. The Prophet's victories - the Battle of Badr and the conquest of Mecca - are celebrated. It is also a time for the healing of quarrels. This is especially associated with the feast at the end of Ramadan. It is customary to greet one's friends by saying, "If I have done you any wrong, please forgive me."

A lady in Djakarta put this into practice. She reached the conclusion that the resentment she held against a friend was in itself wrong — however deeply she felt that she had been injured. She decided to take the opportunity of the feast to set it right on her side. She went to mutual friends and said, "You know how it is between us. Help me." Together they went to the house, and her companions supported her while she apologised for the ill will she had harboured.

The Turkish editor Ahmet Emin Yalman relates a similar incident.

God forgives, and so must we. That is the purpose of the Bairams (feasts). Their function is to be an occasion of reconciliation. This is effective. For instance, when I was engaged, there was a division in my fiancee's family. I noticed that a certain relative was never seen in their company, though I did not know the cause. When the next feast came, the family went to call on the man, there was a sweet reconciliation and all was well.

"I must clean my heart," is a phrase often heard in connection with this kind of action.

The instruction in the Quran about Ramadan is as follows. It is reproduced from the leaflet sent out for Ramadan 1974 by the Islamic Cultural Centre, London, giving the times of sunrise and sunset in different cities in the United Kingdom, for the benefit of those keeping the Fast.

Ramadan is the (month) in which was sent down the Quran, as a Guide to mankind. Also clear (signs), for guidance and for judgment (between right and wrong). So every one of you who is present (at his home) during mat month should spend it fasting. But if anyone is ill, or on a journey, the prescribed period (should be made up) by days later. God intends every facility for you. He does not want to put you to difficulties. (He wants you) to complete the prescribed period and to glorify Him.

The feast that follows Ramadan lasts three days. It is known as the *'Eid-ul-fitr* (Feast of the Breaking of the Fast).

Payment Due : It is at the end of Ramadan that the yearly payment of alms or poor-tax (*Zakat)* is made. This is defined as "an obligation prescribed by God on those Muslims, men and women, who possess enough means, to distribute a certain percentage of their annual savings or capital in goods or money among the poor and needy."

The basic traditional percentage is *2½* per cent. In recent years *Zakat* has played a large part in plans for an Islamic economic order and a tax system in line with Islamic tradition.

Proclamation of Human Rights

The fifteenth century of the Islamic era opened on 9 November 1980 AD, (1 Muharram 1401 AH). The year before and the year following this date were a period of intense activity throughout the Muslim world. Behind the turbulent political conflicts of the time Muslim scholars, writers and economists, as well as many of the rank and file of practising Muslims in different walks of life, were seeking to deepen their understanding of their faith. It was an opportunity, said Dr. Inamullah Khan, Secretary General of the World Muslim Congress, "to take stock of the gains and losses of the Muslims in the 1400 years. We should not only talk about our achievements but also our failures and the pitfalls into which we have been falling ... As Islam wants to build an egalitarian and a humanitarian society the two-year Hijra celebration should be for correcting past mistakes in all fields of life, be it educational, cultural, social, not ignoring the very important part that economics play in modern life today."

To bring an eternal message to the attention of mankind involves a continuing battle to clarify its meaning and to purify its expression, in the lives and in the statements of Muslim believers. Two such statements were issued by the Islamic Council of Europe: the *Universal Islamic Declaration,* April 1980, which stressed that "a universal order can be created only on the basis of a universal faith and not by serving the gods of race, colour, territory or wealth"; followed by the *Universal Islamic Declaration of Human Rights,* September 1981, "based on the Quran and the Sunnah and compiled by eminent Muslim scholars, jurists and representatives of Islamic movements and thought."

The Declaration follows the lines of the Declaration of Human Rights, issued in 1948 by the General Assembly of the United Nations. It has 23 clauses:—the Right to Life, to Freedom, to Equality, to Justice, to Fair Trial etc. There is a basic difference of approach. The United Nations Declaration starts with "the recognition of the inherent dignity and of the equal and inalienable rights of all members of the human family." The Muslim Declaration looks to "the Divine source and sanction of these rights." "We, as Muslims, believe ... that each one of us is under a bounden duty to spread the teachings of Islam by word and deed, and indeed in all gentle ways, and to make them effective not only in our individual lives but also in the society around us."

The Rights of Minorities are included. "The Quranic principle, 'There is no compulsion in religion', shall govern the religious rights of non-Muslim minorities." The "Right to found a family" (common to both Declarations) is followed by a section on the rights of married women. Explanatory notes point out that throughout the Declaration "person" refers to both the male and female sexes: and also that each of the Rights expressed carries a corresponding duty.

> "This is a declaration for mankind, a guidance and instruction to those who fear God."
>
> Quran: Sura 3: 138 Al-Imran

A Note on the Illustrations : The oneness of God and the essential unity of His creation are basic to Islamic art, as they are to all Muslim life and thought. This is reflected in an exactness of mathematical design which gives serenity in architecture and undergrades all the arts.

Light is one: yet when broken by a prism it reveals every shade of colour. The millions of mankind are all equal — all sons of Adam, made of clay - yet in that equality there is scope for the differences of human personality, and never in all history have two individuals been identical. So it is with design: mathematically perfect, yet infinitely varied.

This perfection of pattern is given life in different ways: by the flowing lines of the Arabic script, drawn with the master skill of the calligraphed; by the floral designs that recall the "gardens through which rivers flow" so often described in the Quran; by the reshaping of triangle, square, and circle swept, as it were, by the movement of wind or water.

12

Scientific Approach

The study of the rise and decline of intellectual movements is a fascinating and very instructive aspect of the history of scholarship. The matter which surprises most about Islamic civilization is, that in spite of the fact that learning and inquiry were the integral part of the faith, the period of truly creative scientific activity was very short-lived. With one major thrust the scholars and scientists in Islam reached the meridian of their scientific and philosophical achievements; but then there was a sudden-decline. The short period of widespread creative activity was followed by almost permanent intellectual stagnation. Therefore, it would be interesting and intellectually rewarding to search for factors and forces which led to this unfortunate transformation.

Scholarly Percepts

The closing of the doors of ijtihad (independent thinking) was the single most important factor which killed the spirit of inquiry. History of Islamic civilization is strewn with countless political and intellectual calamities, but the one which had extremely disastrous effects, was the suspension of independent reasoning. Since Islam was 'not merely a manifesto for the spiritual salvation of man, but was also a compact code of conduct for all areas of worldly existence, the Quran, and the Prophet, had made special provision for the use of independent reasoning for resolving complex problems of the Muslim community.

Moreover, Islam claimed that it was the final and eternal message of rectitude. In order to fulfil this mission it had to have built-in flexibility so that it could amicably adjust itself to the changing conditions of life. Reason was applauded as the priceless gift of God, which had to be used for the betterment and uplift of the moral and spiritual standards. Innovation was to be respected as long as it did not conflict with the fundamentals of the faith.

The Quran says :

> And if any tidings, whether of safety or fear, come unto them, they noise it abroad whereas if they had referred it to the messenger and such of them as are in authority, those among them who are able to think out the matter would have known it.

According to Ahmad Galwash the word in the Quranic verse is yastanbitana which is derived from *Istanbat* meaning search of hidden meaning through the effective use of human reason. There is also an authentic saying of the Prophet, which has been frequently quoted in support of Ijtihad. The tradition is as follows; He (the Prophet) was sending a judge to take charge of legal affairs in Al-Yeman, and asked him on what he would base his legal decisions "On the Quran" he replied. "But if that contains nothing to the purpose?" "Then upon your usage." "But if that also fails you?" "Then I will follow my own opinion." And the Prophet approved his purpose. Ahmad Galwash defined ijtihad as "The exercise of judgement to meet the new circumstances". A renowned Muslim scholar of Pakistan, Abul Ala Maududi, has given the following definition of the term:

> The whole of this legislative process which makes the legal system of Islam dynamic and makes its development and evolution in the changing circumstances possible results from a particular type of academic research and intellectual effort, which in the terminology of Islam is called ijtihad. Literally the word ijtihad means to put in the maximum effort to ascertain in a given problem or issuing the injunction of Islam and its real intent.

Vesey-Fitzgerald has explained the concept of ijtihad in Islam as follows :

> The mujtahids are the earliest expounders and architects of the law; and ijtihad (the word literally means hard-striving or strenuousness) is the mental discipline of their profession. The word connotes a power of making law, of deducing new principles and applying them to the new facts. In theory, as we have already said this mental discipline resulted in the discovery of the law of God on the basis of revelation according to the accepted categories of the usul-ul-fiqh.

There is no precise historical evidence to show how, where and by whom the doors of ijtihad were finally closed. The opinion commonly held among scholars is that in the evolution of Islamic theology there reached a stage when learned theologians under threat from the rulers or for other selfish reasons were trying to put superimposed or distorted interpretations over Islamic principles. In this way ijtihad became a tool to justify the nefarious designs of the rulers. So the scholars thought that if the process of interpretation was allowed to continue, the time would come when in the bewildering maze of interpretations the true spirit of Islam would be lost. The only way to stop such a tragedy was to declare that the era of independent reasoning in Islam had ended and Islamic Shariah was perfected for all times to come.

The infiltration of the Hellenic thought and unabated passion of Muslim philosophers to Hellenize Islam was also considered a powerful threat to the faith which might have compelled the religious scholars to decry independent reasoning. Many Muslim scholars of the Greek thought had adopted duplicity of attitude to stave off popular criticism. Among their own circle they would profess faith in the sophisticated doctrines of the Hellenic philosophy, but while interacting with the masses they used to advocate the superiority of revelation, or would interpret regulations of Shariah in a manner that they would not seem contrary to the Greek thought.

After closing the doors of ijtihad, the Muslims became a community of muqalladin (blind followers). Search for precedents, and memorizing quotations from the predecessors became the hallmark of scholarships. Later in Islamic history occasionally a stray voice could be heard in defense of ijtihad, but on the whole the kingdom of thought and letters remained denuded of creativity. The most challenging and outstanding defense of ijtihad was done by Shah Wali Ullah, who ranks among the greatest religious scholars of Islam on the Indo-Pakistan sub-continent. His treatise entitled Iqd-ul-Jadid fi Ahkamal-Ijtihad wal Taqlid was a powerful effort to reintroduce independent thinking in Islam. It is only in the twentieth century however that scholars in the Muslim countries, have seriously advocated ijtihad as means for the rejuvenation of Islamic civilization. Muhammad Abduh, the late Grand Mufti of Egypt and Sir Muhammad Iqbal the poet philosopher of Pakistan, were the landmark figures of this century, who repeatedly warned the Muslims that unless independent reasoning was once again introduced as a basic ingredient of research and enquiry, Islam could not be salvaged out of its present day socio-political difficulties.

Recent Explanation : A more recent explanation of Ijtihad has been done by Muhammad Asad in the following words:

> And this is where ijtihadi legislation rightfully comes in. To be more precise the legitimate field of the community's law-making activity presses (a) details in cases and situations where the Shariah provides a general principle but no detailed ruling and (b) principles and details with regard to matters which are Mubah that is, not covered by Shariah laws at all. It is this method that the Quran has referred to in the words (for every one of you we have ordained a Divine Law and an open road). This Divine Law (Shariah) outlines the area within which Muslim life may develop, within this area an 'open road' (Minhaj) for temporal legislature which would cover contingencies deliberately left untouched by the *nasus* of the Quran and Sunnah.

Sometimes ijtihad is divided into two categories. Absolute Ijtihad (Ijtihad Mutlaq) which means independent reasoning on critical issues. It can lead to innovative solution to the problems which are new, and for which there are no precedents in fiqh (jurisprudence). In this process one can bypass the established schools of thought, and the sanctified consensus called (Ijmah) of the *Ulama*. The second category is labelled as Relative Ijtihad, which is merely rejuvenation or revivification of the old principles of Shariah to handle new situations.

Even a cursory review of the history of Muslim scholarship leaves no doubt that the closing of the doors of Ijtihad was a major educational tragedy in Islam. The conditions of learning became so stagnant, and the climate of thought so reactionary, that not to speak of creating something absolutely new for the advancement of knowledge, scholars allowed the existing fund of religious and scientific knowledge to stagnate to an extent that much of it became obsolete. Instead of being of any help in resolving the problems it became an insurmountable roadblock to any kind of dynamic thinking.

Rise of Scholars : The rise of *Ulama* (religious scholars) as a very closed and powerful elitist group is also listed as a major factor which created numerous barriers to independence of research and expansion of knowledge in Islam.

The social and intellectual history of Islam shows that during the first hundred years of its existence the *Ulama* (scholars) did not acquire any significant role in the Muslim society. One reason could be that during this period there were large numbers of people who had either direct association with the Prophet, the sole fountain head of knowledge, or they were instructed by those who had the privilege of imbibing wisdom directly from him. Historians of Islam would say that as long as Sahaba (Companion of the Prophet, and the younger generation closely associated with them, lived, the need for scholars as a special class did not arise. Moreover, during this period most of the knowledge was communicated by word of mouth, and there was not enough written material to impart it through organized instruction. Political chaos, resulting from internecine tribal feuds could be another factor which might have hindered the growth of formal religious instruction.

Cultivation of Knowledge : With the passage of time, however, as the earlier generations of Muslims died, need was felt of putting in writing that which was formerly being communicated by word of mouth. Territorial expansion, and contacts with Byzantum, and

Persian Civilizations showed that for intellectual and spiritual health of society, cultivation of knowledge, through formal educational structures was a basic necessity. Moreover, to accommodate new socio political realities Laws of Islam were being interpreted and reinterpreted so fast, that without expert guidance it was difficult to know the true spirit of religion. It is also to be kept in mind that knowledge and learning thrive only under conditions of peace and prosperity. The earlier period of Islamic history was racked with internal feuds and external wars, and in that state of chronic instability nothing could be accomplished in terms of intellectual refinement.

Educational Development

The rise of Abbasides (749-1258 A.D.) marked the sudden upsurge of intellectual activity. Centralization of Caliphate authority, consolidation and streamlining of administration under Persian administrators, who rose to high positions under the new dynasty, opened an era of peace and order in the kingdom. The result was that under the liberal royal patronage, for the first time, art, science, letters and philosophy got a chance to flourish widely among the populace. The introduction of Greek learning made knowledge more complex and need was felt to organize formal institutes to impart education. It was in these circumstances that learning and teaching became a profession, and *Ulamas* (scholars) emerged as a separate professional class in the Muslim society. Its members went through rigorous training and prolonged induction into numerous branches of secular and religious knowledge, and after the completion of studies became the religious mentors of the community. The masses in general remained ignorant, and the same was true of the rulers who had the ability to govern and administer, but lacked understanding of the religious law which, in theory at least, was the basis of state legislation. Most of them lacked the competence to know the exact meanings of these laws, and very often even if they understood the legal and moral implications of Shariah, dynastic squabbles, court intrigues, wars and pursuit of pleasures would not leave enough time with them to watch the implementation of religious law. All these factors resulted in the emergence of *Ulama* as a class of specialists whose guidance was constantly sought by the rulers and the ruled.

Islam had abolished priestcraft as a profession, but in due course *Ulama* became a powerful aristocracy of knowledge, and they remained so for a long time in the history of Islamic civilization. Their influence and authority further increased, when numerous institutions, borrowed from conquered lands, needed their approval in the form of consensus (Ijma) as specialists of religious law.

The Ijma (consensus of the learned) has been a subject of acute controversy in the history of Muslim jurisprudence. In view of its being one of the major sources of legitimacy, it was a very powerful weapon in the hands of the religious class to maintain its supremacy. Claude Cahen calls it 'the dictatorship of the *Ulama*' in the Muslim society. Their influence in the Muslim society, however, was not steady or uniform. It used to vary from dynasty to dynasty and sometimes from one king to another in the same dynasty. For instance, during the Mutizala supremacy under Al-Mamun, the *Ulama*s were eclipsed by philosophers, but immediately after the decline of the Mutazalite doctrine, the *Ulama* reemerged as a potent social and political force in the Abbaside kingdom.

Many of them became top administrators of the state, and occupied important positions at the seats of higher learning and in Judiciary. As Muftis (Jurists) they gave Fatwas (Authoritative Interpretations) to determine the right and wrong of public policy and as Qadis (Judges) they presided over courts of law to resolve religious disputes and other litigations relating to civil and criminal justice in Islam. Very often they also administered charitable endowments for the general benefit of the community.

Afaf Lutfi Al Sayyid Marsot has given the following reasons for the expansion of the role of *Ulama* in a Muslim society.

Basic Function : The basic functions of the *Ulama* were to teach Islam and interpret, that is to be the teachers, lawyers, qadis, and religious mentors. But since almost every aspect of daily life was regulated by the Shariah (holy law) or required a ruling in the light of Shariah the services of the *Ulama* became necessary in every walk of life, political, social and economic, and they were called upon to play a vast variety of parts.

In due course the *Ulama* because of their all-pervading influence almost became a ruling class. One thing fortunate, however, was that this class did not become hereditary. Anybody irrespective of caste or colour, who had attained a certain level of scholarship in religious laws could be recruited into their ranks.

Constructive Role : The history of *Ulama*s shows that as a class at one stage they played a very constructive role. Some of them were bold enough to uncover the fallacies of the Muslim rulers. They acted as a loyal opposition to the government in power. They were the custodians of the religious laws and were expected to keep its fundamentals free from spiritual and moral contamination. They were consulted by Sultans practically in all matters relating to religion and politics.

While each Muslim was obliged to tread the path of rectitude, *Ulamas* installed themselves as the custodians of religious morality for the society as a whole. They were expected to tame those propensities among individuals which produced heresies, and endangered the purity of canonical law.

Their role, as the enlightened critics of the rulers, however, did not last for a long time. Wisdom and knowledge did not save them from the corrupting influences of wealth and power. They exploited the widespread and deepseated religious sentiments of the Muslim masses—a tendency which unfortunately became the permanent feature of the *Ulamas* as a class during the later periods of Islamic history. This deterioration in the standard of integrity among religious scholars was a common topic of discussion in the literature on Islamic ethics. They became hirelings or parasites of the rulers. Al-Ghazzali who was an eye witness to the unholy alliance between the princes and the *Ulamas* made the following remarks:

> And the third thing to avoid is not to mix with princes and Sultans, and not to see them, for seeing them and sitting with them is great mischief, and if you are impelled to do this, avoid praising them and commending them, for Allah The Exalted is angered when an oppressor and an impious man is praised, and whoever has called for the lengthening of their lives has delighted that Allah be disobeyed in his land.

Keddie has made the following comments on the role of *Ulamas* in Egypt after 1500 A.D. :

> An important role of the *Ulama* has been to justify the *status quo* and to guard both themselves and secular rulers from attacks by the dissatisfied or dispossessed. They formed an important part of the ideological underpinning of the rulers, needed to justify submission to existing landlords and government agents. They thus helped perpetuate the hierarchical and traditional order of things by teaching submission even to unjust rulers and maintaining that the hierarchical social order was both natural and good.

It was not only in Egypt, but in the rest of the Muslim kingdoms also, that the religious scholars showed marked signs of degeneration in their caliber and moral integrity. Inducements of wealth, and lust for power made the vast majority of them merely lackeys of the rulers. In theory they still continued to enjoy the privileges which had hallowed their role in the past, but in practice the latter image was only a pale reflection of their former grandeur.

They loved *status quo,* and would not hesitate to sacrifice all their convictions at the alter of expediency. Many of them suffered permanently from the crisis of the conscience, because there was a conspicuous gap between the theory and practice of their profession. In theory they were still a beacon light of prudence and religious wisdom for the masses, but in practice their knowledge had become shallow. Constant dependence on rulers killed their creativity and independent thinking.

They had acquired the reputation as time-servers, opportunists, and bearers of double moral standards. By repeated compromises with the glaring breaches of the law they had forfeited the confidence of the masses. Ariel Heyd has given the following picture of the eighteenth century *Ulama* in the Ottoman Empire, which was more or less typical of their class in most Muslim kingdoms in the Middle Ages.

Lack of Unity : Lack of unity among them was one of the fundamental causes for this. Not only, as mentioned above, were the leading '*Ulama*' families and high Mollas separated by a deep gulf from the rank and file, but within the leadership itself the struggle for promotion to the highest positions led to constant intrigues. These became particularly violent when in the eighteenth century an excessively large number of Muderrises and Mollas were appointed because of favouritism and nepotism, thus increasing the number of candidates for the few top positions in the corps. Hence it should not be surprising that a Molla was often willing to yield to the Sultan's wishes and even agree to innovations of Western origin, as the price for gaining ascendancy over a rival. Moreover, the prestige of the '*Ulama*' had declined greatly during preceding generations because of the growing corruption in their ranks. Posts were given or even sold to unsuitable men, such as followers and servants of high '*Ulama*'.

In some cases people who were not even able to read their names were appointed Qadis. The venality of the judges had become proverbial. While in olden times, a leading 'Alim' lamented, people came to the Qadi to complain of oppression by the governor and his subordinates, it was now the other way round. Instead of the '*Ulama*' restraining the Government from infringing upon the holy law, the Sultan had to issue innumerable Firmans warning the judges not to violate the Shariah.

Since to be an Alim (religious scholar) brought a lot of power and prestige, it was the desire of every young man to enter the ranks of this profession. The result was that scholarship became a playground for fortune-hunters. In short, when Muslim scholars became functionaries of the state, they lost their independence, and in order to maintain their position, very often they had to sell their conscience. When scholarship became a marketable commodity it lost much of its pristine dignity, and its custodians then naturally became a subject of adverse comments and popular ridicule. In theory, from platform and pulpit, religious scholars continued to preach in a convincing manner that 'pen is mightier than the sword,' but in practice the pen was subservient to the one who wielded the sword.

Another possible cause for the decline of scientific enquiry in Islam could be the ultimate triumph of the science of theology over other sciences. It was noticed earlier, great scientists like Abu Nasr al Farabi (258/870-339/950), Abu Raihan-al-Beruni (362/973-462/1051) and Abul Walid Muhammad ibn Rushd (520/1126-595/1198) in spite of their great passion for science, and deep interest in rationalism, never questioned at least publicly, the importance of religion as the ultimate source of knowledge and enlightenment. But the typical orthodox circles never trusted them, and a simmering controversy between religion and science remained an integral part of the scholarly debate and discussion in every part of the Muslim world. It was however religion which in the end won the battle, and science was condemned as something which produced agnostics and sowed seeds of distrust and doubt among the simpleminded people. The theologian who led this triumphant crusade was Al-Ghazzali. In his writings he launched a scathing criticism against scientists and philosophers.

Doyen of Scholars : Even a cursory glance at the history of Islamic scholarship can show that Al-Ghazzali had the largest following in the Muslim lands. He earned the reputation of being the doyen of religious scholars and his encyclopaedic production *Ihya-ul-Ulum al Din*—(The Revivification of Religious Science) has been a popular textbook of theology throughout the sweep of centuries and his fame as a leading exponent of truly Islamic point of view has remained undiminished. In the religious literature of Islam he is generally referred as *Hujjat-ul-Islam* (Proof of Islam). It is an agnomen which is not given to any other theologian in Islam. In his writings he vehemently criticized the rationalist philosophers who preceded him and called them unbelievers. Aristotle and Plato in his opinion were unbelievers and all Muslim scholars who were influenced by them were also thrown out of the fold of Islam.

We must therefore reckon as unbelievers both these philosophers themselves and their followers among the Islamic philosophers such as Ibn Sina, al Farabi and others.

This criticism is greatly elaborated by him in his famous work entitled *Tahafut al Falasifa.* (The Incoherence of the Philosophers of the Philosophers). In it he unleashed biting criticism against practically every aspect of scientific thought which in his opinion, cast any doubt on the fundamentals of religion. Abu Rushd wrote a strong reply in support of science in his treatise entitled "The Incoherence of the Incoherence", but it failed to dislodge Al-Ghazzali's influence from vast majority of Muslims. Al-Ghazzali had integrated various streams of Islamic thought so skilfully and with such knowledge and insight that it was difficult to refute his argument easily. He blended philosophy with religion in such a manner that supremacy of the religion could not be questioned. His *Ihyal-Ulum al Din* became the most popular book after the Quran. One thirteenth century writer pointed out if all the books on the religion of Islam were destroyed, Ihya alone was sufficient to make up the loss. For a devout Muslim it remained a treasure house of eternal spiritual wisdom and made Shariah the most desirable way of harvesting goodness in life. The victory of the science of theology was not an unmixed blessing. Instead of doing some creative thinking to maintain the dynamic character of the doctrine, theologians wasted their talent and energies in endless debate and discussion on trivial issues regarding grammar, choice of words, use of terms, syntax and other etymological rules.

The dependence of the scholar on the patronage of their royal masters, in due course became another factor which proved extremely detrimental to the advancement of knowledge. In fact, it became the major source of corruption among them and ultimately eroded their integrity. The tradition of the scholars depending entirely on the funds and facilities provided by the rulers developed very early in Islamic history. Academies and schools, where secular and religious knowledge was imparted, were built and maintained at state expense. In times of peace and prosperity, or of decay and anarchy, the Muslim rulers were always anxious to extend their patronage to scholars and men of science.

Al-Mamun (815-833) the Abbaside Caliph established his famous academy called "Bait-ul-Hikma" (House of Wisdom) at Baghdad which became one of the major sources of the dissemination of philosophical knowledge in the Muslim empire. The history of this "House of Wisdom" shows that the scholars associated with it were mostly non-Arab and its library consisted mostly of Greek and Persian books. Later the Persian rulers of Buwaid dynasty and Fatimid rulers of Egypt established similar academies, where instruction was imparted in every conceivable branch of human knowledge.

Islamic University : Just a quarter of a century before the sack of Baghdad by Halaqu Khan a university called Mustansiriyah was founded in this city in 1234 A.D. G. Le Strange has given the following comprehensive account of the intellectual climate and physical environments of this institution :

> We are told that in outward appearance, in stateliness of ornament and sumptuousness of furniture, in spaciousness and in the wealth of its pious foundations, the Mustansiriyah surpassed everything that had previously been seen in Islam. It contained four separate law-schools, one for each of the orthodox sects of the Sunnis, with a professor at the head of each, who had seventy-five students (faqih) in his charge, to whom he gave instruction gratis. The four professors each received a monthly salary, and to each of the three hundred students one gold dinar a month was assigned. The great kitchen of the college further provided daily rations of bread and meat to all the inmates. According to Ibn-al-Furat there was a library in the Mustansiriyah with rare books treating of the various sciences, so arranged that the students could easily consult them, and those who wished could copy these manuscripts, pens and paper being supplied by the establishment. Lamps for the students and a due provision of olive oil for lighting up the college are also mentioned, likewise storage places for cooling and drinking water; and in the great entrance hall stood a clock doubtless some form of clepsydra, announcing the appointed times of prayer, and marking the lapse of the hours by day and by night. Inside the college a bath house . . . was erected for the special use of the students, and a hospital ... to which a physician was appointed, whose duty it was to visit the place every morning, prescribing for those who were sick; and there were great store-chambers in the *Madrasa* provided with all requisites of food, drink, and medicines.

Network of Libraries : Widespread network of large and well-equipped private and public libraries, and flourishing book trade also provided eloquent testimony to the strength and calibre of intellectual activity that characterized practically every Muslim kingdom. Book collection was a great hobby with the aristocracy and an important symbol of its social prestige. Palaces of the princes and chambers of aristocrats boasted of vast collections of books on all subjects. In due course mosques and madrasas also started having libraries of their own.

"There was, however, no uniform pattern of royal patronage to religious and secular knowledge. It used to differ from ruler to ruler. It mostly depended on the personal proclivities of the patron. If he was inclined to rational and abstract philosophical thought, his leanings towards secular knowledge would be obvious, but if he was a devout orthodox Muslim, religious learning definitely would interest him more. For instance, under Mamun, secular and rational knowledge had precedence because the ruler himself was a staunch supporter of rationalism. Similarly under Seljuk rulers when defenders of religious orthodoxy like Nizam-ul-Mulk came at the helm of the affairs, government's primary concern was to support and strengthen the instruction of religious science, Nizam-ul-Mulk during his term as Prime Minister of the most powerful Muslim kingdom of the day, established a network of madrasas. (religious schools), the most important of which were in Baghdad and Nishapur. They were generally attached to the mosques and their objective was to propagate true Islamic learning so that defenses against heresies could be fortified.

Scholars and students in these schools received government stipends and the state also provided financial and administrative support to these institutes. Abu zubayr, a famous Arab traveller, visited Baghdad in 1184 A.D. and found that in the eastern part of the city alone there were thirty madrasas. He has given the following description of these colleges:

> The ordinary mosques in both the eastern and the western parts cannot be estimated, much less counted. The colleges are, about thirty, and all in the eastern part, and there is not one of them that does not outdo the finest palace. The greatest and the most famous of them is the Nizamiyah which was built by Nizam-ul-Mulk and restored in 1506 A.D. These colleges have large endowments and tied properties that give sustenance to the faqihs who teach in them and dispensed on the scholars.

Over and above the facilities provided for the cultivation of knowledge, each Muslim ruler had an overwhelming desire to adorn his court with renowned scholars. He provided them with pensions, and gave free access to state libraries and observatories. The scholars in turn gave him medical and astrological advice, and were very often instrumental in building weapons of war. They also helped him to resolve problems of public policy which needed knowledge and prudence.

Accumulation of Talent : Kings vied with each other in their efforts to accumulate talent and scholarship in their courts. Luster and radiance of scholarship around the throne was considered essential to increase the international reputation and prestige of the dynasty. For physicians, scientists, poets and artists attachment to the court was a coveted prize, because this was a shortcut to professional fame and social prestige. This close relationship between rulers and Muslim scholars remained a permanent feature of the history of Muslim scholarship.

Practically all the leading scientists and philosophers of Islam were attached to the royal courts. Al-Kindi was attached to the court of Caliph Mamun, whom he served in various capacities, the most important of them being that of a consultant and tutor to the princes. This opportunity had tremendous bearing on Al-Kindi's achievements, because it enabled him to meet the best minds in the realm, and he was able to use the biggest and the most useful libraries of the Muslim world.

Fakhr-ad-Din Razi was attached to the court of Sultan Muhammad Ibn Tukush surnamed Khwarizm Shah in Khorasan.

Ibn Sina spent most of his professional life as a courtier. His career in this respect was very adventuresome. Reputation and ambition took him to various courts. It would be interesting to reproduce the detailed account of his intellectual and professional adventures in various princely courts recorded by Ibn-Khallikan.

Unmatched Talent : The emir Nuh Ibn Mansur as-Samani, prince of Khorasan, having heard, during a fit of sickness, of Abu Ali Ibn Sina talent, sent for him and was restored to health under his treatment. Abu Ali was then received into the favour of that prince, and he frequented his library, which was of incomparable richness, as it contained not only all the celebrated works which are found in the hands of the public, but others not to be met with anywhere else, and of which not only the titles but the contents were unknown. Here Abu Ali discovered treatises on the sciences of the ancients and other subjects the essence of which he extracted, and with the greater part of which sciences he became acquainted. It happened, some time afterwards, that this library was consumed by fire, and Abu Ali remained the sole depository of the knowledge which it contained.

Some persons even said that it was he who set fire to the library, being induced to do so for the reason that he alone was acquainted with its contents, and that he wished to pass off as his own the information which he had there acquired. He had not reached his eighteenth year when he had completely mastered all the sciences to the attainment of which he had directed his studies. At the age of twenty-two, he lost his father, in the vicissitudes of whose fortune he had partaken, and with whom he acted as admil for the Sultan. When the affairs of the Samanide dynasty fell into disorder, Abu Ali left Bukhara and proceeded to Korkanj, the capital of Khwarizm, where he frequented the court of Khwarizm Shah Ali Ibn Mamuri Ibn Muhammad. He wore the dress of a jurisconsult with the talisman, and obtained a monthly stipend for his support. He afterwards departed from Korkanj and visited Nasa, Abiward Tus, and other cities, during which period he paid his court to the emir Shams-al-Maali Kabus Ibn Washmakir. When Kabus was arrested and confined in the castle where he died, (a circumstance of which we shall give the particulars in his life,) Abu Ali went to Kihistan, where he had a severe illness, and then returned to Jurjan. From Jurjan Abu Ali proceeded to Rai and was attached to the court of Majd-ad Dawlat son of Fakhral Dawlat. He went afterwards to Kazwin and then to Hamadan where he became wazir to Shamsal-Dawlat.

Similarly Ibn Rushd after the completion of his studies as a physician and jurist was attached to courts at Corodova and Marrakush, and under Al-Mansur (1186-1199) he was given the highest rank among the courtiers. The same can be said practically about the rest of the scholars and scientists who have earned a permanent place in the history of Islamic civilization.

The relationship between scholars and their royal patrons, however, was never smooth or peaceful.

Fortunes of the scholar were linked with the destiny of the ruling dynasty. A change of ruler would very often mean humiliation, imprisonment and even death for all courtiers including the scholars. The result was that treachery and intrigue were the common features of the court life. Scholars were chased in and out of courts frequently. Many of them seemed to be fortune hunters as they moved from court to court either in search of better worldly gains or looking for safety against a whimsical master. Naturally such instability must have hampered the creative energies of many a Muslim scholar. Moreover in spite of the greatest of efforts, their objectivity must have been marred by views of the patron. Such constraints must have dissuaded many scholars from uncovering truth with confidence and integrity. Under these circumstances the scope of independent thinking was considerably curtailed.

Holy Prophet's Tradition

The Prophet had said that 'the learned are the heirs of the Prophets,' but as ill-luck would have it most of them in Islam became hirelings of the heirs to the thrones. They were expected to be men of integrity, piety and independent thinking. Their main job was to be the moral and religious mentors of the community. Dispensation of truth and wisdom, without fear and favour, was the cardinal characteristic of their profession. These ideals, however, were shattered to a vast extent, once the scholars and scientists had placed themselves under intellectual captivity of the royal patronage. They fell low in popular prestige.

Although dependence on royal patronage was a universal trend among Muslim scholars, occasionally a disenchanted soul used to raise a voice of protest against the baneful effects of such a practice. In his Revivification of the Sciences of Religion, Al-Ghazzali unrolled a discussion on the relationship of scholars and rulers and his conclusion was that dependence of scholars on princes was a pernicious practice. It was a source of moral and religious corruption, and against self-respect and independence which distinguished a scholar from other human beings. Knowledge in his opinion was a sacred trust which should not be easily betrayed and traded with ordinary worldly gains.

The courts of princes, in his opinion were great temptations which enticed scholars to tell lies and practice duplicity. They supported policies and decisions which they knew to be untrue, and against reason and religion.

It was for this reason that Al-Ghazzali advised the *Ulama* to stay away from the princes as much as they could. In his *Nasihat ul Maluk* (Counsel for Kings) he says :

> Know that you can have three sorts of relations with princes, governors, and oppressors. The first and worst is that you visit them, the second and better is that they visit you, and the third and surest that you stay far from them, so that neither you see them nor they see you—There is also the Hadith 'The *Ulama* are God's trustees for the servants of God, so long as they do not mix with the rulers, and if they do that, they have betrayed the prophets; beware of them and stay far from them'. Sufyan-al-Thawri said "In Hell there is a valley entirely inhabited by Quran readers who used to visit kings." Muhammad Ibn Salama said, "A fly on a pile of excrement is finer than a Quran reader at the door of those people."

Rumi, the famous mystic and poet of Iran also pointed out that receiving robes and favours from princes was derogatory to the dignity of scholarship.

Another possible corrupting influence in the history of Muslim scholarship could be the tendency among Muslim scholars to be slavishly subservient to the precedent. Students spent considerable part of their educational career in searching passages from the writings of the leading authors of the past. This wasteful intellectual exercise must have frustrated the abilities, and crippled the creative urges of many a brilliant mind. Scholars spent countless hours of patient and anxious research to find out some evidence in support of their thesis from the writings of their forerunners. The result was that most of their works were crowded with quotations and references from the past, which made their reading very often an insufferable intellectual drudgery. Probably they were inhibited against creative thinking, and whenever anything new struck them they would like to shift its responsibility on someone else.

As the distance between the earlier writers and later scholars increased this passion for authoritative references to former works kept on consuming more and more time of the researchers.

Heaps of Books : With the passage of time the volume of literature in each field of human knowledge had increased so much, that it became difficult for a student to sort out the real from the spurious. Year after year he burnt his midnight candle to examine and assimilate truth out of the bewildering maze of interpretations and distortions, which very often left him confused and frustrated. Historical perspectives provide richness and depth to research, but it should be only means to an end and not an end in itself. Unfortunately for most Muslim scholars search for historical evidence became an end in itself. The tragedy was further compounded when some of the authorities of the past were permanently declared to be sacrosanct, and whose ideas were accepted uncritically. This kind of captivity of the past adversely affected the creative ability. In a dynamic and creative civilization, authorities which have outlived their usefulness, are always replaced by new ones. This creates an atmosphere of intellectual freedom, and creates willingness to question the retention of such propositions which no longer help men to resolve their problems of life. In the history of Muslim scholarship, such an attitude, however, did not last for a long time. After the initial outburst of creativity, the majority of later scholars stagnated because they failed to replace the old authorities when their thesis had become defunct and inoperative. This intellectual tyranny of the past was a major calamity which wrecked originality in Muslim scholarship.

The discrepancies which stemmed out from fruitless search for authorities, ' and the blockade of mind which resulted from undue reverence to their expositions, were further aggravated by faulty documentation. In the absence of printing, the great works of scholarship were circulated in manuscript form in various parts of the Muslim world. Copies were made by a professional copyist called (the Katib). Although these copyists were professionals, and fairly knowledgeable in various sciences, still in making copies of manuscripts there were always unavoidable omissions and additions. Moreover scholars had the habit of writing comments on the margins of the books, and as the works passed from generation to generation, at some stage, the reader could confuse the marginal comments of the other readers with the text of the original author. Very often at one place, there would be only one manuscript and the researcher had no opportunity of comparing its contents with another's copy. These limitations created considerable confusion and hindered dispassionate and objective research. The world of scholarship in Islam was also plagued with considerable plagerism, and it is mentioned that authors used to indulge in numerous unethical practices in humiliating and denigrating their rivals. Some of them used to write bad books and attribute them to great authors so that their reputation could be ruined. Very often, renowned writers in order to avoid carping criticism of vindictive and unfair critics, used to write anonymous books.

Intellectual Dishonesty : Obviously this kind of intellectual dishonesty multiplied difficulties of research in natural and social sciences manifold. Research workers always remained suspicious regarding their sources, and spent a lot of time in sorting out genuine information from the doubtful one. The absence of printing not only greatly increased the chances of this intellectual dishonesty, but also created scarcity of books. Muslim scholars always complained about the non-availability of the books, the serious-minded and honest among them had to spend a considerable part of their life in travelling from place to place in search of manuscripts which were distributed over wide areas of the Muslim world. This inability persisted for a long time, and must have been a tremendous strain on the time and resources of the authors.

Bibliography

Abdullah, Muhammad : *Islamic Prayers,* Idara Ishaat-e-Diniyat, New Delhi, 1999.

Acquinas, St. Thomas : *The Political Ideas of Islam,* Hafner Publishing Company, New York, 1953.

Adair and Yazbeck Haddad : *Islamic Values in the United States,* Oxford, New York, 1997.

Adams, C.C. : *Islam and Modernism in Egypt,* Oxford University Press, New York, 1953.

Ahmad, Khurshid : *Islam : its Meaning and Message,* Islamic Council of Europe, London, 1976.

Ahmad, M.M.Z. : *Mystical Tendencies in Islam in the Light of the Quran and Traditions*, Daya Publishing House, Delhi, 1986.

Ahmad, Moinuddin : *Religions of Mankind,* Kitab Bhavan, New Delhi, 1994.

Antonio Cassese : *The Self-determination of Peoples,* Columbia University, New York, 1981.

Antony G.N. Flew : *Wants or Needs : Choices or Commands,* Paris, 1953.

Arbery : *Sufism*, George Allen & Unwin Ltd., London, 1996.

Arnold and Guillaume : *The Legacy of Islam,* Oxford University Press, London, 1949.

Arnold, Sir Thomas : *The Caliphate,* MacMillan, London, 1965.

Arnold, T. W. : *Preaching of Islam*, London, 1913.

—— : *Principles of Islam*, Luzac & Co., London, 1913.

Arnold, Toynbee : *The World and the West,* Macmillan, London, 2000.

Asborn Eide : *Human Rights in World Society,* Oslo, 1977.

Aurobindo, Sri : *The Foundations of Islamic Culture*, New York, 1973.

Bar Hebraeus : *Chronicon Ecclesiasticum*, Louvain, 1872.

Baral, Lok Raj : *Regional Migrations, Ethnkity and Security,* Bombay, 1995.

Barkatullah, M. : *Khilafat,* MacMillan, London,1924.

Basham, A. L. : *A Cultural History of India,* Oxford, New York, 1975.

Basil, King : *The Conquest of Fearm,* Illias Pub., Islamabad, 2000.

Batty and Morgan : *War its Conduct and Legal Results,* Feroz Pub., Lahore, 2000.

Baumstark, A. : *Ceschichte der Syrischen Literatur*, Bonn, 1922.

Bawer, Raymond : *The New Man in Soviet Social Psychology,* Oxford, New York, 1990.

Beckett, Katharine Scarfe : *Perception of the Islamic Word,* Cambridge University Press, New Delhi, 1992.

Berger, M. : *Islam in Egypt Today : Social and Political Aspects of Popular Religion,* MacMillan, London, 1970.

Bergestrasser, G. : *Risalat Hunayn ibn Isltaq*, Leipzig, 1925.

Berkes, N. : *Turkish Nationalism and Western Civilization,* Allen & Unwin, London, 1959.

Berkey, Jonothan P. : *The Formation of Islam : Religion and Society in the Near East,* Cambridge University Press, New Delhi, 1990.

Bertram, Thomas : *Arabia Felix,* Oxford, New York, 2003.

Bevan, E. R. : *House of Seleucus*, Allen & Unwin, London, 2001.

Bhatia, H. S. : *Studies in Islamic law, Religion and Society*, Deep & Deep Publications, New Delhi, 1997.

Bhawany : *Revolutionary Study of National Development,* Allen & Unwin, London, 2001.

Binder, L. : *Religion and Politics in Pakistan,* University Press. Berkeley, 1961.

Boer, T. J. : *Geschichte der Philosophie im Islam*, Stuttgart, 1901.

Browne, E. G. : *History of Arabian Polity*, Cambridge, 1921.

Caetani, L. : *Annali dell' Islam*, Milano, 1905.

Cajori, F. : *A History of Muslims*, New York, 1954.

Carra, De Vaux : *Penseurs d' Islam*, A. & B. Pub., Paris, 1921.

Carre, Olivier : *Islam and the State in the World Today*, Manohar Publisher, New Delhi, 1989.

Chaghatai, M. A. : *Muslim Monuments of Ahmadabad through their Inscriptions*, Deccan College Research Institute, Pune, 1942.

Chiragh, Ali : *The Proposed Political Legal and Social Reform under Muslim Rule*, Popular Prakashan, Bombay, 1883.

Clothey, W. : *Images of Man : Religious and Historical Process in South Asia*, New Era Publications, Madras, 1984.

Commissariat, M. S. : *A History of Gujarat*, Longman's Green & Co., Bombay, 1938.

Dhagamwar, Vasudha : *Law, Power and Justice : Protection of Personal Rights under Islam*, Bombay, 2001.

Dhaul, Laxmi : *The Sufi Shrine of Ajmer*, Rupa & Co., New Delhi, 1987.

Dieterici, F. : *Alfarabi's Philosophische Abhandlungen*, Mac & Jac Pub., Leiden, 1890.

Dinet and Salman : *Life of Muhammad (PBUH)*, Feroz Pub., Lahore, 2003.

Divine, Epiphany : *Man and Transformation*, MacMillan, London, 1964.

Dorothy, Vaugham : *Europe and the Turks*, Oxford, New York, 2004.

Doughty, C.M. : *Travels in Arabia Deserta*, MacMillan, London, 1923.

Drfyer, J. L. E. : *History of the Planetary Systems*, Cambridge, New York, 1903.

Duchesne, L. : *Early History of the Christian Church*, London, 1914.

Dutt, Nalinaksha : *Early Monastic Buddhism*, Calcutta, 1941.

El-Beladhuri : *Kitab futuh al-buldan, Liber expugnationis regionum*, London, 1868.

Hauser : *Ueber das Kitab al-hijar*, Erlangen, 1922.

Heath, T. L. : *Aristarchus of Samos*, Oxford, 1913.

Hffele, C, J. : *History of the Christian Church Councils*, Edinburgh, 1871.

Hogarth, D. G. : *The Nearer East*, London, 1905.

Houtsma, T. and Others : *Encyclopaedia of Islam*, London, 1934.

Inge, R. : *Philosophy of Plotinus*, London, 1918.

Inostranzev : *Iranian Influences on Moslem Literature*, Bombay, 1918.

Isaac, Asimove : *Exploring the Earth & the Cosmos*, Crown Publishers, New York, 1989.

Izutsu, Toshihdo : *A Comprehensive Study of the Key Philosophical Concepts of Sufism and Taoism*, University Press, Tokyo, 1966.

Karnal, A. Faruqui : *Islam : Today and Tomorrow*, Deep & Deep Pub., New Delhi, 1989.

Karpinski, L.C. : *Algebra of al-Khwarizmi*, Oxford, New York, 1915.

Kaur, R. : *Islamic Co-operation and Unity*, Deep & Deep Publications, New Delhi, 1993.

Keddie, Nikki, R. : *Saints and Sufis, Muslim Religious Institutions since 1500*, University of California Press, California, 1972.

Khaja, Khan : *Studies in Tasawwuf*, University of Madras, Madras, 1923.

Khalifa, Abdul Hakim : *The Islamic Ideology*, Fortune Books, London, 1993.

Khalifa, Abdul Hakim : *The Prophet (PBUH) and His Message*, Islamic Pub., Lahore, 1996.

Khan, Inayat : *Mysticism of Sound*, Pilgrims Book House, New Delhi, 1997.

King, L.W. and Thompson, H.R. : *Sculptures and Inscriptions of Darius the Great on the Rock of Behistan*, Oxford, London, 1907.

Lambton, A.K.S. : *Islam and World,* Oxford, New York, 1956.

Landau, R. : *The Philosophy of the Ibn Arabi,* Century Pub., London, 1959.

Laroui, Abdullah : *The Crisis of the Arab Intellectual,* University of California Press, California, 1976.

Meherhof, H. : *New Light on Hunayn ibn Ishaq*, in *Isis*, 1956.

Merivale, C. : *History of the Romans under the Empire*, London, 1896.

Mommsen, T. : *Provinces of the Roman Empire*, London, 1909.

Muir, Sir William : *The Caliphate, its Rise, Decline, and Fall,* London, 1891.

Muni, S.D. and Kalim Bahadur : *Domestic Conflicts in South Asia,* South Asia Publishers, New Delhi, 1986.

Murthy, T.S. : *Assam: the Difficult Years,* Himalayan Books, New Delhi, 1983.

Myron Weiner : *Sons of the Soil: Migration and Ethnic Conflict in India,* University Press, Prineton, 1978.

Nicholson, R.A. : *Literary History of the Arabs*, London, 1922.

Poole, Lane, S. : *The Mohammedan Dynasties*, London 1895.

Purgiter : *Ancient Indian Historical Tradition*, 1922.

Ray, Samirendra : *Judicial Review and Fundamantal Rights,* Eastern Law House, Kolkata, 2002.

rvine, W. : *Later Mughals*, Deep & Deep Pub., New Delhi, 1971.

Saxena, K.P. : *Human Rights: Perspective and Challenges,* Lancers Books, New Delhi, 1996.

Smith, D. E. : *History of Iran and Turkey*, New York, 1923-25.

Smith, V.A. : *Early History of India*, Oxford, 1914.

Socrates : *Ecclesiatica Historia*, Oxford, 1844.

Stapleton & Azo-Hussain : *Polity in Iraq and Persia*, Calcutta, 1927.

Steele, R. : *Practical Diplomacy,* New Delhi, 1952

Tarn, W. W. : *The Greeks in Bactria*, Cambridge, 1938.

Thomas, J. : *Selections Illustrating the History of Greek Polity,* 1941.

Warmington, E. H. *: The Commerce between the Roman Empire and Arabs*, 1939.

Wiberg, J. : *The Anatomy of the Brain in the Works of Galen and 'Ali' Abbas, Janus*, 1914.

Wiedemann, E. : *Uber Thabit ibn Qurra, sein Leben und Wirken*, Erlangen, 1922.

Winer, L. : *Contributions towards a History of Arabico-Gothic Culture*, New York, 1917.

Zaehner, R.C. : *Hindu and Muslim Mysticism,* Oxford, London, 1960.

Zafeeruddin, M.M. : *System of Modesty and Chastity in Islam,* Idara Ishaat-e-Diniyat Pvt. Ltd, New Delhi, 1995.